Sing Grammar

싱그래머

Sing Grammar
싱그래머

초판1쇄 발행　2015년 10월 30일
초판2쇄 발행　2016년 8월 25일
제2판1쇄 발행　2021년 3월 1일
제2판2쇄 발행　2022년 6월 25일

지은이 김지연 | **펴낸이** 이찬규 | **펴낸곳** 북코리아
등록번호 제03-01240호 | **전화** 02-704-7840 | **팩스** 02-704-7848
이메일 ibookorea@naver.com | **홈페이지** www.북코리아.kr
주소 13209 경기도 성남시 중원구 사기막골로 45번길 14 우림2차 A동 1007호
ISBN 978-89-6324-684-0 03740
값 20,000원

KOMCA 승인필

지루한 문법책은 가라!

싱~긋 웃게 만드는 싱그래머로 배우자!

제2판
최신 팝송 20곡
추가 수록!

Sing Grammar
싱그래머

영어 팝송 총 80곡 수록!
하루 1곡씩 80일 만에 영문법 완벽 마스터!

김지연 지음

북코리아

시작하며

지루한 문법책은 가라!
싱~긋 웃게 만드는
싱그래머로 배우자!

- **챗GPT 시대, 완벽한 AI?**
더욱 중요해진 것은 감성 영어!

언어에도 인공지능 기능이 도입되면서 우리는 원하는 표현을 뚝딱 생성해낼 수 있는 시대에 살고 있다. 디지털 기기만 있으면 검색의 번거로움 없이 실시간으로 상대방의 언어를 이해하며, 하려는 말을 상대방의 언어로 생성해낼 수 있게 되었다. 이에 번역 AI만 있다면 더 이상 영어공부가 필요 없다거나, 영어 학습과 영어 교수의 필요성에 의문을 제기하는 사람들도 있다.

나 또한 대표적인 인공지능 챗GPT로 필요한 표현을 검색하고 이용해보면서 놀라운 빅데이터 수집능력과 정확한 문장 생성 능력에 감탄을 금치 못하였다. 이대로 인간의 언어능력마저 AI가 대신할 수 있게 되는 시대가 온 것일까. 성실하게 영어를 공부해온 학습자로서 영어 학습에 대한 두려움과 좌절감이 느껴지는 순간이기도 하였다.

하지만, 이 새롭고도 막강한 기능을 갖춘 언어 인공지능을 사용해본 결과, 결코 우리 인간의 능력을 대체할 수 없는 영역이 있다는 것을 알게 되었다. 그것은 바로 우리 인간이 가진 '감성'이었다! 과연 다양한 문화적 배경을 가진 복잡다단한 개인의 감정을 AI 언어가 대신해낼 수 있을까? AI로는 감정을 효과적으로 전달하기 위한 언어의 미묘한 차이를 표현하는 데 분명 한계가 있다고 생각한다.

그러기에, 언어 인공지능은 우리의 언어 사용에 도움을 줄 수 있는 도구로 활용하면 될 것이고, 우리의 감성을 효과적으로 표현해낼 수 있는 언어능력은 꾸준히 개발시켜야 할 것이다. 결국 앞으로는 자신의 감정을 정확하게 표현하는 능력이 매우 중요해질 것이며, 감성이 녹아 있는 영어 팝송이 영어 학습에 매우 효과적일 것이라는 결론에 도달하게 되었다.

- **《싱그래머》의 출발! 영문법 수업의 기적을 보다!**

교실에서 학생들을 가르치면서 학습자들이 가장 힘들어하는 영문법을 가르치는 시간은 영어교사로서도 가장 부담이 되는 영역이자 고민이 되는 시간이었다. 문법 수업을 지루해하는 학생들이 고개를 떨구는 모습을 보며 자괴감을 느끼기를 여러 번…. '어떻게 하면 엉어 문법을 신나고 재미있게 가르칠 수 있을까'를 고민하였고, 팝송과 함께 영문법을 가르치면 어떨까 하는 생각이 바로 이 책 《싱그래머》의 출발이었다.

영어 팝송에 녹아 있는 문법을 빈칸으로 두어 노래를 들려주었고, 학생들은 저절로 영어 가사를 따라가며 빈칸에 들어갈 문법에 집중하고 있었다. 반복적으로 등장하는 문법 형식을 채워나가며 문장 안에서의 문법의 기능에 관심을 기울였고, 팝송을 듣고 난 뒤 학습하게 되는 문법 개념을 더욱 잘 이해하게 되었다. 문법은 팝송에 흐르는 스토리와 함께 더욱 효과적으로 머릿속에 각인되었고, 문제 풀이까지 자연스럽게 이어져 문법 적용 능력을 갖추게 되는 효과가 있었다. 팝송과 함께한 싱그래머 수업은 더 이상 지루하고 힘든 45분 독무대가 아니었다. 공부가 놀이가 되는 시간이었고, 영문법이 즐거워지는 순간이었다. 나는 이것을 싱그래머가 이루어낸 '영어 문법 학습의 기적'이라고 감히 말한다.

- **《싱그래머》와 함께 팝송을 부르며 영어 문법 능력 키우기!**
  감성 역량을 끌어올려 미래 핵심역량 함양!

싱그래머 수업을 하다 보면 가르침이 보람과 감사함으로 다가오는 순간이 있다. 팝송으로 영어 문법 능력을 향상하고, 더불어 감성까지 풍부해진 학생들을 마주할 때가 그렇다. 학생들은 가슴 아픈 이별 노래나 애절한 마음을 담은 사랑 노래를 통해 문법을 알아가면서 풍부한 감정을 쌓아나간다.

싱그래머 학습은 최근에 더욱 가치 있게 평가받는 감성 역량을 끌어올릴 수 있기에, 영어 능력 향상과 함께 미래 핵심역량을 함양할 수 있는 효과적인 도구로 사용될 수 있을 것이다.

- **《싱그래머》 제2판이 나오다!**

《싱그래머》가 나온 이후 지난 5년간 독자들로부터 피드백을 받았고, 나 또한 《싱그래머》로 제자들과 교실 수업을 하면서 보완해야 할 부분을 고민하게 되었다. 기존 60종의 문법항목에 20종을 추가해 총 80종의 영문법을 팝송과 함께 학습할 수 있도록 구성해서 더욱 체계적이고 완성도 있는 교재로 제작하였다. 특히 팝송 선정 시, ① 한국인에게 사랑받는 유명 팝송 중에서 주요 문법이 잘 녹아 있고, ② 반복된 가사 속에 문법 문형이 지속적으로 등장해 학습자들의 뇌에 효과적으로 각인되며, ③ 노랫말이 자극적이지 않고 비속어를 담고 있지 않아 교육적으로 가치 있는 노래들로 구성하였다.

- **교사에게는 효과적인 교수-학습 도구!**
  학습자들에게는 영문법 울렁증 극복 도구!

팝송을 도입해 영문법을 가르치는 것은 영어 학습에 활력을 불어넣을 뿐만 아니라, 감성 풍부한 노랫말을 통해 영어 문법을 자연스럽게 노출시키는 효과가 있다.

따라서 《싱그래머》는 영어를 가르치는 교수자에게 효과적인 교수 자료로 활용될 수 있을 것이다. 아울러 영문법 기초가 부족하거나 영문법에 막연한 울렁증을 겪고 있는 학생들에게는 문법을 쉽게 이해하며 기초부터 탄탄하게 실력을 쌓아갈 수 있는 최고의 학습서가 될 것이다.

《싱그래머》의 효과적 활용으로 대한민국 영어 학습자들에게 영문법이 더욱 친근해지고, 영문법이 이해되고, 영문법이 쉬워지길 바란다.

2022년 6월

저자 김지연

차례

I. Basic

II. Intermediate

III. Advanced

Sing Grammar 이렇게 활용하세요!

1. 수준 체크!

Basic, Intermediate, Advanced level 순으로 순차적으로 노래와 함께 문법학습을 진행

차례

I. Basic

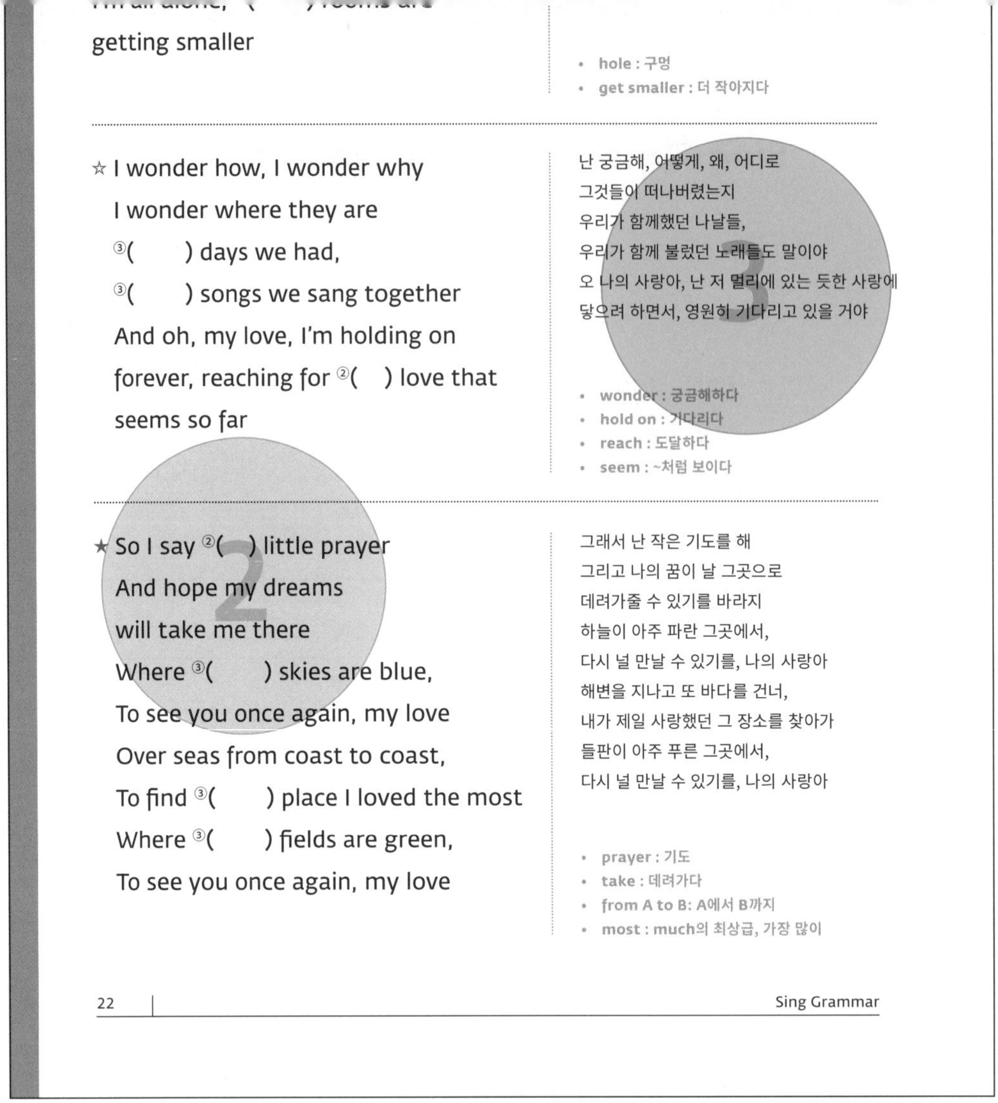

getting smaller

- hole : 구멍
- get smaller : 더 작아지다

☆ I wonder how, I wonder why
I wonder where they are
③(   ) days we had,
③(   ) songs we sang together
And oh, my love, I'm holding on
forever, reaching for ②( ) love that
seems so far

난 궁금해, 어떻게, 왜, 어디로
그것들이 떠나버렸는지
우리가 함께했던 나날들,
우리가 함께 불렀던 노래들도 말이야
오 나의 사랑아, 난 저 멀리에 있는 듯한 사랑에
닿으려 하면서, 영원히 기다리고 있을 거야

- wonder : 궁금해하다
- hold on : 기다리다
- reach : 도달하다
- seem : ~처럼 보이다

★ So I say ②( ) little prayer
And hope my dreams
will take me there
Where ③(   ) skies are blue,
To see you once again, my love
Over seas from coast to coast,
To find ③(   ) place I loved the most
Where ③(   ) fields are green,
To see you once again, my love

그래서 난 작은 기도를 해
그리고 나의 꿈이 날 그곳으로
데려가줄 수 있기를 바라지
하늘이 아주 파란 그곳에서,
다시 널 만날 수 있기를, 나의 사랑아
해변을 지나고 또 바다를 건너,
내가 제일 사랑했던 그 장소를 찾아가
들판이 아주 푸른 그곳에서,
다시 널 만날 수 있기를, 나의 사랑아

- prayer : 기도
- take : 데려가다
- from A to B: A에서 B까지
- most : much의 최상급, 가장 많이

22 | Sing Grammar

2. 팝송 듣고 빈칸 채우기!

노래를 들으면서 빈칸을 채우고, 가사 속 문법에 더욱 주목

3. 가사 의미 파악!

가사 해석 및 어휘와 표현을 보면서 팝송의 의미를 더욱 잘 이해

4. 핵심 문법 이해!

해당 팝송이 담고 있는 문법 개념을 학습하며 문법 이해

5. 가사 예문 파악!

핵심 문법이 녹아있는 문장만을 따로 떼어 문법을 효과적으로 각인

35 부가의문문

부가의문문이란

- 상대방에게 어떤 사실을 확인하거나 동의를 구할 때 문장 끝에 덧붙이는 의문문으로 '그렇지?'라는 의미를 나타낸다.

부가의문문 만드는 법		
형태	앞문장이 긍정이면 부정으로 앞문장이 부정이면 긍정으로	- Math is difficult, **isn't it**? - You are not angry, **are you**?
주어	앞문장의 주어를 대명사로 바꿈	- Justine is a good teacher, **isn't he**? - Jessica didn't come to the gym, **did she**?
동사	be동사나 조동사는 그대로, 일반동사는 do/does/did로	- The food was terrible, **wasn't it**? - We can dance together, **can't we**? - Your parents live in LA, **don't they**? - Bruno doesn't wear glasses, **does he**? - Jina didn't finish her project, **did she**?
축약	부정의 부가의문문은 축약형	- You are good at speaking English, **aren't you**?

가사 예문

I thought we were holding on, aren't we?

우린 잘 견뎌내고 있다고 생각했는데, 그렇지 않니?

(*부가의문문이 주로 주절의 시제를 따르나, 문맥상 그렇지 않을 수도 있음)

7. 문법 적용 문제풀이!

문법 실전문제를 풀면서 적용능력을 기르고, 학습의 완성도를 향상

6. 잠깐, 집중!

심화내용이나 예외가 적용되는 부분에 집중하며 문법지식을 확장

Attention!

앞서 언급된 명사를 생략하고 a few / a little과 few / little만 쓸 수도 있다!

- "How many countries have you visited?" "**A few.**" (A few = a few countries)
- "Would you like some coffee?" "Yes, just **a little.**" (a little = a little coffee)

6

Q1 다음 문장의 빈칸에 a few / few 또는 a little / little을 써 넣으시오.

1. I have ________ questions about my surgery today.
2. Gambling attracts desperate people who have ________ money.
3. I found ________ mistakes on your essay. You did a great job!
4. I cannot move this box for myself. Can you give me ________ help?

Q2 〈보기〉의 명사와 a few / few 또는 a little / little을 사용하여 문장을 완성하시오.

〈보기〉 minutes friends break rain

7

1. Sera just moved to this school, so she has ____________.
2. I had to work overtime yesterday, so I need ____________.
3. I have something to tell you. Would you stop by my office for ____________?
4. Because we had ____________ and it was dry this summer, the price of crops has jumped.

Question 2 **1.** few friends **2.** a little break **3.** a few minutes **4.** little rain

I
Basic

1 Just the way you are — Bruno Mars

Oh ①(   ) eyes, ①(   ) eyes
Make the stars look like ②(   )'re not shining
①(   ) hair, ①(   ) hair
Falls perfectly without her trying
③(   )'s so beautiful, And ④( ) tell her everyday

그녀의 눈, 그녀의 눈은
별들이 빛나지 않는 것처럼
보이게 만들죠
그녀의 머리카락, 그녀의 머리카락은
그녀가 애쓰지 않아도 완벽히 흘러내려요
그녀는 너무 아름다워요,
난 매일 그녀에게 말하죠

- look like~ : ~처럼 보이다

Yeah ④( ) know, ④( ) know
When I compliment her, she won't believe me
And ⑤(   )'s so, ⑤(   )'s so sad to think
she doesn't see what ④( ) see
But every time she asks ⑥(   )
Do I look okay, I say

나는 알아요, 나는 알아요
내가 그녀를 칭찬해도, 그녀는 날 믿지 않을 거란 걸
그것은 너무나 슬퍼요, 그녀가 내가 보는 것을 못 본다고 생각하면
하지만 그녀가 매번 자기 모습이 괜찮냐고
나에게 물어보면 난 말하죠

- compliment : ① 칭찬하다 ② 칭찬
- won't : will not의 축약형

★ When ④( ) see ⑦(   ) face
There's not a thing that I would change
Cause you're amazing
Just the way ⑧(   ) are
And when you smile, the whole world stops and stares
for a while Cause girl, you're amazing
Just the way ⑧(   ) are

내가 당신의 얼굴을 볼 때
단 한 가지도 바꾸고 싶은 게 없어요
왜냐하면 당신은 놀랍거든요
당신 그대로도
당신이 웃을 때, 전 세계가 멈추고 한동안
빤히 쳐다보죠
왜냐하면 당신은 놀랍거든요
그저 당신 모습 그대로도

- amazing : 놀라운
- way : 길, 방식
- for a while : 잠시 동안

①(　　) lips, ①(　　) lips I could kiss them all day if she'd let me ①(　　) laugh, ①(　　) laugh ③(　　) hates but I think it's so sexy ③(　　)'s so beautiful And I tell her everyday	그녀의 입술, 그녀의 입술은 그녀가 허락하면 매일 입맞춤할 텐데 그녀의 웃음, 그녀의 웃음 그녀는 싫어하지만 난 매력적이라고 생각해요 그녀는 너무나 아름다워요 그리고 난 매일 그녀에게 말하죠 • **let~ :** ~에게 허락하다 • **so :** 매우
Oh you know, you know, you know I'd never ask you to change If perfect is what you're searching for, then just stay the same So don't even bother asking If you look okay, You know I say	당신은 알죠 당신은 알죠 내가 당신에게 바뀌길 요구하지 않을 거란 걸 완벽함이 당신이 찾는 거라면, 그냥 그대로 있어 주세요 물어볼 필요도 없이 당신이 당신 괜찮냐고 나에게 물어보면 난 말하죠 • **search for :** 찾다 • **bother :** 괴롭히다

★ Repeat

The way you are The way you are Girl, you're amazing Just the way you are	당신 모습 그대로 당신 모습 그대로 당신은 놀라워요 그저 당신 모습 그대로도

★ Repeat

1 인칭대명사

인칭대명사란

- 사람이나 동물, 사물의 이름을 대신하여 지칭하는 말이다.
- 1인칭(I), 2인칭(you), 3인칭(he, she, it)으로 나눌 수 있고, 문장에서 어떤 역할을 하느냐에 따라 주격, 소유격, 목적격으로 쓰인다.
- 소유대명사는 각 인칭에 따른 '~의 것'으로 나타낸다.

	단수				복수			
	주격 (~은/는/이/가)	소유격 (~의)	목적격 (~을/를)	소유 대명사 (~의 것)	주격 (~은/는/이/가)	소유격 (~의)	목적격 (~을/를)	소유 대명사 (~들의 것)
1인칭	I (나는)	my (나의)	me (나를)	mine (나의 것)	we (우리는)	our (우리의)	us (우리를)	ours (우리의 것)
2인칭	you (너는)	your (너의)	you (너를)	yours (너의 것)	you (너희들은)	your (너희들의)	you (너희들을)	yours (너희들의 것)
3인칭	he (그는)	his (그의)	him (그를)	his (그의 것)	they (그들은/그것들은)	their (그들의/그것들의)	them (그들을/그것들을)	theirs (그들의 것)
	she (그녀는)	her (그녀의)	her (그녀를)	hers (그녀의 것)				
	it (그것은)	its (그것의)	it (그것을)	–				

가사 예문

Her eyes, her eyes make the stars look like they're not shining.
그녀의 눈, 그녀의 눈은 그것들이(별들이) 빛나지 않는 것처럼 보이게 만들죠.

Q1 다음 밑줄 친 부분을 바르게 고치시오.

1. A: Whose book is that? B: It's her. → ________
2. A: What is you favorite sport? B: Soccer is my favorite sport. → ________
3. I want to see him, but he doesn't want to see my. → ________
4. Joy and I are very good friends. Our like each other. → ________

Q2 다음 우리말과 뜻이 같도록 빈칸에 알맞은 말을 쓰시오.

1. 네 방이 너무 지저분해. 너는 방을 청소해야 해.

→ ________ room is so messy. ________ should clean your room.

2. 우리의 여름 방학은 정말 좋았어. 너희 것(방학)도 좋았니?

→ ________ summer vacation was so nice. Was ________ good, too?

3. 내일은 그녀의 생일이야. 나는 그녀를 위해 깜짝 파티를 준비할 거야.

→ Tomorrow is ________ birthday. I will prepare a surprise party for ________.

4. 나는 나의 미국 친구들이 그리워. 나는 이번 크리스마스에 그들을 방문할 거야.

→ I miss ________ American friends. I will visit ________ this Christmas.

Q3 다음 문장의 빈칸에 들어갈 적절한 표현을 쓰시오.

1. I like your coat. Where did you buy ________?
2. I can't find my glasses. Did you see ________?
3. Mike is good at music. ________ plays the piano and guitar very well.
4. My parents and I went to the art festival. ________ saw many beautiful paintings there.

Fill in the Blank ① her ② they ③ she ④ I ⑤ it ⑥ me ⑦ your ⑧ you

Question 1 **1.** hers **2.** your **3.** me **4.** We

Question 2 **1.** Your, You **2.** Our, yours **3.** her, her **4.** my, them

Question 3 **1.** it **2.** them 또는 mine **3.** He **4.** We

2 My love | Westlife

①(   ) empty street,
①(   ) empty house,
②(   ) hole inside my heart,
I'm all alone, ③(   ) rooms are getting smaller

텅 빈 거리,
텅 빈 집,
내 맘에 생겨난 공허함,
난 홀로 있는데도, 공간은 점점 작아져만 가네

- **hole :** 구멍
- **get smaller :** 더 작아지다

☆ I wonder how, I wonder why
I wonder where they are
③(   ) days we had,
③(   ) songs we sang together
And oh, my love, I'm holding on forever, reaching for ②(   ) love that seems so far

난 궁금해, 어떻게, 왜, 어디로
그것들이 떠나버렸는지
우리가 함께했던 나날들,
우리가 함께 불렀던 노래들도 말이야
오 나의 사랑아, 난 저 멀리에 있는 듯한 사랑에
닿으려 하면서, 영원히 기다리고 있을 거야

- **wonder :** 궁금해하다
- **hold on :** 기다리다
- **reach :** 도달하다
- **seem :** ~처럼 보이다

★ So I say ②(   ) little prayer
And hope my dreams
will take me there
Where ③(   ) skies are blue,
To see you once again, my love
Over seas from coast to coast,
To find ③(   ) place I loved the most
Where ③(   ) fields are green,
To see you once again, my love

그래서 난 작은 기도를 해
그리고 나의 꿈이 날 그곳으로
데려가줄 수 있기를 바라지
하늘이 아주 파란 그곳에서,
다시 널 만날 수 있기를, 나의 사랑아
해변을 지나고 또 바다를 건너,
내가 제일 사랑했던 그 장소를 찾아가
들판이 아주 푸른 그곳에서,
다시 널 만날 수 있기를, 나의 사랑아

- **prayer :** 기도
- **take :** 데려가다
- **from A to B:** A에서 B까지
- **most :** much의 최상급, 가장 많이

I try to read, I go to work
I'm laughing with my friends
But I can't stop to keep myself from thinking,
Oh, no

난 책도 좀 보고, 일도 나가고
친구들과 웃기도 하지
하지만 계속 너를 생각하는 내 자신을 멈출 수가 없어
오, 안돼

- **stop A from B: B로부터 A하는 것을 멈추다**

☆ Repeat

★ Repeat

To hold you in my arms
To promise you my love
To tell you from my heart
You're all I'm thinking of
I'm reaching for ③(   ) love that seems so far

널 내 품에 안고
나의 사랑을 너에게 약속할게
내 진심을 너에게 말하는데
난 온통 네 생각뿐이라는 걸
난 저 멀리 있는 듯한 사랑을 향해 달려갈 거야

- **hold** : 포옹하다
- **promise** : 약속하다

★ Repeat × 2

2 a, an, the

a, an

- a, an은 셀 수 있는 명사의 단수형 앞에 쓰여서, '하나(one)', '불특정한 하나', '~마다/~당'을 나타낸다.

① I eat **an** apple everyday. → 하나

② He is **a** student. → 불특정한 하나

③ I get a medical check-up once **a** year. → ~마다

- 발음이 자음인 단어 앞에는 a, 발음이 모음인 단어 앞에는 an을 붙인다.

발음이 자음으로 시작되는 명사 또는 명사구 앞	**a** book, **a** car, **a** desk, **a** teacher, **a** mirror, **a** river, **a** pretty girl, **a** bad boy, **a** beautiful park
발음이 모음으로 시작되는 명사 또는 명사구 앞	**an** apple, **an** umbrella, **an** artist, **an** egg, **an** old man, **an** expensive clothes, **an** interesting story

the

- the는 특정한 것, 앞에 나온 명사를 다시 받을 때 쓰이며, 명사의 단수, 복수형에 관계없이 쓸 수 있다.

① It's too cold. Close **the** door, **please.** → 특정한 것을 가리킬 때

② **The** earth moves around **the** sun. → 세상에서 유일한 것

③ **The** boy on the stage is my son. → 수식받는 명사 앞에

④ She plays **the** piano for 30 minutes everyday. → 악기 이름

⑤ I like a girl. **The** girl lives next to my house. → 앞에 나온 명사를 다시 받을 때

가사 예문

An empty street, an empty house, a hole inside my heart,
텅 빈 거리, 텅 빈 집, 내 맘에 생겨난 공허함,

I'm all alone, the rooms are getting smaller.
난 홀로 있는데도, 공간은 점점 작아져만 가네.

Q1 빈칸에 a, an, the 중 알맞은 말을 쓰시오.

1. Take ____ umbrella with you today.
2. ____ State of Liberty in NY is the symbol of freedom.
3. My father bought ____ skinny jean for me, but the jean was too small.

Q2 다음 문장의 밑줄 친 부분을 바르게 고치시오.

1. A old lady carries a heavy bag. → ____________
2. I have a dog, Berry. A dog is so cute. → ____________
3. My family visits my grandma twice the month. → ____________

Q3 다음 밑줄 친 a의 쓰임이 〈보기〉와 같은 것은?

〈보기〉 My family goes camping twice a month.

① She doesn't have a car.
② Brendon is a middle school student.
③ A dog is a faithful animal.
④ I send him an e-mail once a week.
⑤ Rome was not built in a day.

Fill in the Blank ① An ② A ③ The
Question 1 **1.** an **2.** The **3.** a
Question 2 **1.** An old lady **2.** The dog **3.** twice a month
Question 3 ④

3	Uptown girl	Westlife

Uptown ①(   )
She's been living in her uptown ②(   )
I bet she never had a backstreet ③(   )
I bet her mama never told her why
I'm gonna try for an uptown ①(   )

부잣집 아가씨
그녀는 부자동네에서 살아왔죠
제가 확신하건데, 그녀는 뒷골목 건달을 만나본 적 없을 거예요
제가 확신하건데, 그녀의 엄마는 왜 그래야 하는지 말해주지 않았을 거예요
저는 부잣집 아가씨를 한번 사귀어볼 거예요

- has been living : 살아오고 있다
- uptown : 부유층 지역의
- bet : 확신하다
- try : ① 노력하다 ② 시도하다 ③ 시도

★ She's been living in her white bread ②(   ) as long as anyone with hot ④(   ) can
And now she's looking for a downtown ⑤(   )
That's what I am

뜨거운 열정을 가진 사람이 견디기에는 너무 오래 그 편한 세상에서 살아왔죠
이제 그녀는 도시의 남자를 찾고 있어요
그게 바로 저랍니다

- white bread world : 백인 상류 사회 (비유)
- as long as~ : ~하는 한
- look for~ : ~를 찾다

And when she knows what she wants from her ⑥(   ),
And when she wakes up and makes up her ⑦(   ),
she'll see I'm not so tough
Just because I'm in ⑧(   ) with an uptown ①(   )
You know I've seen her in her uptown ②(   )

인생에서 찾고 싶은 게 무엇인지 알게 되면,
정신을 차리고 마음을 결정하게 되면,
그녀는 제가 그렇게 거칠지 않나는 걸 알게 될 거예요
왜냐하면 전 부잣집 아가씨와 사랑에 빠져 있기 때문이죠
부자동네에서 그녀를 본 적이 있어요

She's got a ⑫(   )

She's getting tired of
her high class ⑨(   )s and
all her ⑩(   )s from her uptown
⑪(   )s
She's got a ⑫(   )

그녀는 부자 남자친구들로부터 받은 선물들과
최고급의 장난감들에 싫증을 내고 있죠
이제 그녀는 선택을 할 수 있어요

- make up one's mind : 마음을 결정하다
- get tired of~ : ~에 싫증나다
- class : 계층
- choice : 선택

Uptown girl
You know I can't afford to buy her
⑬(   )s
But maybe someday when my ⑭(   )
comes in,
she'll understand what kind of ③(   )
I've been and then I'll win
And when she's walking,
she's looking so fine
And when she's talking,
she'll say that she's mine
She'll say I'm not so tough
Just because I'm in love with
an uptown ①(   )

부잣집 아가씨
알다시피, 저는 그녀에게 진주를 사줄
능력은 없어요
하지만 언젠가 제가 부자가 되면
그녀는 제가 어떤 남자였는지 알게 될
거예요 그러면 저는 그녀의 사랑을 얻게
되겠죠
그녀가 걸어갈 때 그녀는 너무 멋져 보여요
그녀가 얘기를 할 땐 그녀는 제 사랑이라고
말을 할 거예요
그녀는 제가 그렇게 거칠지 않다고
말할 거예요
부잣집 아가씨와 사랑에 빠져 있기 때문이죠

- You know : 알다시피
- pearl : 진주
- can't afford to~ : ~할 여력이 없다
- when one's ship comes in : 부자가 되면(비유)
- be in love with~ : ~와 사랑에 빠져 있다

★ Repeat

Uptown ①(   ) She's my uptown
①(   )
You know I'm in ⑧(   ) with an
uptown ①(   )

부잣집 아가씨 그녀는 나의 부잣집
아가씨예요
전 부잣집 아가씨와 사랑에 빠졌어요

3 명사

명사란

- 사람이나 동물, 사물, 장소 등의 '이름'을 나타내는 말로, 크게 셀 수 있는 명사와 셀 수 없는 명사로 나누어진다.

셀 수 있는 명사	보통명사	일반적인 사물의 이름을 나타내는 명사로서, 단수와 복수로 나타냄	computer, desk, book, fruit, tree, letter, boy, mountain, animal, school, building, teacher, pencil, friend, cat, toy, sea, ship
	집합명사	사람이나 사물의 집합체를 나타내는 명사	family, class, people, nation, audience, team, staff, crowd, committee
셀 수 없는 명사	물질명사	정해진 모양이 없는 물질을 나타내는 명사	water, bread, milk, air, money, paper, sugar, meat, salt, butter, rice, cake, time, pizza, rain, food, cheese
	고유명사	하나뿐인 사람, 사물, 장소를 나타내는 고유한 이름	Incheon international airport, Gangnam, Time Square, Korea, Obama, Mr. Smith, Jennifer, BTS, Statue of Liberty
	추상명사	추상적인 개념을 나타내는 명사	love, beauty, happiness, peace, freedom, advice, justice, kindness, success, knowledge, wisdom, advice, experience

가사 예문

Uptown girl, She's been living in her uptown world.

부잣집 아가씨, 그녀는 부자동네에서 살아왔죠.

I bet she never had a backstreet guy.

제가 확신하건데, 그녀는 뒷골목 건달을 만나본 적 없을 거예요.

I bet her mama never told her why.

제가 확신하건데, 그녀의 엄마는 왜 그래야 하는지 말해주지 않았을 거예요.

Attention!

셀 수 없는 명사의 경우 a/an 또는 복수형 -s를 쓸 수 없다!

I'm very thirsty. I want to drink **water**! (a water → X, water → O)

In Korea, we have much **rain** in summer. (rains → X, rain → O)

Q1 다음 명사들 중 나머지 넷과 종류가 다른 것을 골라 동그라미 하시오.

1. pencil / bag / sea / mountain / love
2. meat / bread / paper / friend / sugar
3. beauty / computer / peace / freedom / thought
4. Nation / Ms.Kim / Busan / G-dragon / Empire State Building
5. family / team / knowledge / audience / crowd

Q2 다음 문장에서 틀린 부분을 찾아 바르게 고치시오.

1. She is from a Canada. ________ → ________
2. Do you want a coffee? ________ → ________
3. He is an English teachers. ________ → ________
4. Can you pass me the salts, please? ________ → ________
5. Can you give me an advice? ________ → ________
6. I don't have much times. I'll call you back. ________ → ________

Fill in the Blank ① girl ② world ③ guy ④ blood ⑤ man ⑥ time ⑦ mind ⑧ love ⑨ toy ⑩ present ⑪ boy ⑫ choice ⑬ pearl ⑭ ship

Question 1 **1.** love **2.** friend **3.** computer **4.** Nation **5.** knowledge

Question 2 **1.** a Canada → Canada **2.** a coffee → coffee **3.** teachers → teacher **4.** salts → salt **5.** an advice → some advice 또는 any advice **6.** times → time

4 Reach | S club 7

When the world leaves you feeling
blue, You can count on me,
I will be there for you
When it seems all your ①(   ) and
②(   ) are a million ③(   ) away,
I will re-assure you
We've got to all stick together,
Good ④(   ), there for each other
Never ever forget that I've got you and
you've got me, so

세상이 너를 우울한 채로 있게 내버려둘 때,
넌 나한테 기대도 돼, 내가 널 위해 곁에 있을게
너의 모든 희망과 꿈이 너무나 멀게만 보일 때,
내가 너에게 그 꿈과 희망을 재확인시켜줄게
우린 꼭 함께해야 해
좋은 친구들은 서로를 위해 있어
그것을 절대 잊지 마
나에게는 네가 있고 너에게는 내가 있어,
그러니까

- **blue** : 우울한
- **count on~** : ~를 의지하다
- **million** : ① 백만 ② 수많은
- **reassure** : 재확인시키다
- **We've got to~** : 우리는 ~해야 한다
- **stick together** : 서로 들러붙다
- **each other** : 서로서로
- **so** : 그러므로 (= **therefore**)

★ Reach for the ⑤(   )
Climb every mountain higher
Reach for the ⑤(   )
Follow your heart's desire
Reach for the ⑤(   )
And when that rainbow's shining
over you,
That's when your ②(   ) will
all come true

별에게 손을 뻗어봐
모든 산을 더 높이 올라가봐
별에게 손을 뻗어봐
너의 마음속 바람을 따라가봐
별에게 손을 뻗어봐
그리고 저 무지개가 너를 비출 때,
그때는 너의 꿈이 이루어질 거야

- **reach for~** : ~를 향해 닿다
- **higher** : 더 높은
- **desire** : 소망
- **dreams come true** : 꿈이 이루어지다

There's a place waiting just for you
It's a special place where your ②(   )
all come true

너만을 기다리고 있는 곳이 있어
그곳은 너의 모든 꿈이 이루어지는
특별한 곳이지

Fly away, Swim the ocean sea
Drive that open road,
Leave the past behind you
Don't stop, gotta keep moving
Your hopes gotta keep building
Never ever forget that I've got you and you've got me, so

멀리 날아봐, 저 푸른 대양을 헤엄쳐봐
뻥 뚫린 도로를 달려봐,
지나간 과거는 뒤로한 채
멈추지 말고, 계속 움직여
너의 꿈은 계속 커가는 중이니까
절대 한순간도 잊지 마, 나에게는 네가 있고
너에게는 내가 있어, 그러니까

- **wait for~ :** ~를 기다리다
- **leave :** 떠나다
- **past :** 과거
- **gotta = got to** (해야 한다)
- **keep ~ing :** ~를 계속하다
- **follow :** 따르다

★ Repeat

Don't believe in all that you've been told
The sky's the limit, you can reach your goal
No-one knows just what the future holds
There ain't nothing you can't be
There's a whole world at your ⑥(   )
I said reach, Climb every mountain (reach)
Reach for the moon (reach)
Follow that rainbow and your ②(   ) will all come true

네가 들었던 말을 모두 믿지는 마
오직 하늘만이 한계야(한계란 없어),
넌 너의 꿈에 도달할 수 있어
아무도 미래가 어떻게 될지 몰라
네가 이룰 수 없는 건 아무것도 없어
세상은 너의 발 앞에 있어
내가 말했지 펼치라고, 모든 산을 올라가 (뻗어)
달까지 가보는 거야 (뻗어)
무지개를 따라가 그러면 너의 꿈은 이루어질 거야

- **goal :** 목표
- **feet :** foot의 복수형

★ Repeat × 2

4 명사의 복수형

명사의 복수형이란

- 셀 수 있는 명사는 두 개 이상일 경우 복수형으로 나타낸다. 복수형을 만드는 방법에는 규칙변화와 불규칙변화가 있다.

- There are **two books** on the desk. (O)
- There are two book on the desk. (X)

명사의 복수형을 만드는 법

규칙 변화	**① 대부분 명사 →**	**명사 + -s**	book → books, desk → desks, pencil → pencils, egg → eggs, bag → bags, car → cars, girl → girls
	② -o, -s, -x, -sh, -ch로 끝나는 명사 →	**명사 + -es**	potato → potatoes, bus → buses, box → boxes, dish → dishes, church → churches, bench → benches
	③ 자음 + y로 끝나는 명사 →	**y를 i로 바꾸고 + -es**	city → cities, lady → ladies, baby → babies, candy → candies, country → countries
	④ -f, -fe로 끝나는 명사 →	**f, fe를 v로 바꾸고 + -es**	knife → knives, leaf → leaves, wolf → wolves
불규칙 변화	**단수와 복수 형태가 같은 경우**		series → series, species → species, crossroads → crossroads
	단수와 복수 형태가 다른 경우		child → children, mouse → mice, man → men, woman → women, tooth → teeth, ox → oxen, foot → feet

가사 예문

When it seems all your hopes and dreams are a million miles away,
I will reassure you.

너의 모든 희망과 꿈이 너무나 멀게만 보일 때, 내가 너에게 그 꿈과 희망을 재확인시켜줄게.

Q1 다음 괄호 안의 표현 중 알맞은 것을 고르시오.

1. The two (baby / babys / babies) are sleeping on the sofa.
2. Can you put some (potato / potatos / potatoes) in my soup?
3. My mom grows many (flower / flowers / floweres) in the garden.
4. Ladies and (gentleman / gentlemen / gentlemans), welcome to the show.
5. Caterpillars eat the young (leaf / leafs / leaves) of this plant. (caterpillar : 애벌레)

Q2 다음 문장에서 틀린 명사 형태를 찾아 바르게 고치시오.

1. Watch out! The bus are coming. ________ → ________
2. He used two knife to cut the big fish. ________ → ________
3. How many country are there in Europe? ________ → ________
4. Three child are running on the playground. ________ → ________
5. Many woman are standing in line to get the free coupon. ________ → ________
6. Can you buy me some pencil on your way back home? ________ → ________

Fill in the Blank ① hopes ② dreams ③ miles ④ friends ⑤ stars ⑥ feet

Question 1 **1.** babies **2.** potatoes **3.** flowers **4.** gentlemen **5.** leaves

Question 2 **1.** bus → buses **2.** knife → knives **3.** country → countries **4.** child → children
5. woman → women **6.** pencil → pencils

5 Friend — Mocca

☆ If anyone can fill my world with ①(　　) and ②(　　　　　) and cast away all of my ③(　　　　　),
Always there beside me when I am down and never left my face with a ④(　　　),

누군가 내 세계를 기쁨과 행복으로 채우고
내 모든 외로움을 날려버릴 수 있다면,
내가 우울할 때 항상 내 옆에 있어서
절대 내가 인상을 찌푸린 채 내버려 두지 않는다면,

- fill A with B : A를 B로 채우다
- cast away~ : ~를 물리치다
- loneliness : 외로움
- frown : ① 얼굴을 찌뿌리다 ② 불쾌함

★ It's you! Yes, it is you, my friend who can make it all come true
It's you! Yes, it is true a friend in need is a friend indeed

바로 너야! 그래, 바로 너, 모든 게 현실이 되게 할 수 있는 내 친구
바로 너야! 그래, 필요로 할 때 있어 주는 친구가 진정한 친구지

- make it : (바라던 일을) 성공하다, 해내다
- come true : 이루어지다, 실현되다
- a friend in need is a friend indeed : 필요할 때 있어 주는 친구가 진정한 친구다

☆ Repeat

★ Repeat

When you're around, I wrap myself
in a pearly smile
When you're around, you light the bulb
inside my head
When you're around, I wrap myself
in a pearly smile
When you're around, I dance and sway
and kiss the ground

네가 곁에 있을 때, 난 진주 같은 미소를 짓지
네가 곁에 있을 때, 넌 내 머릿속을 환히
밝히지
네가 곁에 있을 때, 난 진주 같은 미소를 짓지
네가 곁에 있을 때, 난 춤추고 흔들다가
넘어지지

- **wrap** : ① 싸다 ② 포장하는 랩
- **pearly** : 진주 같은
- **light** : ① 빛 ② 불을 붙이다 ③ 밝은
- **bulb** : 전구
- **sway** : ① 흔들다 ② 흔들림

☆ Repeat

★ Repeat

When you're around, I wrap myself
in a pearly smile
When you're around, you light the bulb
inside my head
When you're around, I wrap myself
in a pearly smile
When you're around, I laugh and
sing out strong and loud

네가 곁에 있을 때, 난 진주 같은 미소를 짓지
네가 곁에 있을 때, 넌 내 머릿속을 환히
밝히지
네가 곁에 있을 때, 난 진주 같은 미소를 짓지
너와 함께 있을 때, 난 웃고 우렁차게 노래
부르지

- **sing out** : 크게 노래하다

5 셀 수 없는 명사

샐 수 없는 명사란

- 셀 수 없는 명사란 감정이나 공기처럼 일정한 형태가 없는 명사를 말한다.
- 물질명사, 고유명사, 추상명사가 이에 해당한다.
- 셀 수 없는 명사 앞에 a, an을 쓸 수 없으며, 뒤에 –s를 붙일 수 없다.
- 항상 단수 취급하여 동사의 수를 일치시킨다.

물질명사

- 형체는 있지만 일정하지 않은 명사이다.

water, juice, milk, coffee, beer, salt, sugar, butter, paper, wood,
meat, bread, rice, pizza, cake, chocolate, food, ice, air, money

- 물질 명사는 그것을 담는 용기나 단위로 셀 수 있다.

• a glass of water	• a cup of coffee	• a bottle of beer
• a carton of milk	• a piece of cake	• a slice(piece) of pizza
• a piece(sheet) of paper	• a can of soda	• a loaf of bread
• a spoonful of sugar	• a bowl of rice	• a box of cereal

- Would you drink **a glass of water**?
  물 한잔 마시겠어요?
- I'd like to order **two pieces of cheese cake** and **three cups of coffee**.
  저는 치즈케이크 두 조각과 커피 세 잔을 주문할게요.

고유명사

- 하나뿐인 사람이나 사물의 이름이다.

King Sejong, Beatles, Tom, Einstein, Pororo, Samsung, Apple, Queen,

BTS, Korea, Mt. Everest, Han River, Niagara Falls, New York, NIKE

- **Pororo has** many adventures with his friends.
  뽀로로는 친구들과 여러 가지 모험을 한다.
- **BTS is** giving a speech about love at the United Nations now.
  BTS는 지금 유엔본부에서 사랑에 관한 연설을 하고 있어.

추상명사

- 눈에 보이지 않고 형태가 없는 감정이나 개념이다.

beauty, knowledge, feeling, joy, happiness, anger, loneliness, love, freedom,

information, advice, peace, success, kindness, jealousy, youth, honesty, trust

- **Knowledge is** power. 아는 것이 힘이다.
- **Honesty is** the best policy. 정직이 최상의 방책이다.

가사 예문

If anyone can fill my world with joy and happiness and cast away all of my loneliness, It's you!

누군가 내 세계를 기쁨과 행복으로 채우고 내 모든 외로움을 날려버릴 수 있다면, 그건 바로 너야!

Q1 다음 우리말과 의미가 같도록 문장을 완성하시오.

1. 우리는 파티에서 와인 세 병을 마셨다.

→ We drank ________________ at the party.

2. 나는 종이 한 장 위에 중요한 정보를 적었다.

→ I noted the important information on ________________.

3. 올리비아는 할머니를 위해 치킨 수프 한 그릇을 샀다.

→ Olivia bought ________________ for her grandmother.

4. 나는 오늘 아침으로 두 조각의 토스트와 한 잔의 우유를 마셨다.

→ I had ______________ and ______________ for breakfast today.

5. 커피가 좀 쓰네요. 설탕 한 스푼 넣어주실 수 있나요?

→ This coffee is a little bit bitter for me. Can you put ________________ in it?

Q2 다음 문장에서 어법상 어색한 부분을 찾아 바르게 고치시오.

1. We need some moneys to pay the bill. ________ → ________
2. I am thirsty. Can I have some waters? ________ → ________
3. Would you give me some advices about the job? ________ → ________
4. James bought five bottles of beers at the liquor store. ________ → ________
5. The main character, Pororo, are a cute little blue penguin.

________ → ________

Fill in the Blank ① joy ② happiness ③ loneliness ④ frown

Question 1 **1.** three bottles of wine **2.** a piece of paper **3.** a bowl of chicken soup **4.** two pieces of toast, a glass of milk **5.** a spoonful of sugar

Question 2 **1.** moneys, money **2.** waters, water **3.** advices, advice **4.** beers, beer **5.** are, is

6 City of stars | La La Land OST

①(   )(   )(   ),
Are you shining just for me?
①(   )(   )(   ),
There's so much that I can't see
Who knows?
I felt it from the first embrace I shared with you

별들의 도시여,
오직 나를 위해서 빛나는 건가요?
별들의 도시여,
너무나 밝아서 바라볼 수가 없네요
누가 알까요?
당신과 나누었던 첫 번째 포옹에서 그것을 느꼈다는 것을요

- **shining :** 빛나는, 반짝이는
- **There is/There are ~ :** ~이 있다
- **embrace :** ① 포옹 ② 껴안다

That now, Our dreams,
They've finally come true
①(   )(   )(   ),
Just one thing everybody wants
There in the bars and through the
②(   )(   )(   )(   )
(   ),
It's love
Yes, all we're looking for is love from someone else

이제 우리의 꿈들은
마침내 이루어졌어요
별들의 도시여,
모든 사람이 원하는 것은 한 가지예요
바 안과 붐비는 레스토랑의 연기 속에서도,
그건 사랑이죠
맞아요, 우리 모두가 찾고 있는 건
누군가로부터의 사랑이죠

- **come true :** 이루어지다
- **smokescreen :** 연막
- **crowded :** 붐비는
- **look for ~ :** ~를 찾다

A rush
A glance
A touch
A dance

끌림
눈빛
손길
춤

- **rush :** ① 급히 움직이다 ② 돌진하다 ③ 돌진 ④ 끌림
- **glance :** ① 눈짓 ② 흘긋 보다

To look in ③(   )(   ),
To light up the skies,
To open the world and send me reeling
A voice that says 'I'll be here and you'll be alright.'
I don't care if I know just where I will go
Cause all that I need is this crazy feeling
and ④(   )(   )(   )(   )
I think I want it to stay

누군가의 눈을 들여다보는 것은,
하늘이 맑아지고,
세상이 열리고 나를 황홀하게 만드는 것이에요
'난 여기 있을 것이고, 너는 괜찮을 거야.' 라고 말하는 당신의 목소리가 들려와요
내가 가야 할 길을 알고 있다고 해도 신경 쓰지 않아요
왜냐하면 내가 원하는 건 이 미칠듯한 감정과 내 심장의 쿵쾅거림이니까요
이 느낌대로 머물고 싶어요

- **reel :** ① 얼레 ② 휘청거리다 ③ 마음이 크게 동요하다
- **rat-a-tat :** (의성어) 둥둥, 쾅쾅

①(   )(   )(   ),
Are you shinning just for me?
①(   )(   )(   ),
You never shined so brightly

별들의 도시여,
오직 나를 위해서 빛나는 건가요?
별들의 도시여,
이보다 더 밝게 빛낸 적은 없었죠

6 명사의 소유격

~of

- 일반적으로 사물에 대해서 '~의'라는 표현을 할 때 of를 쓴다.

- Do you know the **title of this song**?
  이 노래의 제목
- Look at the **color of the beach**. It is so beautiful.
  바다의 색깔

~'s + 명사

- 일반적으로 사람이나 동물에 대해서 '~의'라는 표현을 할 때 ~'s를 쓴다.

- I broke **my brother's bike**. He must be angry with me.
  내 형의 자전거
- What is **Professor Kim's office number**? I have something to discuss with her.
  김 교수의 사무실 번호

가사 예문

City of stars, Are you shining just for me?
별들의 도시여, 오직 나를 위해서 빛나는 건가요?

To look in somebody's eyes
누군가의 눈을 들여다본다는 것은

Attention!

~s로 끝나는 복수명사일 경우에는 소유격을 표현할 때 ~'만 쓸 것!

- I visit my **parents' house** every Sunday. (parents's house → X)
- You can put your gym suits in the **students' lockers**. (students's lockers → X)

Q1 다음 밑줄 친 부분의 쓰임이 나머지 넷과 다른 것은?

① Some of my sister's toys are missing.

② Daniel's my daughter's neighborhood.

③ Do you know Mr. Brown's e-mail address?

④ My family went to Lisa's wedding last Sunday.

⑤ There are many artists' paintings in this museum.

Q2 다음 주어진 우리말과 의미가 같도록 빈칸에 알맞은 말을 쓰시오.

1. 이 공기청청기의 가격 얼마인가요? (공기청정기 : air purifier)

→ What's the ______________________?

2. 헨리의 친한 친구는 기안과 시언이야.

→ ______________________ are Gian and Sieun.

3. 너 그 베트남 음식의 이름을 기억하니? (베트남의 : Vietnamese)

→ Do you remember the ______________________?

4. 나의 가족은 조부모님의 정원에서 바비큐파티를 했어.

→ My family had a barbecue party at my ______________________.

Fill in the Blank ① City of stars ② smokescreen of the crowded restaurants ③ somebody's eyes ④ rat-a-tat of my heart

Question 1 ②

Question 2 **1.** price of this air purifier **2.** Henry's close friends **3.** name of the Vietnamese food **4.** grandparents' garden

7	You are the sunshine of my life	Stevie Wonder & Lisa Ono

★ ①(　　)(　　) the sunshine of my life
That's why I'll always be around
①(　　)(　　) the apple of my eye
Forever you'll stay in my heart

당신은 내 인생의 햇살
그게 바로 내가 언제나 당신 곁에 머무는 이유죠
당신은 눈에 넣어도 아프지 않을 소중한 사람
영원히 당신은 내 마음속에 머물 거예요

- **The apple of my eye** : (비유적 표현) 그 어떤 다른 것들보다도 소중한 것
- **Forever** : 영원히

I feel like ②(　　)(　) the beginning
Though I've loved you for a million years
And if I thought ③(　　)(　　)(　　) ending
I'd find myself drowning in my own tears

난 바로 지금이 우리의 시작처럼 느껴져요
수많은 시간 동안 당신을 사랑해왔지만 말이에요
그리고 만약 우리 사랑이 끝났다고 생각되면
난 눈물 속에 빠져 있을 거예요

- **feel like~** : ~처럼 느끼다
- **Though** : 비록 ~하지만
- **I've loved** : 사랑해왔다(현재완료로서 과거부터 지금까지)
- **drown** : 빠뜨리다

①(　　)(　　) the sunshine of my life
That's why I'll always stay around
①(　　)(　　) the apple of my eye
Forever you'll stay in my heart

당신은 내 인생의 햇살
그게 바로 내가 언제나 당신 곁에 머무는 이유죠
당신은 눈에 넣어도 아프지 않을 소중한 사람
영원히 당신은 내 마음속에 머물 거예요

- **That's why~** : 그것이 ~ 이유이다
- **stay** : 머무르다

You must have known that ④(　)(　　) lonely
Because you came to my rescue
And I know that this must be heaven
How could so much love be inside of you?

내가 외로웠다는 걸 당신은 알았겠죠
당신은 나에게로 다가와 날 구원해주었는 걸요
그리고 난 이게 바로 천국일 거라고 생각해요
당신은 어쩜 그렇게도 많은 사랑을 담고 있나요?

- **must have known** : 알았음에 틀림없다
- **lonely** : 외로운
- **rescue** : 구조
- **must be~** : ~임에 틀림없다

①(　　)(　　) the sunshine of my life, yeah
That's why I'll always stay around
①(　　)(　　) the apple of my eye
Forever you'll stay in my heart

당신은 내 인생의 햇살
그게 바로 내가 언제나 당신 곁에 머무는 이유죠
당신은 눈에 넣어도 아프지 않을 소중한 사람
영원히 당신은 내 마음속에 머물 거예요

★ Repeat

7 be동사

be동사란

- be동사는 '~이다', '~있다'라는 뜻이고, 현재형은 주어의 인칭과 수에 따라 am, are, is로 변한다.
- am, are, is의 과거형은 각각 was, were, was이다.

be동사의 형태

	현재형				과거형	
	단수	축약형	복수	축약형	단수	복수
1인칭	**I am** (나는 ~이다)	**I'm**	**We are** (우리는 ~이다)	**We're**	**I was** (나는 ~이었다)	**We were** (우리는 ~이었다)
2인칭	**You are** (너는 ~이다)	**You're**	**You are** (너희들은 ~이다)	**You're**	**You were** (너는 ~이었다)	**You were** (너희들은 ~이었다)
3인칭	**He is** (그는 ~이다)	**He's**	**They are** (그들은 ~이다/ 그것들은 ~이다)	**They're**	**He was** (그는 ~이었다)	**They were** (그들은 ~이었다/ 그것들은 ~이었다)
	She is (그녀는 ~이다)	**She's**			**She was** (그녀는 ~이었다)	
	It is (그것은 ~이다)	**It's**			**It was** (그것은 ~이었다)	

가사 예문

You are the sunshine of my life. That's why I'll always be around.
당신은 내 인생의 햇살. 그게 바로 내가 언제나 당신 곁에 머무는 이유죠.

You are the apple of my eye. Forever you'll stay in my heart.
당신은 눈에 넣어도 아프지 않을 소중한 사람. 영원히 당신은 내 마음속에 머물 거예요.

Q1 다음 빈칸에 be동사를 알맞은 형태로 쓰시오.

1. We ______ Koreans.
2. The book ______ under the table.
3. Eric and Jen ______ my classmates.
4. I took my umbrella this morning because it ______ raining outside.
5. The weather is nice today, but it ______ very cold and windy yesterday.
6. He ______ my English teacher when I was an elementary school student.

Q2 다음 밑줄 친 부분을 줄여 쓰시오.

1. <u>We are</u> very busy now. → ______________
2. <u>They are</u> in the library. → ______________
3. <u>She is</u> so pretty and kind. → ______________
4. <u>You are</u> the sunshine of my life. → ______________
5. <u>It is</u> my mistake. It is not your fault. → ______________
6. <u>He is</u> very popular among South-East Asians. → ______________

Q3 다음 문장에서 <u>틀린</u> be동사의 형태를 찾아 바르게 고치시오.

1. My mom were sick last Sunday. __________ → __________
2. They was in the classroom an hour ago. __________ → __________
3. The song Gangnam Style is popular in 2012. __________ → __________
4. All the windows is open. Can you shut them? __________ → __________
5. The sweater are on sale for half price. I should buy it. __________ → __________

Fill in the Blank ① You are ② This is ③ our love was ④ I was

Question 1 **1.** are(또는 were) **2.** is(또는 was) **3.** are(또는 were) **4.** was **5.** was **6.** was

Question 2 **1.** We're **2.** They're **3.** She's **4.** You're **5.** It's **6.** He's

Question 3 **1.** were → was **2.** was → were **3.** is → was **4.** is → are **5.** are → is

8 You are not alone — Michael Jackson

Another day has gone I'm still all alone
How could this be
You'①(   )(   )(   ) with me
You never said goodbye
Someone tell me why
Did you have to go and leave my world so cold

또 하루가 지나고 난 여전히 혼자예요
어떻게 된 거죠
그대가 여기 내 곁에 없다니
당신은 내게 잘 있으란 말도 하지 않았죠
왜 그랬는지 누군가 내게 알려주세요
떠나야만 했나요 차갑게 날 떠나야만 했나요

- **has gone** : 가버리다
- **alone** : 혼자의
- **have to~** : ~해야 한다
- **leave** : 떠나다

☆ Everyday I sit ask myself
How did love slip away
Something whispers in my ear and says

매일 난 앉아서 나에게 묻죠
어떻게 사랑이 그렇게 조용히 가버릴 수 있는지를
무언가 내 귀에 대고 속삭여요

- **slip away** : 슬그머니 떠나다
- **whisper** : 속삭이다

★ You ②(   )(   )(   ) but I am here with you
Though you're far away I am here to stay
But you ②(   )(   )(   ) I am here with you
Though we're far apart
You're always in my heart but you ②(   )(   )(   )

당신은 혼자가 아니예요 내가 여기에 당신과 함께 있으니
비록 당신은 멀리 있지만 내가 여기에 머물러 있으니
당신은 혼자가 아니예요 내가 여기 당신과 함께 있잖아요
비록 우리가 멀리 떨어져 있지만
당신은 항상 내 맘속에 있으니 당신은 혼자가 아니예요

- **far** : 멀리
- **apart** : 떨어져서

Just the other night I thought
I heard you cry
Asking me to come and hold you
in my arms
I can hear your prayers
Your burdens I will bear
But first I need your hand
Then forever can begin

어느 날 밤이었어요 당신의 울음소리를
들은 것 같았죠
와서 당신을 안아달라고 부탁하는 듯한
난 당신의 기도를 들을 수 있고
당신의 짐을 내가 지겠어요
하지만 우선 당신의 손을 잡고 싶어요
그러면 영원은 시작될 거예요

- **hold :** 안다
- **prayer :** 기도
- **burden :** 짐
- **bear :** 견디다

☆ Repeat

★ Repeat

Whisper three words and
I'll come running, darling
And girl, you know that I'll be there
I'll be there

세 마디만 속삭여주세요 그럼 내가
달려갈게요
그대여, 당신은 내가 그대 곁에 갈 거라는
것을 알고 있죠
내가 그대 곁에 있을 거예요

★ Repeat × 2

8 be동사 부정문

be동사의 부정문이란

- be동사의 부정문은 「be동사(am, are, is) + not~」의 형태이며, '~가 아니다'라는 의미이다.

주어	be동사+not	축약형	
I	am not	I'm not	—
You	are not	You're not	You aren't
He / She / It	is not	He's not / She's not / It's not	He isn't / She isn't / It isn't
We / They	are not	We're not / They're not	We aren't / They aren't

가사 예문

You are not alone, but I am here with you.
당신은 혼자가 아니에요, 내가 여기에 당신과 함께 있으니.

Q1 다음 밑줄 친 부분을 줄여 쓰시오.

1. I am not excited. → ____________________
2. You are not alone. → ____________________
3. They are not my classmates. → ____________________
4. We are not from London. → ____________________
5. He is not busy on weekend. → ____________________

Q2 다음 문장을 부정문으로 바꿔 쓰시오.

1. I am thirsty. → ____________________
2. You are tall. → ____________________
3. It is open on Sundays. → ____________________
4. She is in the hospital. → ____________________
5. They are basketball players. → ____________________

Q3 다음 빈칸에 aren't 가 들어갈 수 없는 것은?

① My English teacher ______ very kind.

② We ______ Facebook friends each other.

③ My brother and I ______ late for school.

④ The clothes on the wall ______ expensive.

⑤ Bob and Mark ______ working at the same company.

Fill in the Blank ① re not here ② are not alone

Question 1 **1.** I'm not **2.** You're not / You aren't **3.** They're not / They aren't
4. We're not / We aren't **5.** He's not / He isn't

Question 2 **1.** I am not thirsty. / I'm not thirsty. **2.** You are not tall. / You aren't tall.
3. It is not open on Sundays. / It isn't open on Sundays.
4. She is not in the hospital. / She isn't in the hospital.
5. They are not basketball players. / They aren't basketball players.

Question 3 ①

9	Marry you	Bruno Mars

☆ It's a beautiful night
We're looking for something dumb to do
Hey baby, I think I wanna marry you
(　)(　) the look in your eyes?
or (　)(　) this dancing juice?
Who cares, baby, I think I wanna marry you

아름다운 밤이에요
우린 뭔가 바보 같은 짓을 하려고 찾고 있죠
내 사랑, 나 당신과 결혼하고 싶나 봐요
당신의 눈빛 때문일까요?
아니면 이 술 때문일까요?
누가 신경 쓰겠어요(무슨 상관이에요),
내 사랑, 나 당신과 결혼하고 싶은가 봐요

- **look for ~** : ~을 찾다
- **dumb** : 멍청한
- **wanna** = **want to**
- **look** : ① 보다 ② 보이다 ③ 외모, 매력

Well, I know this little chapel on the boulevard we can go
No one will know
Oh, come on, girl
Who cares if we're trashed
Got a pocket full of cash we can blow
Shots of Patron and it's on, girl

저 큰길에 우리가 갈 수 있는 조그만
예배당을 알아요
아무도 모를 거예요
어서 대답해줘요
우리가 흠뻑 취한대도 상관할 사람 없어요
날려버릴 수 있는 돈이 주머니에
가득하니까요
비싼 데킬라 몇 잔과 함께 이제 시작이에요

- **chapel** : 예배당
- **boulevard** : 대로
- **trashed** : (속어) 술에 취한
- **Patron** : 데킬라 브랜드

★ Don't say no, no, no, no-no
Just say yeah, yeah, yeah, yeah-yeah
And we'll go, go, go, go-go
If you're ready, like I'm ready

안 된다고 하지 말아요
그냥 예라고 말하세요
그러면 우린 떠날 거예요
당신이 나처럼 준비가 되었다면요

Cause ☆ Repeat

I'll go get a ring
Let the choir bells sing like oooh
So what you wanna do?
Let's just run, girl
If we wake up and you wanna break up,
that's cool
No, I won't blame you
It was fun, girl

가서 반지 하나 사올게요
성가대 종이 오~ 하며 노래하게 만들어요
자, 당신은 뭘 하고 싶어요?
그냥 같이 달아나요
우리가 잠에서 깨어 당신이 헤어지길
원한다면, 괜찮아요
아니요, 당신을 비난하지 않을게요
즐거웠으니까요, 그대여

- **choir :** 성가대
- **break up :** 헤어지다
- **blame :** 비난하다

★ Repeat

☆ Repeat

⁂ Just say I do
Tell me right now, baby
Tell me right now, baby, baby

그저 그러겠다고 말해줘요
지금 당장 말해줘요, 내 사랑
지금 당장 말해줘요, 내 사랑

⁂ Repeat

☆ Repeat

9 be동사 의문문

be동사의 의문문이란

- be동사의 의문문은 평서문의 주어와 be동사의 위치를 바꾼다.
- 「be동사 + 주어~?」의 형태이며, '~이니?'라는 의미를 가진다.

- 평서문: **You are** an English teacher. 당신은 영어 선생님이다.
- 의문문: **Are you** an English teacher? 당신은 영어 선생님인가요?

be동사 의문문에 대한 응답

- be동사의 의문문에 대한 대답은 긍정이면 「Yes, 주어 + be동사」, 부정이면 「No, 주어 + be동사 + not」으로 쓴다.

- A: Are you hungry now? B: Yes, I am. / No, I'm not.
- A: Is he absent from school today? B: Yes, he is. / No, he isn't.
- A: Are they excited about the news? B: Yes, they are. / No, they aren't.

가사 예문

Is it the look in your eyes? or, is it this dancing juice?

당신의 눈빛 때문일까요? 아니면 이 술 때문일까요?

Attention!

be동사 의문문		의문사가 있는 의문문
Are you happy?	vs	**Why** are you happy?
(be동사가 맨 앞으로)		(의문사가 맨 앞으로)

Q1 다음 문장을 의문문으로 바꿔 쓰시오.

1. You are sick. → ____________________
2. This is so exciting. → ____________________
3. They are from Australia. → ____________________
4. The story is interesting. → ____________________

Q2 다음 의문문에 대한 적절한 대답을 쓰시오.

1. Is it expensive? → Yes, ______ ______. / No, ______ ______.
2. Is he good at dancing? → Yes, ______ ______. / No, ______ ______.
3. Are you happy with your life? → Yes, ______ ______. / No, ______ ______.

Q3 다음 우리말과 의미가 같도록 괄호 안의 말을 이용해 질문을 만들고, 적절한 대답을 쓰시오.

1. 미국 드라마는 한국에서 인기가 있니? (American drama / popular)

→ A: ____________________?

B: Yes, ______ ______. / No, ______ ______.

2. 너 이번 주말 바쁘니? (busy / weekend)

→ A: ____________________?

B: Yes, ______ ______. / No, ______ ______.

3. 그녀는 개를 무서워하니? (afraid / dogs)

→ A: ____________________?

B: Yes, ______ ______. / No, ______ ______.

Fill in the Blank Is(is) it

Question 1 **1.** Are you sick? **2.** Is this so exciting? **3.** Are they from Australia?
4. Is the story interesting?

Question 2 **1.** it is / it isn't **2.** he is / he isn't **3.** I am / I'm not

Question 3 **1.** Is American drama popular in Korea? / it is / it isn't
2. Are you busy this weekend? / I am / I'm not
3. Is she afraid of dogs? / she is / she isn't

10 I have a dream — ABBA

☆ I ①(　　　) a dream, a song to sing
To ②(　　　) me cope with anything
If you ③(　　) the wonder of a fairy tale
You can ④(　　　) the future even if you ⑤(　　　)

나에겐 꿈이 있어요, 부를 노래가 있어요
어떤 일이든 극복할 수 있게 도와주죠
만일 당신이 신비로운 요정들의 이야기를 이해한다면
비록 실패한다 하더라도 당신에겐 미래가 있어요

- **cope with :** ~에 대처하다, ~을 극복하다
- **see :** ① 보다 ② 이해하다 ③ 확인하다
- **wonder :** ① 궁금해 하다 ② 경이로움
- **fairy tale :** 동화
- **even if ~ :** 비록 ~일지라도

★ I ⑥(　　　　) in angels
Something good in everything I ③(　　)
I ⑥(　　　　) in angels
When I ⑦(　　　) the time is right for me
I'll ⑧(　　　) the stream
I ①(　　　) a dream

난 천사들을 믿어요
난 보이는 모든 것들 속에 좋은 점만 보아요
난 천사들을 믿어요
그리고 언젠가 날 위한 그 시간이 오면
난 시냇물을 건널 거예요(기회를 잡을 거예요)
나에겐 꿈이 있어요

- **believe in ~ :** ~를 믿다
- **The time is right for ~ :** ~에게 적당한 때가 오면

I ①(　　　) a dream, a fantasy
To ②(　　　) me through reality
And my destination ⑨(　　　　) it worthwhile
Pushing through the darkness still another mile

나에겐 꿈이 있어요, 환상이 있어요
현실을 헤쳐 나갈 수 있게 도와주죠
그리고 나의 목표는 나의 꿈을 가치 있는 것으로 만들어줘요
아직도 남아있는 어둠을 헤치며 나아가도록

- **destination :** 목적지
- **make it worthwhile :** ~을 가치 있는 일로 만들다
- **push through ~ :** ~을 헤치며 나아가다

★ Repeat

※ I'll ⑧(   ) the stream
I ①(   ) a dream

난 시냇물을 건널 거예요(기회를 잡을 거예요)
나에겐 꿈이 있어요

☆ Repeat

★ Repeat

※ Repeat

10 일반동사

일반동사란

- be동사와 조동사를 제외한 주어의 동작이나 상태를 나타내는 모든 동사를 말한다.
- go, come, do, like, love, swim, play, read, study, teach, learn, make 등이 일반동사에 속한다.

일반동사의 형태변화

- 주어가 3인칭 단수가 아닌 경우에는 단수와 복수에 관계없이 동사원형을 쓴다.

- They **speak** English very well.
- I **go** to the library every Saturday.
- You **read** the newspaper after breakfast.

- 주어가 3인칭 단수일 경우에는 형태를 변화시킨다.

- The man **speaks** English very well.
- She **goes** to the library every Saturday.
- He **reads** the newspaper after breakfast.

- 주어가 3인칭 단수일 때 일반동사의 변화

대부분의 동사	동사원형 + -s	comes, plays, needs, drinks, runs, starts, gives, gets
-o, -s, -x, -sh, -ch로 끝나는 동사	동사원형 + -es	goes, passes, fixes, mixes, washes, teaches, watches
자음 + y로 끝나는 동사	y를 i로 바꾸고 + -es	studies, flies, marries, cries, carries, tries, applies, worries
have	has	

가사 예문

I have a dream, a song to sing.

나에겐 꿈이 있어요, 부를 노래가 있어요.

And my destination makes it worthwhile.

그리고 나의 목표는 나의 꿈을 가치 있는 것으로 만들어 줘요.

Q1 다음 괄호 안에서 알맞은 것을 고르시오.

1. He (get / gets) up at 6 o'clock.
2. Jisung (play / plays) soccer very well.
3. Jim and Bob (go / goes) to school by bike.
4. It (start / starts) at 10 o'clock in the morning.
5. We (visit / visits) our grandparents once a month.

Q2 다음 우리말과 의미가 같도록 빈칸에 알맞은 말을 쓰시오.

1. 김 선생님은 우리에게 과학을 가르치신다. → Ms. Kim ________ us science.
2. 그녀는 언니 한 명과 오빠 한 명이 있다. → She ________ one sister and one brother.
3. 나는 공상과학 소설을 아주 좋아한다. → I ________ science fiction novel very much.
4. 아버지는 식사 후에 커피를 마신다.
→ My father ________ a cup of coffee after meals.
5. 르네는 기타를 치고, 그녀의 아이들은 노래를 한다.
→ Renee ________ the guitar, and her children ________ songs.

Fill in the Blank ① have ② help ③ see ④ take ⑤ fail ⑥ believe ⑦ know ⑧ cross ⑨ makes

Question 1 **1.** gets **2.** plays **3.** go **4.** starts **5.** visit

Question 2 **1.** teaches **2.** has **3.** like **4.** drinks **5.** plays, sing

11 Tie the yellow ribbon round the old oak tree | Tony Orlando & Dawn

I'm coming home
I've done my time
Now I've got to know what is and isn't mine
If you received my letter telling you I'd soon be free
Then you'll know just what to do
If you still want me
If you still want me

난 집으로 가고 있답니다
형기를 다 마치고
이젠 무엇이 내 것이고 무엇이 아닌지를 알아야 하겠죠
곧 풀려날 거라고 쓴 내 편지를 당신이 받았다면
당신이 어떻게 해야 할지 알 거예요
아직도 당신이 날 원한다면
아직도 당신이 날 원한다면

- **have got to :** ~을 해야 한다
- **receive :** 받다

★ Oh, tie a yellow ribbon round the old oak tree
It's been three long years
Do you still want me?
If I (　　) (　　) a ribbon round the old oak tree
I'll stay on the bus
forget about us
Put the blame on me
If I (　　) (　　) a yellow ribbon round the old oak tree...

오, 오래된 떡갈나무에 노란색 리본을 달아주세요
3년이란 긴 세월이 흘렀죠
당신은 아직도 날 원하나요?
만약 내가 오래된 떡갈나무 주위에 리본을 볼 수 없다면
난 버스에서 내리지 않을 거예요
그리고 서로를 잊기로 해요
모든 잘못은 내게 있으니까요
만약 내가 오래된 떡갈나무 주위에 노란색 리본을 볼 수 없다면…

- **round :** ① 둥근 ② ~ 주위에
- **oak tree :** 떡갈나무
- **It's been** = **It has been**
- **put the blame on :** ~에게 책임을 지우다

Bus driver, please look for me
'Cause I couldn't bear to see
what I might see
I'm really still in prison
And my love, she holds the key
A simple yellow ribbon's what I need to set me free
I wrote and told her, please...

버스 기사 아저씨, 내 대신 좀 봐 줄래요
차마 그걸 내 눈으로 볼 수가 없네요
나는 아직도 감옥에 있는 거나 마찬가지예요
내 사랑, 그녀가 열쇠를 쥐고 있지요
내가 자유로워지기 위해 필요한 건 단지 노란 리본이랍니다
나는 편지를 써서 그녀에게 말했었죠
제발…

- **bear** : 견디다
- **what** : (관계대명사로) ~것
- **prison** : 감옥
- **set free** : 자유롭게 하다

★ Repeat

Now the whole damn bus is cheering
And I can't believe I see
A hundred yellow ribbons round the old oak tree
I'm coming home

지금 버스 안이 온통 난리예요
내가 보고 있는 걸 믿을 수가 없네요
오래된 떡갈나무에 걸려 있는 수많은 노란 리본들
난 지금 집으로 가고 있답니다

- **damn** : 제기랄(감탄사)
- **cheer** : 응원하다

11 일반동사 부정문

일반동사 부정문이란

- 일반동사 부정문은 주어에 따라 동사원형 앞에 don't(do not) 또는 doesn't(dose not)를 써서 만든다.

주어	부정문	예문
3인칭 단수가 아님 (I/You/We/They)	주어 + don't(do not) + 동사원형~.	I **don't** like coffee.
3인칭 단수 (He/She/It)	주어 + doesn't(does not) + 동사원형~.	He **doesn't** like coffee.

가사 예문

If I don't see a ribbon around the old oak tree, I'll stay on the bus.
만약 내가 오래된 떡갈나무 주위에 리본을 볼 수 없다면, 난 버스에서 내리지 않을 거예요.

Attention!

일반동사 과거형의 부정문은 **did not(didn't)**으로!

일반동사 과거형의 부정문은 주어와 상관없이 「did not(didn't) + 동사원형」 형태이다.

He went to the party. → **He did not(didn't)** go to the party.

Q1 다음 괄호 안에서 알맞은 것을 고르시오.

1. He (don't / doesn't) eat fast food.
2. I was tired, but I (don't / doesn't / didn't) sleep well last night.
3. Jenny and Jacob (don't / doesn't) like to listen to the loud music.
4. Korean students (don't / doesn't) use their cell phones in the classroom.

Q2 다음 우리말과 의미가 같도록 괄호 안의 말을 이용하여 문장을 완성하시오.

1. 그들은 학교에서 교복을 입지 않는다. (wear / school uniforms / at school)

→ ______________________________

2. 그 비행기는 정시에 도착하지 않았다. (arrive / on time)

→ ______________________________

3. Zara는 오늘 아침 그녀의 개를 산책시키지 않았다. (walk her dog / this morning)

→ ______________________________

4. 그는 식사 후 디저트 먹는 것을 좋아하지 않는다. (eat dessert / after meals)

→ ______________________________

Q3 다음 문장을 부정문으로 바꿔 쓰시오.

1. They want to try new things. → ______________
2. Yumi helps her mom do the laundry. → ______________
3. The dog protected her master from a danger. → ______________
4. We share our ideas to make a better choice. → ______________

Fill in the Blank don't see

Question 1 **1.** doesn't **2.** didn't **3.** don't **4.** don't

Question 2 **1.** They do not (don't) wear school uniforms at school. **2.** The airplane did not (didn't) arrive on time. **3.** Zara did not (didn't) walk her dog this morning. **4.** He does not (doesn't) like to eat dessert after meals.

Question 3 **1.** They do not (don't) want to try new things. **2.** Yumi does not (doesn't) help her mom do the laundry. **3.** The dog did not (didn't) protect her master from a danger. **4.** We do not (don't) share our ideas to make a better choice.

12 I remember — Mocca

I remember the way you glanced at me
Yes, I remember
I remember when we caught a shooting star
Yes, I remember

나는 당신이 날 힐끗 보았던 것을 기억해요
그래요, 난 기억해요
나는 우리가 유성을 잡았을 때를 기억해요
그래요, 난 기억해요

- **the way~ :** ~하는 방식
- **glance at~ :** ~를 힐끗 보다
- **shooting star :** 유성

★ I remember all the things that we shared,
and the promise we made just you and I
I remember all the laughter we shared,
all the wishes we made upon the roof at dawn

나는 우리가 함께 나눈 모든 것을 기억해요,
그리고 당신과 나 우리 둘이 만들었던 그 약속도
나는 우리 함께 나눈 모든 미소를 기억해요,
새벽에 지붕 위에서 빌었던 모든 소원들도

- **promise :** 약속
- **laughter :** 웃음
- **make wishes :** 소원을 빌다
- **at dawn :** 새벽에

( )( )( ) when we were dancing in the rain in that December?
And I remember when my father thought you were a burglar

당신은 그해 12월에 우리가 빗속에서 함께 춤추던 때를 기억하나요?
그리고 나의 아버지가 당신을 도둑으로 오해했던 일도 난 기억해요

- **burglar :** 도둑

★ Repeat

Yes, ★ Repeat

I remember the way you read your books
Yes, I remember the way you tied your shoes
Yes, I remember the cake you loved the most
Yes, I remember the way you drank your coffee
I remember the way you glanced at me
Yes, I remember when we caught a shooting star
Yes, I remember when we were dancing in the rain in that december and the way you smile at me
Yes, I remember

나는 당신이 책을 읽어주던 것을 기억해요
그래요, 나는 당신이 신발 끈을 묶던 것도 기억해요
그래요, 나는 당신이 가장 좋아하던 케이크도 기억해요
그래요, 나는 당신이 커피 마시던 모습도 기억해요
나는 당신이 날 힐끗 보던 모습도 기억해요
그래요, 나는 우리가 유성을 잡았던 때를 기억해요
그래요, 나는 그해 12월 우리가 빗속에서 함께 춤추며 당신이 내게 웃음 지어주던 그 모습도 기억해요
그래요, 나는 기억해요

12 일반동사 의문문

일반동사의 의문문이란

- 일반동사 의문문은 주어에 따라 문장 맨 앞에 Do 또는 Does를 붙여 만든다.

주어	의문문	긍정의 대답	부정의 대답
3인칭 단수가 아님 (I/You/We/They)	Do + 주어 + 동사원형~ ?	Yes, 주어 + do.	No, 주어 + don't.
3인칭 단수 (He/She/It)	Does + 주어 + 동사원형~ ?	Yes, 주어 + does.	No, 주어 + doesn't.

- A: **Do** you eat breakfast every morning? B: Yes, I do. / No, I don't.
- A: **Does** she eat breakfast every morning? B: Yes, she does. / No, she doesn't.

가사 예문

Do you remember when we were dancing in the rain in that December?

당신은 그해 12월에 우리가 빗속에서 함께 춤추던 때를 기억하나요?

Attention!

일반동사 과거형의 의문문은 Did로 시작!

일반동사 과거형 의문문은 「Did + 주어 + 동사원형~ ?」의 형태이며, Did 뒤에는 동사원형을 취한다.

- **Did you go** to the party yesterday? (O)
- Did you went to the party yesterday? (X) (went → go)

Q1 다음 괄호 안에서 알맞은 것을 고르시오.

1. (Do / Does / Did) you usually go to work by subway?
2. (Do / Does / Did) you send an email to your boss this morning?
3. (Do / Does / Did) Amanda take a yoga lesson every Friday?

Q2 다음 문장을 의문문으로 바꿔 쓰시오.

1. She lives in Busan. → ______________________
2. You keep a diary everyday. → ______________________
3. Josh and David graduate this year. → ______________________
4. Your sister helped with your homework. → ______________________
5. Chris grows an apple tree in his garden. → ______________________

Q3 다음 우리말과 의미가 같도록 괄호 안의 말을 이용하여 문장을 완성하시오.

1. 너의 팀은 금메달을 땄니? (win / the gold medal) → ______________________
2. 너는 어제 콘서트에 갔었니? (go / to the concert) → ______________________
3. 너는 저 문제 이해하니? (understand / that question)

→ ____

4. 그 식당은 일요일에 여니? (open / on Sunday)

→ ____

5. 그녀는 매일 공원에서 산책하니? (take a walk / in the park)

→ ____

Fill in the Blank Do you remember

Question 1 **1.** Do **2.** Did **3.** Does

Question 2 **1.** Does she live in Busan? **2.** Do you keep a diary everyday?
3. Do Josh and David graduate this year? **4.** Did your sister help with your homework?
5. Does Chris grow an apple tree in his garden?

Question 3 **1.** Did your team win the gold medal? **2.** Did you go to the concert yesterday?
3. Do you understand that question? **4.** Does the restaurant open on Sunday?
5. Does she take a walk in the park everyday?

13 Close to you

Carpenters

①(   )(   )(   ) suddenly (   )
every time you are near?
Just like me, they long to be close
to you
②(   )(   )(   )(   ) down from
the sky every time you walk by?
Just like me, they long to be close
to you

당신이 가까이 있을 때면 왜 매번 새들이
갑자기 나타날까요?
바로 나처럼, 그들도 당신 곁에 머물고
싶은가 봐요
당신이 걸어 지나갈 때면 왜 매번 별들이
하늘에서 쏟아질까요?
바로 나처럼, 그들도 당신 곁에 머물고
싶은가 봐요

- **suddenly** : 갑자기
- **appear** : 나타나다
- **every time** : 매번
- **like~** : ~처럼
- **walk by** : 걸어 지나가다
- **long to~** : ~를 간절히 바라다

☆ On the day that you were born
the angels got together
and decided to create a dream come
true
So they sprinkled moon dust in your
hair of gold
and starlight in your eyes of blue

당신이 태어나던 날
천사들이 모여서
꿈을 실현시키고자 결정했죠
그래서 천사들은 달빛을 당신 금발에
그리고 별빛을 당신의 푸른 눈에 뿌렸죠

- **decide** : 결정하다
- **get together** : 모이다
- **come true** : (꿈이) 실현되다
- **sprinkle** : 흩뿌리다
- **starlight** : 별빛

★ That is why all the girls in town
follow you all around
Just like me, they long to be
close to you

그래서 동네 모든 소녀들이 당신 곁을
맴도는가 봐요
바로 나처럼, 그들도 당신 곁에 머물고
싶은가 봐요

☆ Repeat

★ Repeat

Just like me, they long to be close to
you
Wa, close to you
Wa, close to you
Ha, close to you
La, close to you

바로 나처럼, 그들도 당신 곁에 머물고
싶은가 봐요
당신 가까이
당신 가까이
당신 가까이
당신 가까이

13 의문사가 있는 의문문

의문사가 있는 의문문이란

- 의문사는 who(누구), what(무엇), which(어느), when(언제), where(어디), how(어떻게), why(왜)를 말하며, 특정한 정보를 묻기 위해 사용된다.

- 의문사가 있는 의문문의 경우, 의문사를 문장의 가장 앞에 위치시킨다.

- **What** is your name?
- **How** do you go to school?
- **When** is your birthday?

가사 예문

Why do birds suddenly appear every time you are near?
당신이 가까이 있을 때면 왜 매번 새들이 갑자기 나타날까요?

Why do stars fall down from the sky every time you walk by?
당신이 걸어 지나갈 때면 왜 매번 별들이 하늘에서 쏟아질까요?

Q1 다음 문장의 빈칸에 들어갈 알맞은 의문사를 쓰시오.

1. A: ________ is my bag? B: It's under the table.
2. A: ________ is that gentleman? B: He's my boss.
3. A: ________ were you late for school? B: Because I missed the bus.
4. A: ________ was your trip? B: It was wonderful.
5. A: ________ do you leave for US? B: I'll leave on June 10th.
6. A: ________ did you do during the vacation? B: I traveled Europe.

Q2 다음 대화의 빈칸에 알맞은 말을 쓰시오.

1. 왜 너는 그렇게 행복해하니? → ________ are you so ________?
2. 언제 영화가 시작하니? → ________ does the movie ________?
3. 어디서 너는 열쇠를 찾았니? → ________ did you ________ your key?
4. 어떤 계절을 너는 가장 좋아하니? → ________ season do you ________ most?
5. 너는 여가시간에 무엇을 하니? → ________ do you ________ in your free time?

Q3 우리말과 같은 뜻이 되도록 주어진 표현을 이용하여 문장을 완성하시오.

1. 그녀는 어디에 사니? (live) → ____________________
2. 제주의 날씨는 어떤가요? (weather / in Jeju) → ____________________
3. 너는 어젯밤에 어디에 갔었니? (go / last night) → ____________________
4. 네가 가장 좋아하는 가수는 누구니? (favorite singer) → ____________________
5. 당신의 휴대폰 번호는 무엇인가요? (cell phone number) → ____________________

Fill in the Blank ① Why do birds, appear ② Why do stars fall

Question 1 **1.** Where **2.** Who **3.** Why **4.** How **5.** When **6.** What

Question 2 **1.** Why, happy **2.** When, start **3.** Where, find **4.** Which, like **5.** What, do

Question 3 **1.** Where does she live? **2.** How is the weather in Jeju? **3.** Where did you go last night? **4.** Who is your favorite singer? **5.** What is your cell phone number?

14	Beautiful Sunday	Daniel Boone

Sunday morning up with the lark
I think I'll take a walk in the park
Hey hey hey, (   )'( ) a (   )(   )

일요일 아침에 종달새와 같이 일찍
일어나서
공원을 산책하려고 해요
이봐요, 정말 아름다운 날이에요

• lark : 종달새

I've got someone waiting for me
And when I see her I know that she'll say
Hey hey hey, (   )'( ) a (   )(   )

나를 기다리는 사람이 있어요
그녀는 나를 보고 이렇게 말을 할 거예요
이봐요, 정말 아름다운 날이에요

• wait for : ~를 기다리다

★ Hi hi hi, beautiful Sunday
This is my my my beautiful day
When you said said said said that you loved me
Oh, my my my (   )'( ) a (   )
(   )

안녕, 아름다운 일요일이에요
오늘은 나의 아름다운 날이에요
당신이 나를 사랑한다고 말했던
오, 나의 아름다운 날이에요

• say(말하다)-said-said

Birds are singing, you by my side
Let's take a car and go for a ride
Hey hey hey, (   )'( ) a (   )(   )

새들도 노래하고, 당신은 내 곁에 있어요
차를 타고 함께 드라이브 가요
이봐요, 정말 아름다운 날이에요

- **side : ~곁**
- **take a car : 차를 타다**
- **go for a ride : 드라이브 가다**

We'll drive on and follow the sun
Making Sunday go on and on
Hey hey hey (   )'( ) a (   )(   )

우리는 드라이브를 하면서 태양을 따라갈 거에요
계속해서 멋진 일요일을 만들 거에요
이봐요, 정말 아름다운 날이에요

- **follow : 따르다**
- **We'll = We will**

★ Repeat × 2

14 비인칭 주어 it

비인칭 주어 it이란

- 날짜, 시간, 계절, 날씨, 요일, 거리, 명암 등을 나타낼 때 비인칭 주어 it을 쓴다.
- 이때, it은 '그것'이라고 해석하지 않는다.

비인칭 주어 it의 쓰임

날짜	**It**'s August 10th. **It**'s my birthday today.
시간	**It**'s already 11 o'clock but he didn't come home yet.
계절	I love the spring - **it**'s a wonderful time of the year.
날씨	Is **it** still raining outside?
요일	Thanks God, **It**'s Friday.
거리	**It**'s about 400 kilometers from Busan to Seoul.
명암	**It** gets dark very early in winter time.

가사 예문

Hey hey hey, it's a beautiful day.
이봐요, 정말 아름다운 날이에요.

Attention!

'그것'이라는 대명사 it과 비인칭 주어 it의 쓰임을 구분할 것!

A: How about this yellow skirt?
B: **It** looks good. I'll take **it**.
→ 대명사 (그것)

A: How long does **it** take to get to the airport?
B: **It** takes about 30 minutes by taxi.
→ 비인칭 주어 ('그것'이라고 해석하지 않음)

Q1 다음 it의 쓰임이 나머지 넷과 다른 것은?

① It's 11:30 a.m.

② It's spring now.

③ It is a nice present.

④ It was wonderful day.

⑤ It is becoming dark outside.

Q2 다음 우리말과 뜻이 같도록 빈칸에 알맞은 말을 쓰시오.

1. 아침 8시이다. → ______ ______ ______ a.m.
2. 오늘이 목요일이니? → ______ ______ ______ today ?
3. 봄에는 날씨가 따뜻하다. → ______ ______ ______ in spring.
4. 버스로 한 시간 걸린다. → ______ ______ an ______ by ______.
5. 오늘은 3월 1일이다. → ______ ______ ______ ______ today.
6. 뉴욕에서 LA까지 비행기로 얼마나 걸리니?

→ ______ ______ does ______ ______ from NY to LA by airplane?

Fill in the Blank It's beautiful day

Question 1 ③

Question 2 **1.** It is 8 **2.** Is it Thursday **3.** It is warm **4.** It takes, hour, bus **5.** It is March 1st
6. How long, it take

15 Upside down

A-teens

My grades are down ①(　　) A's ②(　)
D's
I'm way behind ③(　) history
I lost myself ③(　) fantasies ④(　) you
and me together
I don't know why - I - I
but dreaming's all I do
I won't get by - I - I ⑤(　) mere
imagination

내 성적이 A에서 D로 떨어졌어
난 역사에서 많이 처져 있어
난 너와 내가 함께 있는 환상 속에서
넋을 잃었지
나도 왜 그런지는 모르겠지만 난 꿈만 꿔
난 상상만으로는 살아갈 수 없어

- **grade** : 성적
- **from A to B**: A에서 B까지
- **way behind** : 매우 처진
- **lose oneself** : 이성을 잃다
- **fantasy** : 환상
- **get by** : 살아가다
- **mere** : 단지
- **imagination** : 상상

★ Upside down
Bouncing off the ceiling
Inside out
Stranger ②(　) this feeling
Got no clue what I should do
But I'll go crazy if I can't get
⑥(　　)(　) you

엉망진창
천장에서 떨어져 튀어 오르고 있어
뒤죽박죽
이런 느낌은 처음인 걸
뭘 해야 할지 전혀 모르겠어
하지만 네 곁으로 갈 수 없다면 난 미쳐버릴 거야

- **bounce** : 튀다
- **ceiling** : 천장
- **off** : ~로부터 떨어져서
- **clue** : 단서

My teacher says to concentrate
So what? his name was Peter the Great
The kings and queens will have to wait
Cuz I don't have forever
I wish that I - I - I could walk right up
②(　) you

선생님은 정신 차리라고 말씀하시지
그럼 어쩌라는 거예요?
그의 이름은 피터 대왕
왕과 왕비는 기다려야 할 걸
왜냐하면 난 영원히 집중 안 할 거거든
난 내가 너에게 곧바로 갈 수 있길 원해

Each time I try - I - I the same old hesitation

그럴 때마다 난 망설이기만 하지

- **concentrate :** 집중하다
- **Cuz = Because**
- **hesitation :** 망설임

★ Repeat

Somehow someday
You will love me, too
One day will be the day when all my dreams come true

어떻게든 언제든
너도 날 사랑하게 될 거야
언젠가는 내 모든 꿈들이 실현되는
그날이 올 거야

- **dreams come true :** 꿈이 실현되다

★ Repeat × 2

But I'll go crazy if I can't get
⑥(　　　)(　　) you
But I'll go crazy if I can't get
⑥(　　　)(　　) you

하지만 네 곁으로 갈 수 없다면 난 미쳐버릴 거야
하지만 네 곁으로 갈 수 없다면 난 미쳐버릴 거야

15 전치사

• 명사나 대명사 앞에 위치하여 시간, 위치, 원인, 수단 등을 나타낸다.

시간의 전치사

at	+ 시각	**at** 8:30, **at** night, **at** that time
in	+ 월/년/계절	**in** March, **in** 2009, **in** spring
on	+ 날짜/요일/특정한 날	**on** April 1st, **on** Thursday, **on** Thanksgiving
before	~전에	Please check your email **before** noon.
after	~후에	Winter comes **after** fall.
until	~까지	You should be at home **until** 10 o'clock.
during	~동안	He worked at the nursing home **during** summer.
for	~동안	She traveled Europe **for** 15 days.
since	~이래로	He hasn't eaten anything **since** yesterday.

장소의 전치사

in	~안에	My mother is cooking **in** the kitchen.
on	~위에	The little girl sits **on** her father's shoulder.
under	~아래에	Write your name **under** your picture.
down	~아래로	He ran **down** the stairs to open the door.
from	~로부터	How do you get **from** here to Haeundae beach?
to	~에, ~까지	She stood up and walked **to** the window.
near	~가까이에	Can I find a post office **near** here?
by	~옆에	Jane went and sat **by** Patrick.
around	~주위에	He planted beautiful flowers **around** his house.
behind	~뒤에	Joan parked her car **behind** the tree.
in front of	~앞에	Let's meet **in front of** the bus station.
next to	~옆에	Who is that guy **next to** her?
across	~맞은편에	There is a pizza store **across** the street.
between	~사이에	Which one is cheaper **between** these two?

기타 전치사

for	~를 위해서	Josh, Someone left a message **for** you.
by	~의해, ~타고	The picture was painted **by** Vincent Van Gogh. They travelled to Chicago **by** train.
of	~의	I liked the last scene **of** the movie.
to	~에	Don't show these letters **to** anyone else.
with	~와 함께	I always wear these shoes **with** this dress.
about	~에 관하여	What are you talking **about**?
because of	~때문에	His clothes were wet **because of** the rain.

Attention!

특정한 전치가가 쓰인 관용적인 표현은 꼭 외워두자!

- be full of~ : ~로 가득차다
- be famous for~ : ~로 유명하다
- be late for~ : ~에 늦다
- be good at~ : ~를 잘하다
- be known for~ : ~로 알려져 있다
- look for~ : ~를 찾다
- be afraid of~ : ~를 두려워하다
- be proud of~ : ~를 자랑스러워하다
- be familiar with~ : ~에 친숙하다
- look at~ : ~를 보다
- be mad at~ : ~에게 화나다

가사 예문

I'll go crazy if I can't get next to you.

만약 네 곁으로 갈 수 없다면 나는 미쳐버릴 거야.

Q1 다음 괄호 안에서 알맞은 표현을 고르시오.

1. The concert starts (in / on / at) five.
2. Her family goes to church (in / on / at) Sundays.
3. King Sejong invented Korean alphabet (in / on / at) 1443.
4. Children say 'trick or treat' (in / on / at) Halloween in order to get sweets.

Q2 다음 빈칸에 공통으로 들어갈 표현을 〈보기〉에서 고르시오.

〈보기〉 for at with next to

1. I hate to sit _______ smokers.
   The bookstore is just _______ the bakery.
2. This is a gift _______ you.
   Jinhae is famous _______ its cherry blossoms.
3. I am not familiar _______ that subject.
   Can you go _______ me to the party?
4. The man is looking _______ the stars through a telescope.
   Tedra worked for 10 years _______ the company.

Q3 다음 우리말과 의미가 같도록 괄호 안의 표현을 이용하여 문장을 완성하시오.

1. 그는 계산기를 가지고, 그 문제를 풀었다. (calculator)
→ He solved the question _______________.
2. 나는 친구들 앞에서 바보처럼 보이고 싶지 않았다. (friends)
→ I didn't want to look stupid _______________.
3. 너는 오전 9시 이전에 공항에 도착해야 해. (airport)
→ You should arrive _______________ before 9 am.
4. 12월에 그 여객선은 주말에만 운행한다. (weekends)
→ In December, the ferry is in service only _______________.

Fill in the Blank ① from ② to ③ in ④ of ⑤ on ⑥ next to
Question 1 **1.** at **2.** on **3.** in **4.** on
Question 2 **1.** next to **2.** for **3.** with **4.** at
Question 3 **1.** with the calculator **2.** in front of my friends **3.** at the airport **4.** on weekends

16 Summer nights

John Travolta & Olivia Newton-John

Summer loving ①(   ) me a blast
Summer loving ②(   ) so fast
I ③(   ) a girl, crazy for me
③(   ) a boy cute as can be
Summer days drifting away
to oh oh those summer nights

여름날의 사랑이 날 강타했지
여름날의 사랑은 너무나 순식간에 찾아왔어
나한테 푹 빠져버린 여자애를 만났거든
너무나 사랑스런 남자애를 만났지
여름날은 흘러 흘러
여름밤으로 흘러가지

- **blast** : 돌풍
- **crazy for~** : ~에게 반한
- **drift away** : 떠내려가다

Tell me more, tell me more
④(   ) you get very far?
Tell me more, tell me more
Like does he have a car

더 말해줘, 더 말해줘
그 사람하고 얼마나 진척된 거야?
더 말해줘, 더 말해줘
그가 차를 가지고 있는지 뭐 그런 거 말이야

She ⑤(   ) by me, she got a cramp
He ⑥(   ) by me, ⑦(   ) my suit damp
I ⑧(   ) her life, she nearly ⑨(   )
He ⑩(   ) off splashing around,
Summer sun something's begun,
but oh oh those summer nights

그녀가 내 옆에서 수영하고 있었는데,
쥐가 난 거야
그가 옆으로 달려와서, 내 옷을 적셔 놓았어
난 그녀의 생명을 구한 거야, 그녀는 거의
빠져 죽을 뻔했는데
그는 물을 튀기며 내 앞에서 자랑하더라고,
여름 태양이 있는 그곳에서 뭔가 시작된 거야,
하지만 그 여름밤들은

- **cramp** : 쥐, 마비
- **damp** : 축축한
- **drown** : 익사하다
- **show off** : 과시하다
- **splash** : 물을 뿌리다, 첨벙대다

Tell me more, tell me more
⑪(　　) it love at first sight?
Tell me more, tell me more
④(　　) she put up a fight?

더 말해줘, 더 말해줘
첫눈에 반한 사랑이었니?
더 말해줘, 더 말해줘
그녀가 싫어하진 않든?

- **love at first sight :** 첫눈에 반한 사랑
- **put up a fight :** 저항하다

⑫(　　) her bowling in the arcade
We ⑬(　　) strolling
⑭(　　) lemonade
We ⑮(　　) out under the dock
We ⑯(　　) out till ten o'clock
Summer fling don't mean a thing
but oh oh those summer nights

그녀를 볼링장에 데려갔어
우린 산책도 하고 레모네이드도 마셨지
부둣가에서 사랑도 나누고
밤 10시까지 그렇게 밖에 있었지
여름날 한순간의 즐거움은 대단한 건
아니지만,
그 여름밤들은

- **arcade :** 아케이드, 게임센터
- **stroll :** 산책하다, 어슬렁거리다
- **make out :** 사랑하다
- **fling :** (심각하지 않은) 짧은 즐김

Tell me more, tell me more
But you don't gotta brag
Tell me more, tell me more
Cause he sounds like a drag

더 말해줘, 더 말해줘
하지만 허풍떨긴 없기야
더 말해줘, 더 말해줘
그 남자는 질질 끄는 사람 같아

- **brag :** 허풍떨다
- **drag:** 질질 끄는 사람

He ⑦(　　) friendly holding my hand
She ⑦(　　) friendly down in the sand
He ⑪(　　) sweet, just turned eighteen
Well, she ⑪(　　) good
You know what I mean?
Summer heat, boy and girl meet

내 손을 잡은 그는 친근했어
그녀는 백사장 아래에서 친근했지
그는 너무 다정하고, 이제 막 18살이 되었어
음, 그녀는 정말 좋았어
무슨 말인지 알지?
뜨거운 여름날, 소년과 소녀가 만난 거야

but oh oh those summer nights

하지만 그 여름밤들은

- **friendly :** 친근하게
- **just :** 바로, 막

Tell me more, tell me more
How much dough ④(   ) he spend?
Tell me more, tell me more
Could she get me a friend?

더 말해줘, 더 말해줘
그 사람 돈은 얼마나 썼니?
더 말해줘, 더 말해줘
그녀가 나에게도 한 명 소개해줄까?

- **dough :** (속어) money
- **spend :** 소비하다

It ⑰(   ) colder
That's where it ends
So I ⑱(   ) her we'd still be friends
Then we ⑮(   ) our true love vow
Wonder what she's doing now

계절이 바뀌면서
우리도 떠날 수밖에 없었지
대신 우린 떨어져도 마음만은 항상 함께 있을 거라고 나는 말했어
그러고 우리는 서로 진정한 사랑의 맹세를 했지
그녀는 지금 뭘 하고 있을지 궁금하네

- **vow :** 맹세, 서약

Summer dreams ripped at the seams,
but oh those summer nights...
(Tell me more, tell me more)

여름의 꿈들은 그렇게 끝나 버린 거야,
하지만 그 뜨거웠던 여름밤들은…
(말해줘, 좀 더 말해보라고)

- **rip :** 갈라지다
- **seam :** 경계선

16 동사의 과거형

동사의 과거형이란

• 과거의 행동이나 상황, 역사적 사실 등을 나타낼 때 쓰는 동사의 형태이다.

be동사와 일반동사의 과거형태

1. be동사의 과거형

am / is → was	are → were

2. 일반동사의 과거형

규칙 변화	① 대부분의 동사 → -ed	wanted, visited, opened, helped, called, happened
	② e로 끝나는 동사 → -d	loved, liked, lived
	③ 자음+y로 끝나는 동사 → y를 i로 고치고 -ed	studied, tried, cried
	④ 모음+y로 끝나는 동사 → 동사원형 -ed	played, enjoyed, stayed
	⑤ 단모음+단자음으로 끝나는 동사 → 자음을 한 번 더 쓰고 -ed	stopped, dropped, planned

불규칙 변화	do → did	go → went	get → got	run → ran
	make → made	know → knew	eat → ate	come → came
	meet → met	have → had	lose → lost	see → saw
	find → found	teach → taught	buy → bought	write → wrote
	drive → drove	read → read	send → sent	keep → kept
	drink → drank	sleep → slept	break → broke	sing → sang
	take → took	give → gave	swim → swam	leave → left

가사 예문

Summer loving had me a blast.
여름날의 사랑이 날 강타했지.

Summer loving happened so fast.
여름날의 사랑은 너무나 순식간에 찾아왔어.

Q1 다음 빈칸에 괄호 안의 단어를 알맞은 형태로 바꿔 쓰시오.

1. He _______ very fast to catch the bus. (run)
2. I _______ him when I was a high school student. (like)
3. Megan _______ a cup cake for her mom's birthday. (make)
4. James _______ the news article on the internet this morning. (read)
5. Evan _______ to doctor's office yesterday because he was very sick. (go)

Q2 다음 빈칸에 알맞은 말을 〈보기〉에서 골라 알맞은 형태로 바꿔 쓰시오.

〈보기〉 buy be enjoy write study

1. She _______ music in State University of New York two years ago.
2. Brooklyn _______ an email to her friend in Los Angeles last night.
3. Jacob _______ some bread and milk on his way home from work.
4. The weather was not good, but the students _______ playing soccer.
5. I _______ late for the meeting because I had a car accident on the highway.

Fill in the Blank ① had ② happened ③ met ④ Did ⑤ swam ⑥ ran ⑦ got ⑧ saved ⑨ drowned ⑩ showed ⑪ Was ⑫ Took ⑬ went ⑭ drank ⑮ made ⑯ stayed ⑰ turned ⑱ told

Question 1 1. ran 2. liked 3. made 4. read 5. went

Question 2 1. studied 2. wrote 3. bought 4. enjoyed 5. was

17 Raindrops keep falling on my head — B.J. Thomas

Raindrops (   ) (   ) on my head
And just like the guy whose feet are too big for his bed, nothing seems to fit
Those raindrops (   ) (   ) on my head
They keep falling

빗방울이 내 머리 위에 떨어지고 있어요
발이 너무 커서 침대가 맞지 않는 사람처럼,
아무것도 내게 맞는 것이 없어 보여요
빗방울이 내 머리 위에 떨어지네요
계속 떨어지네요

- **raindrops :** 빗방울
- **fit :** ① (꼭)맞다, 적합하다 ② 건강한
- **keep ~ing :** 계속해서 ~하다

So I just did me some talking to the sun
And I said I didn't like the way he got things done
He's sleeping on the job
Those raindrops (   ) (   ) on my head
They keep falling

그래서 난 태양에게 몇 마디 했죠
그가 일하는 방식이 마음에 들지 않는다고
태양이 게으름을 피워서 비가 온다고
빗방울이 내 머리 위에 떨어지고 있어요
계속 떨어지네요

- **did me some talking to~ :** (구어) ~와 이야기를 나누었다 = had a word with~
- **the way~ :** ~하는 방식
- **get things done :** 일을 해내다
- **sleep on the job :** (비유) 게으르다

But there's one thing I know
The blues they send to meet me won't defeat me
It won't be long till happiness steps up to greet me

하지만 내가 아는 한 가지가 있죠
그들이 나를 우울하게 만들어도 나를 좌절시킬 수는 없어요
조금만 시간이 지나면 행복한 마음이 나를 반기며 다가올 거에요

- **The blues:** (비유) 우울함
- **defeat :** ① 좌절시키다 ② 패배
- **won't be long till~ :** ~때까지 오래 걸리진 않을 거야
- **step up :** 앞으로 나오다

★ Raindrops keep falling on my head
But that doesn't mean my eyes will
soon be turning red
Crying's not for me
Cause, I'm never gonna stop the rain
by complaining
Because I'm free
Nothing's worrying me

빗방울이 내 머리 위에 계속 떨어지네요
하지만 그렇다고 해서 내 눈시울은 붉어지지
않는답니다
난 울지 않거든요
투덜거린다고 비가 멈추지는 않기 때문이죠
난 자유로워요
어떤 것도 나를 걱정시킬 수 없답니다

- **complain** : 불평하다

It won't be long till happiness steps up
to greet me

조금만 시간이 지나면 행복한 마음이 나를
반기며 다가올 거예요

★ Repeat

17 현재진행형

현재진행형이란

- 현재 진행 중인 동작을 나타내는 말로 '~하고 있다', '~하고 있는 중이다'의 표현이다.
- 「am/are/is + 동사원형 + ing」로 나타낸다.

- 동사원형 + ing 만드는 법

1. 대부분의 동사 → 동사원형 + ing	wait → waiting turn → turning	play → playing listen → listening
2. 「단모음 + 단자음」으로 끝나는 동사 → 자음 한 번 더 쓰고 -ing	sit → sitting run → running	stop → stopping get → getting
3. 「자음 + e」로 끝나는 동사 → e를 없애고 -ing	waste → wasting take → taking	drive → driving come → coming

A: Hello, James. It's Jennifer.

B: Hi, Jennifer. Can I call you later? I**'m brushing** my teeth.

현재진행형 부정문 / 현재진행형 의문문

- 현재진행형 부정문 : 「am/are/is + not + 동사원형 + ing」
  - Alyssa **is not doing** the laundry. She is talking on the phone.
- 현재진행형 의문문 : 「Am/Are/Is + 주어 + 동사원형 + ing?」
  - It smells so good. **Are you cooking** now?

가사 예문

Raindrops are falling on my head.

빗방울이 내 머리 위에 떨어지고 있어요.

Q1 다음 우리말과 의미가 같도록 괄호 안의 표현을 이용하여 문장을 완성하시오.

1. 너 지금 뉴스를 보고 있니? (watch)

→ _______ you _______ the news now?

2. 그는 정원의 식물에 물을 주고 있다. (water)

→ He _______ _______ the plants in his garden.

3. 실례합니다만, 무엇을 찾고 계신가요? (look for)

→ Excuse me, _______ _______ you _______ for?

4. 컴퓨터 게임을 하는 게 아니에요. 저는 숙제를 하고 있는 중이에요. (play)

→ I _______ _______ _______ computer games. I am doing my homework now.

Q2 주어진 표현을 이용하여 아래 문장의 질문과 대답을 완성하시오.

1. A: ______________________________? B: I'm eating spaghetti. (what / you / eat)

2. A: ______________________________? B: Yes, they are. (they / play / basketball)

3. A: Are the children sleeping now? B: No, _______ _______.

4. A: Are you having a good time at this party? B: Yes, _______ _______.

Fill in the Blank are falling

Question 1 **1.** Are, watching **2.** is watering **3.** what are, looking **4.** am not playing

Question 2 **1.** What are you eating **2.** Are they playing basketball **3.** they aren't **4.** I am

18 Any dream will do

Sarah Brightman

I closed my eyes, drew back the curtain
To see for certain what I thought I knew
Far far away someone ①(   )(   )
But the world ②(   )(   )
Any dream will do

난 커튼을 걷고, 눈을 감았지
내가 안다고 생각했던 걸 확실히 보기 위해서
저 멀리서 누군가 울고 있었지만
세상은 잠들어 있었네
어떤 꿈도 이루어질 거야

- **draw back the curtain :** 휘장을 걷다
- **weep :** 울다

I wore my coat with golden lining
Bright colours shining wonderful and new
And in the east
the dawn ③(   )(   )
And the world ④(   )(   )
Any dream will do

난 황금 안감을 댄 옷을 입었지
밝은 색깔이 빛나고 멋지고 새로웠어
동쪽에서는
새벽이 밝아오고
세상은 깨어나고 있었네
어떤 꿈도 이루어질 거야

- **lining :** 안감
- **dawn :** 새벽

A crash of drums, a flash of light
My golden coat flew out of sight
The colours faded into darkness
I was left alone

요란한 드럼 소리, 번쩍이는 불빛
내 황금 옷은 사라져버렸네
점점 어두워져 가고
난 홀로 남겨졌네

- **crash :** 요란한 소리
- **fly-flew-flown** (날다)
- **out of sight :** 보이지 않는
- **fade into darkness :** 희미해져 암흑이 되다

May I return to the beginning
The light is dimming and the dream is, too
The world and I, we are still waiting
Still hesitating, any dream will do

날 처음으로 돌아가게 하소서
빛은 희미해지고 꿈도 그러하네
세상과 나, 우린 아직 기다리고 있지
우린 아직 망설이고 있지만,
어떤 꿈도 이루어질 거야

- **dim :** 희미하게 하다
- **hesitate :** 망설이다

A crash of drums, a flash of light
My golden coat flew out of sight
The colours faded into darkness
I was left alone

요란한 드럼 소리, 번쩍이는 불빛
내 황금 옷은 사라져버렸네
점점 어두워져 가고
난 홀로 남겨졌네

- **fade :** 희미해지다
- **be left :** 남겨지다

May I return to the beginning
The light is dimming and the dream is, too
The world and I, we are still waiting
Still hesitating,
any dream will do
any dream will do
any dream will do

날 처음으로 돌아가게 하소서
빛은 희미해지고 꿈도 그러하네
세상과 나, 우린 아직 기다리고 있지
우린 아직 망설이고 있지만,
어떤 꿈도 이루어질 거야
어떤 꿈도 이루어질 거야
어떤 꿈도 이루어질 거야

18 과거진행형

과거진행형이란

- 과거진행 중인 동작을 나타내는 말로 '~하고 있는 중이었다'의 표현이다.
- 「was/were + 동사원형 + ing」로 나타낸다.

  A: Why didn't you pick up the phone?

  B: I'm sorry. I **was washing** dishes.

과거진행형 부정문 / 과거진행형 의문문

- 과거진행형 부정문 : 「was/were + not + 동사원형 + ing」

  A: Why did the policeman stop you?

  B: I **was not wearing** a seatbelt when I **was driving**.

- 과거진행형 의문문 : 「(의문사) Was/Were + 주어 + 동사원형 + ing?」

  A: **What were you doing** last night around 9 p.m.? You didn't answer my phone.

  B: Oh, I was at home, but I **was taking** a bath then.

가사 예문

Far far away someone was weeping.
멀리 저 멀리서 누군가 울고 있었네.

And in the east the dawn was breaking, and the world was waking.
동쪽에서는 새벽이 밝아오고, 세상은 깨어나고 있었네.

Q1 다음 우리말과 의미가 같도록 괄호 안의 표현을 이용하여 문장을 완성하시오.

1. 우리는 일을 마치기 위해서 서로 돕고 있었다. (help)

→ We _______ _______ with each other to finish the work.

2. 그녀는 벼룩시장에서 중고 물건을 팔고 있었다. (sell)

→ She _______ _______ the used products in the flea market.

3. 네가 그곳에 도착했을 때, 그들은 무엇을 하고 있었니? (do)

→ What _______ _______ _______ when you arrived there?

4. Ashton이 자전거에서 떨어졌을 때, 그는 헬멧을 쓰고 있지 않았다. (wear)

→ Ashton _______ _______ _______ a helmet when he fell from the bike.

Q2 주어진 표현을 이용하여 아래 문장의 질문과 대답을 완성하시오.

1. A: ______________________ at 6:00 p.m. yesterday? (what / you / do)

   B: I was exercising at the gym.

2. A: ______________________ in the morning there? (it / rain)

   B: No, it wasn't.

3. A: What was Isabella doing then?

   B: She ______________________ at that time. (prepare dinner)

4. A: Were they fighting with each other when their teacher came in?

   B: Yes, _______ _______.

Fill in the Blank ① was weeping ② was sleeping ③ was breaking ④ was waking

Question 1 **1.** were helping **2.** was selling **3.** were they doing **4.** was not wearing

Question 2 **1.** What were you doing **2.** Was it raining **3.** was preparing dinner **4.** they were

19 Isn't she lovely — Stevie Wonder

Isn't she ①(　　　)?
Isn't she ②(　　　　　)?
Isn't she ③(　　　　)?
Less than one minute ④(　　)

그녀는 정말 사랑스럽지 않나요?
그녀는 정말 놀랍지 않나요?
그녀는 정말 소중하지 않나요?
태어난 지 1분도 채 안 됐어요

- **precious :** 소중한
- **less than~ :** ~보다 더 적은

I never thought through love we'd be
making one as ①(　　　) as she
But isn't she ①(　　　) made from love?

결코 생각지 못했어요
사랑을 통해서 우리가
그녀만큼 사랑스러운 아이를 탄생시킬
거라곤
근데 정말 사랑스럽지 않나요?
사랑으로 태어난 이 아이가

- **through :** ~을 통하여
- **as A as B :** B만큼 A한

Isn't she ⑤(　　　)?
Truly the angel's ⑥(　　)
Boy, I'm so ⑦(　　　)
We have been heaven ⑧(　　　)
I can't believe what God has done
Through us he's given life to one
But isn't she ①(　　　) made from love?

그녀는 정말 예쁘지 않나요?
정말로 천사의 최고 걸작이에요
와우, 난 너무 행복해요
우린 하늘의 축복을 받은 거예요
신께서 하신 일을 믿을 수가 없어요
우리를 통해 그 아이에게 생명을 주셨어요
근데 정말 사랑스럽지 않나요?
사랑으로 태어난 이 아이가

- **truly :** 진실로
- **blessed :** 축복받은

Isn't she ①(   )?
Life and love are the ⑨(   )
Life is Aisha
The meaning of her name

그녀는 정말 사랑스럽지 않나요?
생명과 사랑은 같아요
생명은 '아이샤'라고 하죠
그게 그녀 이름의 뜻이에요

Londie, it could have not been done
Without you who conceived the one
That's so very ①(   ) made from love

론디, 이 일은 불가능했을 거예요
그 아이를 품어준 당신이 아니었다면
그건 사랑으로 만들어진 너무나 사랑스러운 일이죠

- **conceive:** ① 생각해내다, 착안하다
② (아이를) 품다

19 형용사

형용사란

- 형용사는 '~한, ~는, ~인'의 뜻으로 명사의 앞 뒤에서 명사를 꾸미거나, 명사를 보충 설명하는 역할을 한다.

형용사의 용법

1. 한정적 용법	형용사가 명사의 앞뒤에서 그 명사를 수식한다. - This is a **lovely** picture. (사랑스러운 – picture라는 명사를 꾸밈) - I want to do something **exciting**. (신나는 – something이라는 명사를 꾸밈)
2. 서술적 용법	형용사가 주어나 목적어를 보충 설명한다. - I am very **hungry**. (배고픈 – 주어 I의 상태를 보충 설명함) - The song makes me **happy**. (행복한 – 목적어 me의 상태를 보충 설명함)

형용사의 주요형태

1. -y	lovely(사랑스러운), healthy(건강한), sleepy(졸리는), hungry(배고픈), dirty(더러운)
2. -ful	beautiful(아름다운), wonderful(멋진), helpful(도움이 되는), useful(유용한)
3. -less	useless(쓸모없는), careless(신중하지 못한), powerless(힘 없는), harmless(해가 없는)
4. -able	lovable(사랑스러운), comfortable(편안한), washable(세탁 가능한), breakable(깨지기 쉬운)
5. -ous	famous(유명한), dangerous(위험한), spacious(넓은), nervous(불안한), curious(궁금한)
6. -ing	exciting(신나는), interesting(흥미로운), shocking(충격적인), surprising(놀라운)
7. -ed	excited(흥분된), interested(관심 있는), shocked(충격받은), surprised(놀란)
8. un-	unhappy(불행한), unafraid(두려워하지 않는), unfair(부당한), unable(할 수 없는)

가사 예문

Isn't she lovely?

그녀는 정말 사랑스럽지 않나요?

Attention!

-ing, -ed로 끝나는 형용사는
사람 주어일 경우 -ed 형용사를, 사물 주어일 경우는 -ing 형용사를 사용!

- I was very **shocked** with the news. (사람주어 I → shocked)
- The news was very **shocking** to me. (사물주어 The news → shocking)

Q1 다음 두 문장을 한 문장으로 쓸 때, 빈칸에 알맞은 말을 쓰시오.

1. He is a student. He is smart. → He is a _______ _______.
2. Look at the wave. The wave is high. → Look at _______ _______ _______.
3. Jina saw a movie. The movie was scary and horrible.

→ Jina saw a _______ _______ _______ _______.

Q2 우리말과 의미가 같도록 괄호 안의 표현을 이용하여 문장을 완성하시오.

1. 저는 편안한 소파를 찾고 있어요. (look for / comfortable)

→ ____

2. Brian은 친절하고, 인자한 교사이다. (kind / generous)

→ ____

3. Emily는 더럽고 쓸모없는 물건들을 버렸다. (throw out / things)

→ ____

4. 나는 스카이다이빙을 즐긴다. 그것은 무섭게 보이지만, 꽤 흥미롭다. (scary / quite interesting)

→ ____

Fill in the Blank ① lovely ② wonderful ③ precious ④ old ⑤ pretty ⑥ best ⑦ happy ⑧ blessed ⑨ same

Question 1 **1.** smart student **2.** the high wave **3.** scary and horrible movie

Question 2 **1.** I'm looking for a comfortable sofa. **2.** Brian is a kind and generous teacher.
3. Emily threw out the dirty and useless things.
4. I enjoy skydiving. It looks scary, but it is quite interesting.

20 You call it love — Karoline Kruger

You call it love
There are things I need to say
About the way I feel when your arms
are all around me
You call it love
Words I heard that sound so fine
meaningless each time till you came
and found me

넌 그걸 사랑이라고 부르는가 봐
난 말하고 싶은 게 있어
너의 팔이 나를 포근히 감쌀 때 내가 어떻게
느끼는지 말이야
넌 그걸 사랑이라고 부르는가 봐
너무나 좋게 들렸던 단어들도
내겐 늘 의미 없는 단어들이었어
네가 와서 나를 찾아주기 전까지는 말이야

- **meaningless :** 의미 없는
- **till :** ~때까지

See, the ground is ①(   ) turning,
②(   ), ③(   )
Feel, the way my heart is burning
④(   ) inside of me

봐, 의심할 여지 없이, 땅이 천천히,
어지럽게 돌고 있어
내 안에서 은밀히 불타오르는 나의 마음을
느껴봐

- **dizzily :** 어지럽게
- **easily :** ① 쉽게, 수월하게 ② 의심할 여지 없이

You call it love
All the wishes in my mind soared
into the skies where reflected
in my own eyes
You say it's love variations on the theme
Love was just a dream,
memories of past sighs

넌 그걸 사랑이라고 부르는가 봐
내 마음속 모든 소망들이
하늘 높이 올라가
내 눈 속에 거울처럼 비췄어
넌 말하지 사랑은 여러 가지 빛깔이 있다고
말이야
내겐 단지 사랑이 꿈이었고,
지난날의 한숨에 대한 기억이었어

- **soar into :** 날아오르다
- **reflect :** 비추다
- **variation :** 변화
- **theme :** 주제
- **past :** 지난
- **sigh :** 한숨

See, you love is always around me
Everywhere, in the air
New sensations now surround me
Ocean wide, deep inside

봐, 너의 사랑은 늘 내 곁에 있고
공중 곳곳에 존재해
새로운 느낌이 이젠 나를 둘러싸고 있어
바다만큼 넓게, 그리고 내 마음 깊숙한 곳에서

- **sensation :** 감각
- **surround :** 둘러싸다

You call it love
All my days pass close to you
Grey skies turn to blue
And the sun shines all around me
You call it love
It's a phrase that people say each and every day
Real love's hard to find though

넌 그걸 사랑이라고 부르는가 봐
내 모든 아름다운 날들이 네 곁에서 지내며 흘러가고
회색빛 하늘도 파란 하늘로 변하고
태양이 내 주위를 온통 비추고 있어
넌 그걸 사랑이라고 부르는가 봐
사랑한다는 말은 사람들이 매일같이 하는 말이지만 진정한 사랑은 찾기 힘들지

- **phrase :** 어구, 표현법
- **though :** 비록 ~하지만

See, the ground is ①(   ) turning, ②(   ), ③(   )
Feel, the way my heart is burning from your touch ④(   )

봐, 의심할 여지 없이, 땅이 천천히, 어지럽게 돌고 있어
너의 손길에 의해 불타오르는 나의 마음을 비밀스럽게 느껴봐

- **burn :** 불타다
- **secretly :** 비밀스럽게

You call it love
Now I know it's so much more
Being close to you makes this feeling new that you call it love

넌 그걸 사랑이라고 부르는가 봐
이젠 알겠어 사랑은 내가 알고 있는 것 훨씬 이상이라는 걸 말이야
네 곁에 있으면 네가 사랑이라고 부르는 이 느낌이 새로워져

20 부사

부사란

- 부사는 '~하게'의 뜻으로 동사, 형용사, 다른 부사, 문장 전체를 꾸미는 역할을 한다.

부사의 쓰임

1. 동사 수식	When it is snowy, drive **slowly**. (천천히 – drive라는 동사를 꾸며줌)
2. 형용사 수식	I am **really** sorry. It's my fault. (정말로 – sorry라는 형용사를 꾸며줌)
3. 부사 수식	She dances **very** well. (매우 – well이라는 부사를 꾸며줌)
4. 문장 전체 수식	**Luckily**, we got the concert ticket. (운 좋게도 – 전체 문장을 꾸며줌)

부사의 주요형태

1. 대부분 형용사에 → -ly를 붙임	quick → quickly, nice → nicely, careful → carefully, kind → kindly, slow → slowly, secret → secretly, soft → softly, loud → loudly, clear → clearly, real → really
2. -y로 끝나는 형용사에 → y를 i로 고치고 -ly	happy → happily, easy → easily, dizzy → dizzily
3. -ue로 끝나는 형용사에 → e를 없애고 -ly	true → truly
4. -le로 끝나는 형용사에 → e를 없애고 -y	simple → simply, possible → possibly, gentle → gently
5. 형용사와 형태가 같은 부사	fast(빠른-빨리), early(이른-일찍), near(가까운-가까이), late(늦은-늦게), high(높은-높게), hard(열심인-열심히)

가사 예문

See, the ground is slowly turning, dizzily, easily.

봐, 의심할 여지 없이, 땅이 천천히, 어지럽게 돌고 있어.

Feel, the way my heart is burning, secretly inside of me.

내 안에서 은밀히 불타오르는 나의 마음을 느껴봐.

Attention!

형용사와 형태가 같은 부사에 -ly를 붙이면 전혀 다른 뜻이 됨!

high → **highly** (매우)   late → **lately** (최근에)

near → **nearly** (거의)   hard → **hardly** (거의 ~않는)

Q1 괄호 안의 표현을 이용하여 다음 문장의 빈칸을 채우시오.

1. The turtle runs ______________. (slow)
2. He drove ______________ because the road was slippery. (careful)
3. The baby was sleeping, so she entered the room ______________. (quiet)

Q2 우리말과 의미가 같도록 괄호 안의 표현을 이용하여 문장을 완성하시오.

1. 우리는 그 무거운 박스를 안전하게 옮겼다. (carry / safely)

→ ______________________________

2. 그것은 어려운 문제였다. 하지만 그는 그것을 쉽게 풀었다. (difficult / easily)

→ ______________________________

3. 당신의 말을 잘 못 들었어요. 더 크게 말씀해 주시겠어요? (can't hear / more loudly)

→ ______________________________

Fill in the Blank ① slowly ② dizzily ③ easily ④ secretly

Question 1 **1.** slowly **2.** carefully **3.** quietly

Question 2 **1.** We carried the heavy box safely. **2.** It was a difficult question. But he solved it easily. **3.** I could not (couldn't) hear you well. Could you speak more loudly?

21 Hero — Mariah Carey

(   )'(   ) a hero if you look inside your heart
You don't have to be afraid of what you are
(   )'(   ) an answer if you reach into your soul
And the sorrow that you know will melt away

당신의 마음속을 들여다본다면 그곳에 영웅이 있어요
당신에 대해서 두려워할 필요 없어요
당신의 영혼에 다다른다면 그곳에 답이 있을 거예요
그리고 당신의 슬픔은 녹아내려 사라지게 될 거예요

- **hero :** ① 영웅
  ② (소설, 영화 등의) 남자주인공
- **don't have to be ~ :** ~일 필요 없다
- **be afraid of~ :**~를 두려워하다
- **reach into~ :** ~에 도달하다
- **sorrow :** 슬픔
- **melt away :** 녹아 사라지다

★ And then a hero comes along with the strength to carry on
And you cast your fears aside and you know you can survive
So when you feel like hope is gone
Look inside you and be strong
and you finally see the truth
that a hero lies in you

그리고 영웅은 계속해서 살아갈 수 있는 힘과 함께 올 거예요
그리고 당신은 두려움을 떨쳐내고 견뎌낼 수 있다는 걸 알게 되죠
그러니 희망이 사라진다고 느낄 때
당신의 마음속 안을 들여다보고 강해지세요
그럼 마침내 알게 될 거예요
영웅은 당신 안에 있다는 것을

- **come along with~ :** ~와 함께 오다
- **strength :** 힘
- **carry on :** 계속하다
- **cast something aside :** 무언가를 떨쳐 버리다
- **feel like~ :** ~한 느낌이 있다
- **lie in~ :** ~안에 있다

It's a long road
When you face the world alone
No one reaches out a hand for you to hold
You can find love if you search within yourself
And the emptiness you felt will disappear

아주 머나먼 길이에요
당신이 혼자 세상을 마주하게 될 때
아무도 당신에게 손을 뻗지 않을 때
당신이 만약 자기 스스로를 돌아본다면
사랑을 찾을 수 있어요
그리고 당신이 느꼈던 공허함은 사라질 거예요

- **search :** ① 수색 ② 찾아보다
- **within~ :** ~이내에
- **emptiness :** 공허함
- **disappear :** 사라지다

★ Repeat

Lord knows dreams are hard to follow
But don't let anyone tear them away
Hold on there will be tomorrow
In time you'll find the way

신은 아실 테죠 꿈을 좇는 것이 힘들다는 걸
하지만 누구든 그걸 망가뜨리게 두지는 말아요
기다려봐요 반드시 내일이 있을 거예요
이윽고 당신은 길을 찾게 될 거예요

- **Lord :** 신
- **tear something away :** 무언가를 억지로 떼어내다
- **hold on :** 기다리다
- **in time :** 이윽고 = **eventually**

★ Repeat

that a hero lies in you
that a hero lies in you

영웅은 당신 안에 있다는 것을
영웅은 당신 안에 있다는 것을

21 There is / There are

There is / There are란

- There is(There are)는 '~이 있다'의 의미이다.
- 뒤에 오는 명사가 단수이면 There is(was), 복수이면 There are(were)를 사용한다.

- **There is** a bag on the table. (단수명사 a bag → There is)
- **There are** four seasons in Korea. (복수명사 four seasons → There are)

형태	과거시제	부정문	의문문
There is + 단수명사	There was~	There is(was) not~	Is(Was) there~
There are + 복수명사	There were~	There are(were) not~	Are(Were) there~

가사 예문

There's a hero if you look inside your heart.
당신의 마음속을 들여다본다면 그곳에 영웅이 있어요.

There's an answer if you reach into your soul.
당신의 영혼에 다다른다면 그곳에 답이 있을 거예요.

Attention!

의문문 Is(Are) there~?에 대한 대답

A: **Is there** an egg in the nest? B: Yes, **there is**. / No, **there isn't**.

A: **Are there** some eggs in the nest? B: Yes, **there are**. / No, **there aren't**.

Q1 우리말과 의미가 같도록 주어진 표현을 이용하여 빈칸을 채우시오.

1. 꽃병에 장미 한 송이가 있다. (a rose)

→ ________ ________ ________ ________ in the vase.

2. 메일함에 편지가 있니? (any letter)

→ ________ ________ ________ ________ in the mailbox?

3. 책장에 책들이 많이 있지 않다. (many books)

→ ________ ________ ________ ________ ________ in the bookshelf.

4. A: 이 주위에 편의점 있나요? / B: 아니요, 없습니다.

→ A: ________ ________ any convenient store around here?

B: No, ________ ________.

5. A: 그 모임에 많은 사람들이 있었나요? / B: 예, 있었지요. (many people)

→ A: ________ ________ ________ ________ at the meeting?

B: Yes, ________ ________.

Q2 다음 문장에서 어색한 부분을 찾아 바르게 고치시오.

1. There are a little water in the bottle. __________ → __________
2. Is there many students in the classroom? __________ → __________
3. There isn't a lot of trees in the garden. __________ → __________
4. Were there any vacant seat in the plane? __________ → __________

Fill in the Blank There's

Question 1 **1.** There is a rose **2.** Is there any letter **3.** There are not many books **4.** Is there / there isn't **5.** Were there many people / there were

Question 2 **1.** are → is **2.** Is → Are **3.** isn't → aren't **4.** Were → Was

22 Can't take my eyes off you

Morten Harket

☆ You're just (　　)(　　　) to be true
Can't take my eyes off you
You'd be like heaven to touch
I wanna hold you so much
At long last love has arrived
And I thank God I'm alive
You're just (　　)(　　　) to be true
Can't take my eyes off you

당신은 믿을 수 없을 만큼 너무 아름답네요
당신에게서 눈을 뗄 수가 없어요
당신은 만질 수 있는 천국과 같아요
당신을 너무나도 안고 싶어요
마침내 사랑이 내게 왔어요
그리고 내가 살아있음을 신께 감사합니다
당신은 믿을 수 없을 만큼 너무 아름다워요
당신에게서 눈을 뗄 수가 없어요

- **good :** ① 좋은, 훌륭한 ② 착한 ③ 아름다운
- **take A off B :** B로부터 A를 떨쳐내다
- **At last :** 마침내

Pardon the way that I stare
There's nothing else to compare
The sight of you leaves me weak
There are no words left to speak
But if you feel like I feel
Please let me know that it's real
You're just (　　)(　　　) to be true
Can't take my eyes off you

이렇게 빤히 쳐다보는 걸 용서하세요
당신을 그 누구와도 비교할 수 없어요
당신의 모습은 날 무력하게 만듭니다
뭐라 말할 수 없네요
만약 당신도 나와 같이 느낀다면
그게 사실이라고 알려주세요
당신은 믿을 수 없을 만큼 너무 아름다워요
당신에게서 눈을 뗄 수가 없어요

- **pardon :** ① 용서 ② 용서하다
- **way :** ① 길 ② 방식
- **stare :** 응시하다
- **compare :** 비교하다
- **leave :** ① 떠나다 ② 남기다 ③ 출발하다
- **let A B :** A로 하여금 B하게 하다

★ I love you baby, and if it's quite all right
I need you baby, to warm the lonely night
I love you baby, trust in me when I say

사랑해요, 만약 괜찮다면
난 당신이 필요해요, 이 외로운 밤을 따뜻하게 해줄
사랑해요, 내가 말할 때 날 믿어줘요

- **quite :** 꽤, 상당히

Oh, pretty baby, don't bring me down
I pray
Oh, pretty baby, now that I've found
you, stay
And let me love you baby, let me love
you

아름다운 그대여, 난 당신이 날 져버리지
않길 기도합니다
아름다운 그대여, 이제 당신을 찾았으니,
내 곁에 머물러줘요
당신을 사랑하게 해줘요, 사랑하게 해줘요

- **bring down** : 쓰러뜨리다, 실망시키다

☆ Repeat

★ Repeat

Oh pretty baby, don't bring me down
I pray
Oh pretty baby, now that I found you,
stay
Oh pretty baby, trust in me when
I say
I need you baby, well will you come
my way?
Oh pretty baby, now that I found you,
stay
And let me love you, baby, let me
love you

오 아름다운 그대여, 절 실망시키지
말아주세요
오 아름다운 그대여, 이제야 당신을 찾았으니,
머물러주세요
오 아름다운 그대여, 제 말을 믿어주세요
당신이 필요해요, 내게로 와주지 않을래요?
오 아름다운 그대여, 이제야 당신을 찾았으니,
머물러주세요
그리고 사랑하게 해주세요, 그대여,
사랑하게 해주세요

22 too

too + 형용사/부사

- 필요 이상으로 '너무 ~한'라는 의미를 나타내며 형용사 또는 부사 앞에 too를 쓸 수 있다.

- **Too** much stress is not good for your health.
  너무 많은 스트레스는 건강에 좋지 않아.
- Don't study **too** hard and take some time to enjoy your life!
  너무 열심히 공부하지 말고 너의 삶을 즐길 시간을 좀 가져!

too + 형용사/부사 + (for 사람) to 동사원형

- too + 형용사/부사 다음에 to 동사원형을 쓸 수 있다. 이때, for + 사람을 함께 쓸 수도 있다.

- This question is **too difficult for me to solve**.
  이 문제는 내가 풀기에는 너무 어려워.
- This table is **too heavy for me to move**. Can you help me?
  이 테이블은 내가 옮기기엔 너무 무거워. 도와주겠니?

가사 예문

You're just too good to be true.
당신은 믿을 수 없을 만큼 너무 아름다워요.

Attention!

too를 문장 중간이 아닌 끝에 붙이면, **또한, 역시**라는 뜻이 된다!

I go to the company on weekends, **too**. 나도 역시 주말에 회사에 가.

Q1 괄호 안의 단어를 바르게 배열하여 문장을 다시 쓰시오. (첫 대문자 유의)

1. (too tight / is / to wear / that skirt / for you).

→ ____

2. (too much / harms / computer games / your mind).

→ ____

3. (it / is / too / for us / to / late / go to the party)?

→ ____

4. You are only 13. (a part time job / to / too / you're / young / have).

→ ____

Q2 주어진 우리말과 같도록 올바른 표현을 쓰시오.

1. 걸어 다니기엔 밖이 너무 추워.

→ It's _____ _______ ____ _______ outside.

2. 우리는 결코 배우기에 너무 늙지 않았어요.

→ We are never _____ _______ ____ _______.

3. 진실을 말하기엔 너무 늦었어요.

→ It was _____ _______ ____ _______ the truth.

4. 내가 해야 할 일이 너무 많이 있어요.

→ There is _____ _______ work for me ____ _______.

Fill in the Blank too good

Question 1 1. That skirt is too tight for you to wear. 2. Too much computer games harms your mind. 3. Is it too late for us to go to the party? 4. You are too young to have a part time job.

Question 2 1. too cold to walk 2. too old to learn 3. too late to tell 4. too much, to do

23 Take a chance on me — ABBA

☆ (　) you change your mind, I'm the first in line
Honey, I'm still free
Take a chance on me
(　) you need me, let me know, gonna be around
(　) you've got no place to go when you're feeling down
(　) you're all alone when the pretty birds have flown
Honey, I'm still free
Take a chance on me

만약 당신이 마음을 바꾼다면, 내가 제일 앞에 있을게요
그대여, 난 아직 혼자예요
나에게서 기회를 잡아요
만약 내가 필요하면, 알려주세요, 주변에 있을게요
만약 당신이 우울할 때 갈 곳이 없다면
만약 예쁜 새들이 날아가 버리고 당신이 완전히 혼자라면
그대여, 난 아직 혼자예요
내게서 기회를 잡아요

- **take a chance on ~ :** ~을 운에 맡기고 해보다
- **let someone something :** 누군가에 무엇을 하게 하다

★ Gonna do my very best and it ain't no lie
(　) you put me to the test,
(　) you let me try

나는 정말 최선을 다할 것이고 거짓말이 아니랍니다
만약 당신이 나를 시험한다면,
만약 당신이 내가 노력하게 해준다면

- **do one's best :** 최선을 다하다

Take a chance on me (That's all I ask of you, honey)
Take a chance on me

내게서 기회를 잡아요 (그게 내가 부탁하는 다예요, 그대여)
내게서 기회를 잡아요

- **ask :** ① 묻다 ② 부탁하다

We can go dancing, we can go walking
as long as we're together
Listen to some music, maybe just
talking, get to know you better
'Cause you know
I've got so much that I wanna do when
I dream I'm along with you
It's magic
You want me to leave it there, afraid of
a love affair
But I think you know that I can't let go

우리가 함께 있는 한, 우리는 춤 추러 갈
수도 있고 산책을 하러 갈 수도 있죠
음악을 듣고, 어쩌면 대화를 나누면서,
당신을 더 잘 알게 되겠죠
당신은 알고 있지요
내가 당신과 함께 있는 꿈을 꾸면, 하고 싶은
일이 너무 많다는 걸요
그것은 마법이죠
당신은 사랑에 두려워하는 나를 그저
놔두길 원하죠
하지만 내가 떠날 수 없다는 걸 당신이
안다고 생각해요

- **as long as ~ :** ~하는 한
- **leave :** ① 떠나다 ② 내버려두다
- **afraid of ~ :** ~를 두려워하는

☆ Repeat

★ Repeat

Take a chance on me
Take a chance on me

내게서 기회를 잡아요
내게서 기회를 잡아요

Oh, you can take your time, baby
I'm in no hurry, know I'm gonna get you
You don't wanna hurt me,
Baby, don't worry, I ain't gonna let you

시간을 두고 생각해봐도 좋아요, 그대여
난 서두르지 않아요, 내가 당신을 차지할 것이란
걸 알기에
당신은 내게 상처 주기 싫어하죠,
그대여, 걱정하지 말아요, 당신이 그러지 못하게
할 테니 (날 상처 주게 하지 않을 거예요)

- **wanan = want to**
- **(be) ganna = (be) going to :** ~ 할 것이다

Let me tell you now
My love is strong enough to last when things are rough
It's magic
You say that I waste my time but I can't get you off my mind
No, I can't let go
'Cause I love you so

지금 당신에게 말할게요
상황이 좋지 않아도 사랑은 계속될 만큼 내 사랑은 충분히 강하다는 걸
그것은 마법이에요
당신은 내가 시간을 낭비하고 있다고 말하죠
하지만 난 당신을 마음에서 지울 수가 없어요
당신을 보낼 수 없어요
왜냐면 전 당신을 너무 사랑하니까요

- **last :** ① 마지막의 ② 지속되다
- **rough :** ① 거친 ② 힘든 ③ 대강의
- **waste :** 낭비하다

☆ Repeat

※ Gonna do my very best, baby, can't you see?
Gotta put me to the test, take a chance on me
(Take a chance, take a chance, take a chance on me)

정말 최선을 다할 거예요, 그대여 모르겠나요?
나를 시험에 들게 해서, 나에게서 기회를 잡아요
(기회를 잡아요, 기회를 잡아요, 내게서 기회를 잡아요)

- **see :** ① 보다 ② 알다

Ba ba ba ba baa, ba ba ba ba baa
Honey, I'm still free
Take a chance on me

Ba ba ba ba baa, ba ba ba ba baa
그대여, 난 아직 혼자예요
내게서 기회를 잡아요

※ Repeat

23 If

If

- If는 '만약 ~한다면'의 뜻으로, 조건을 나타내는 절을 이끈다.

- **If** you are tired, you should take a rest.
  만약에 네가 피곤하다면, 너는 휴식을 취해야 해.
- **If** it rains tomorrow, we'll stay at home.
  만약에 내일 비가 온다면, 우리는 집에 머물 것이다.

Unless

- Unless는 '만약 ~이 아니라면'의 뜻으로, if ~ not과 같은 표현이다.

- **If** you do **not** hurry up, you will miss the bus.
  → **Unless** you hurry up, you will miss the bus.

- **If** you did **not** make a reservation, you should wait for your turn.
  → **Unless** you made a reservation, you should wait for your turn.

가사 예문

If you change your mind, I'm the first in line.
만약 당신이 마음을 바꾼다면, 내가 제일 앞에 있을게요.

Q1 다음 문장과 의미가 같도록 주어진 말로 시작하는 문장으로 고쳐 쓰시오.

1. Unless it's urgent, don't call him. (urgent : 긴박한)

→ If ______________________________.

2. If you are not busy, help me please.

→ Unless ______________________________.

3. If you don't have a ticket, you cannot go inside.

→ Unless ______________________________.

4. Unless you made an appointment for the interview, you can't meet him.

→ If ______________________________.

Q2 다음 우리말과 의미가 같도록 괄호 안의 표현을 이용하여 문장을 완성하시오.

1. 만약 네가 건강해지고 싶다면, 담배를 끊어야 한다. (become healthy / stop smoking)

→ ______________________________

2. 만약 네가 무언가를 쉽게 잊는다면, 메모하도록 노력해. (forget easily / write a memo)

→ ______________________________

3. 최선을 다하지 않으면, 좋은 성적을 받을 수 없어. (Unless / do your best / get a good grade)

→ ______________________________

4. 약속을 지키지 않으면, 좋은 인상을 줄 수 없어. (Unless / keep a promise / a good impression)

→ ______________________________

Fill in the Blank If

Question 1
1. it is not urgent, don't call him **2.** you are busy, help me please
3. you have a ticket, you cannot go inside
4. you did not make an appointment for the interview, you can't meet him

Question 2
1. If you want to become healthy, you should stop smoking.
2. If you forget something easily, try to write a memo.
3. Unless you do your best, you cannot get a good grade.
4. Unless you keep a promise, you cannot give a good impression.

24 I will — The Beatles

Who knows how long I've loved you?
Do you know I love you still?
Will I wait a lonely lifetime?
If you want me to,
①( )(   )

내가 얼마나 당신을 오랫동안 사랑해왔는지 누가 알까요?
당신은 내가 여전히 당신을 사랑한다는 것을 알고 있나요?
내가 외로운 한평생을 기다려야 하는 걸까요?
당신이 원한다면,
난 그럴 겁니다

- I've loved~ : ~를 사랑해오고 있다

For if I ever saw you
I didn't catch your name
But it never really matters
①( )(   ) always feel the same

만약 내가 당신을 보고
이름을 기억하지 못하더라도
그건 전혀 문제될 게 없지요
난 항상 변함없을 테니까요

Love you forever and forever
Love you with all my heart
Love you whenever we're together
Love you when we're apart

당신을 영원히 사랑합니다
당신을 내 진심을 다해 사랑합니다
우리가 함께 있는 모든 순간에 당신을 사랑합니다
우리가 헤어져 있을 때에도 당신을 사랑합니다

- matter : 중요하다
- with all my heart : 진심을 다해
- apart : 떨어져 있는

And when at last I find you
②(   )(   )(   ) fill the air
Sing it loud so I can hear you
Make it easy to be near you
For the things you do endear you to me
Ah, you know ①(   )(   )
①(   )(   )

그리고 마침내 내가 당신을 찾을 때
당신의 노래는 허공을 가득 채울 겁니다
크게 노래를 불러서 내가 당신의 목소리를
들을 수 있게 해주세요
당신 가까이에 있을 수 있게 해주세요
당신이 하는 모든 것들이 내가 당신을
사랑하게 만들어요
당신은 내가 당신을 영원히 사랑할 것을
알지요
내가 당신을 영원히 사랑할 것을

- **at last :** 마침내 (= finally)
- **endear :** 애정을 느끼게 하다

24 조동사 will

조동사 will

- 조동사 will은 동사 앞에 놓여서 '~일 것이다'(미래), '할 것이다'(의지), '~하시겠어요?'(권유)의 의미를 지닌다.

조동사 will의 특징

1. 주어의 인칭과 수에 따라 형태가 변하지 않는다.	He **will** throw a party for his parents. (wills(X) → will(O))
2. 조동사 뒤에는 동사원형을 쓴다.	She **will take** part in the campaign. (will takes(X) → will take(O))
3. 부정문 : will 뒤에 not을 쓰며, won't로 줄일 수 있다.	Could you wait for me? It **won't** take that long. (won't = will not)
4. 의문문 : 조동사를 문장 맨 앞에 쓴다.	A: **Will** you join us? / B: Yes, I **will**. / No, I **won't**.

조동사 will의 용법

1. 미래 (~일 것이다)	She **will** be sixteen next year.
2. 의지 (~하겠다)	**I'll** do my best on this final exam. (I'll = I will)
3. 권유 (~하시겠어요?)	**Will** you have some more pizza?

가사 예문

Cause I will always feel the same. 왜냐하면 나는 항상 같은 감정일 테니까요.

Your songs will fill the air. 당신의 노래는 허공을 가득 채울 겁니다.

Attention!

가까운 미래의 계획을 나타낼 때는 be going to로 미래를 표현할 수 있다!

A: What **are** you **going to** do tomorrow? 너 내일 무엇을 할 거니?

B: I **am going to** visit my uncle's house. 나는 삼촌 댁을 방문할 거야.

Q1 다음 문장의 빈칸에 will과 won't 중 알맞은 표현을 쓰시오.

1. A: I have an important meeting tomorrow. _______ you wake me up at six?
   B: Sure. I will.
2. A: The weather forecast says that it _______ rain in the afternoon.
   B: Then, I will go hiking today.
3. A: I have a presentation tomorrow. I'm so worried about that.
   B: Don't be nervous. You _______ do well on the presentation.

Q2 다음 우리말과 의미가 같도록 괄호 안의 단어들을 바르게 배열하시오. (첫 대문자 유의)

1. 공항까지 저를 데려다 주시겠어요? (take / will / you / to the airport / me /?)

→ ____________________

2. 다시는 늦지 않겠습니다. 정각에 교실에 도착하겠습니다.
(won't / I / late / be / again /.) (will / on time / I / in the classroom / be /.)

→ ____________________

3. 나는 이번 주말 캠핑이 정말 기대돼. 우리는 정말 즐거운 시간을 보낼 거야.
(about camping / I'm / this weekend / so excited /.) (fun / we / have / will / so much /.)

→ ____________________

Fill in the Blank ① I will ② Your song will

Question 1 1. Will 2. won't 3. will

Question 2 1. Will you take me to the airport?
2. I won't be late again. I will be on time in the classroom.
3. I'm so excited about camping this weekend. We will have so much fun.

25 Dancing queen

ABBA

You ①(   )(   ), you ②(   )(   )
Having the time of your life
See that girl, watch that scene
Dig in the dancing queen

당신은 춤을 출 수 있어요, 자이브도 출 수 있죠
인생에서 행복한 시간을 가지면서
저 소녀를 봐요, 저 장면을 보세요
댄싱퀸에 빠져봐요

- **jive :** ① 재즈 음악에 맞춰 추는 화려한 춤
  ② 자이브를 추다
- **have the time of one's life :** 인생의 최고의 순간을 보내다
- **dig in~ :** ~에 빠지다

Friday night and the lights are low
Looking out for a place to go where
they play the right music, getting
in the swing
You come to look for a king
Anybody could be that guy
Night is young and the music's high
With a bit of rock music, everything is
fine
You're in the mood for a dance
And when you get the chance

금요일 밤 불빛은 낮게 깔리고
리듬을 타면서, 좋아하는 곡을 연주하는
그런 곳을 찾아 헤매죠
당신은 왕자님을 찾으러 왔죠
어떤 사람이라도 그 사람이 될 수 있어요
아직 초저녁이고 음악은 울려 퍼지고
록 음악 한 소절만 있으면, 모든 게 괜찮아요
당신은 춤출 기분에 빠지죠
그리고 당신에게 춤출 기회가 오면

- **look out for~ :** ~를 찾으려고 애쓰다
- **swing :** 흔들어 움직이다
- **a bit of :** 한 조각의, 다소
- **in the mood for~ :** ~하고 싶은

★ You are the dancing queen
Young and sweet, only seventeen
Dancing queen
Feel the beat from the tambourine,
oh yeah
You ①(　　)(　　　), you ②(　　)(　　)
Having the time of your life
See that girl, watch that scene
Dig in the dancing queen

당신은 댄싱퀸이 되죠
어리고 예쁜 열일곱 소녀
댄싱퀸
탬버린의 비트를 느껴봐요,
당신은 춤을 출 수 있어요, 자이브도 출 수 있죠
인생에서 행복한 시간을 가지면서
저 소녀를 봐요, 저 장면을 보세요
댄싱퀸에 빠져봐요

- **sweet :** ① 달콤한 ② 사랑스러운 ③ 단 것(~s)

You're a teaser, you turn 'em on
Leave 'em burning and then you're gone
Looking out for another, anyone will do
You're in the mood for a dance
And when you get the chance

당신은 남자들을 가지고 놀아요
그들을 열정으로 불타게 하고 사라지죠
다른 사람을 찾아다니면서, 누구든 괜찮아요
당신은 춤출 기분에 빠지죠
그리고 당신에게 춤출 기회가 오면

- **teaser :** 약 올리는 사람, 애태우는 사람
- **turn someone on :** (성적으로) ~의 흥미를 끌다

★ Repeat

Dig in the dancing queen

댄싱퀸에 빠져봐요

25 조동사 can

조동사 can

- 동사 앞에 놓여서 '~할 수 있다'(가능), '~해도 된다'(허락), '~일 수 있다'(추측)의 의미를 지닌다.

조동사 can의 특징

1. 주어의 인칭과 수에 따라 형태가 변하지 않는다.	He **can** speak Chinese. (cans(X) → can(O))
2. 조동사 뒤에는 동사원형을 쓴다.	She can **drive** a car. (drives(X) → drive(O))
3. 부정문 : 조동사 뒤에 not을 쓴다.	I can**not** play the violin.
4. 의문문 : 조동사를 문장 맨 앞에 쓴다.	**Can** I use a cell phone here?
5. 과거형 : could이다.	When I was young, I **could** swim in this river.
6. could는 can보다 공손한 '요청'의 의미이다.	**Could** you tell me how to get to the National museum?

조동사 can의 용법

1. 능력 가능 (~할 수 있다)	I **can** solve this question.
2. 허락 (~해도 된다)	You **can** leave now.
3. 추측 (~일 수 있다)	It **can** be wrong.

가사 예문

You can dance, you can jive. 너는 춤을 출 수 있어, 자이브도 출 수 있지.

Anybody could be that guy. 어떤 사람이라도 그 사람이 될 수 있어요.

Q1 다음 문장에서 밑줄 친 can의 의미로 알맞은 것에 표시하시오.

1. It can't be true. ☐ 능력 ☐ 허락 ☐ 추측
2. Can you speak Chinese? ☐ 능력 ☐ 허락 ☐ 추측
3. People cannot take a picture here. ☐ 능력 ☐ 허락 ☐ 추측
4. Can you help me carry these boxes? ☐ 능력 ☐ 허락 ☐ 추측

Q2 다음 문장의 빈칸에 들어갈 말을 〈보기〉에서 골라 can't(couldn't)를 이용하여 쓰시오.

〈보기〉 imagine eat meet understand

1. She speaks so fast, so I ________ ________ her.
2. I was very full, so I ________ ________ the dessert.
3. I wanted to talk to Jane yesterday, but I ________ ________ her.
4. Nowadays people ________ ________ their lives without Internet.

Q3 다음 문장의 빈칸에 들어갈 말을 〈보기〉에서 골라 can(could)를 이용하여 쓰시오.

〈보기〉 buy see make run

1. I ________ ________ very fast when I was young.
2. If you do your best in your situation, you ________ ________ your dreams come true.
3. Thanks to the nice weather, they ________ ________ the wonderful view from the tower.
4. There is a convenient store across the street. We ________ ________ the cup noodle there.

Fill in the Blank ① can dance ② can jive

Question 1 **1.** 추측 **2.** 능력 **3.** 허락 **4.** 능력

Question 2 **1.** can't understand **2.** couldn't eat **3.** couldn't meet **4.** can't imagine

Question 3 **1.** could run **2.** can make **3.** could see 또는 can see **4.** can buy

26	She	Elvis Costello

① (　　)(　　)(　　) the face I can't forget
A trace of pleasure or regret,
may be my treasure or the price I have to pay
① (　　)(　　)(　　) the song that summer sings,
may be the chill that autumn brings,
may be a hundred different things
within the measure of a day

그녀는 내가 잊지 못하는 얼굴일지 모릅니다
즐거움 또는 후회의 흔적일 수도 있고요,
나의 보물, 어쩌면 내가 치러야 할 대가일 수도 있어요
그녀는 아마도 여름이 부르는 노래일지도 모르고,
어쩌면 가을이 안겨다주는 서늘함일지도 모르고,
어쩌면 하루에도 수백 가지로 변하는 다른 모습일지도 몰라요

- trace : 흔적
- pleasure : 기쁨
- regret : 후회
- chill : 서늘함

① (　　)(　　)(　　) the beauty or the beast,
may be the famine or the feast,
may turn each day into a heaven or a hell,
① (　　)(　　)(　　) the mirror of my dreams,
A smile reflected in a stream,
② (　　)(　　)(　　)(　　) what she may seem inside her shell,

그녀는 미녀이거나 어쩌면 야수일지도 몰라요
빈곤이거나 풍성함일 수도 있고요,
하루하루를 천국으로 또는 지옥으로 바꿀지도 몰라요
그녀는 내 꿈을 비추는 거울일지도 모르고,
시냇물에 비친 그녀의 미소,
그녀의 속마음은 어쩌면 겉보기와는 다를지도 몰라요

- famine : 굶주림
- feast : 축제
- reflect : 반영하다
- shell : 껍데기

She who always seems so happy
in a crowd
whose eyes can be so private and so
proud,
no one's allowed to see them
when they cry
①(   )(   )(   ) the love that cannot
hope to last,
may come to me from shadows of
the past,
that I'll remember till the day I die

그녀는 많은 사람들 안에서 항상 행복해
보일 거예요
그 눈빛은 비밀스럽고 자존심에 차 있지만,
아무도 그녀가 눈물 흘리는 걸 보지는
못했죠
어쩌면 그녀는 영원히 계속되기를
바랄 수 없는 사랑일지도 몰라요,
과거의 그림자로부터 벗어나 나에게 올지도
모르죠,
난 죽는 날까지 그녀를 기억할 거예요

- **crowd** : 군중
- **is allowed to~** : ~하도록 허락되다
- **shadow** : 그늘
- **till** : ~까지

①(   )(   )(   ) the reason I survive
The why and wherefore I'm alive
The one I'll care for through the rough
and ready years
Me, I'll take her laughter and her tears
and make them all my souvenirs
For where she goes I've got to be
The meaning of my life is
She, she, she

그녀는 어쩌면 내가 살아가는 이유랍니다
그녀가 있기에 내가 있어요
거칠고 긴 세월 동안 내가 돌보아야 할
단 한 사람이랍니다
나는요, 난 그녀의 웃음과 눈물을 모두
받아들일 거예요
그리고 그것들을 모두 소중한 나의 선물로
간직할 거예요
그녀가 어디로 가든지 나도 함께할 거예요
내 삶의 의미는 그녀, 그녀, 그녀이니까요

- **reason** : 이유
- **survive** : 생존하다
- **wherefore** : (고어) 그런 이유로
- **through** : ~를 통하여
- **rough** : 거친
- **laughter** : 웃음
- **care for** : 돌보다
- **souvenir** : 기념품

26 조동사 may

조동사 may

• 조동사 may는 동사 앞에 놓여서 '~해도 좋다'(허락), '~일지도 모른다'(추측)의 의미를 지닌다.

조동사 may의 특징

1. 주어의 인칭과 수에 따라 형태가 변하지 않는다.	She **may** change her mind. mays (X) → may (O)
2. 조동사 뒤에는 동사원형을 쓴다.	My homeroom teacher **may be** upset. may is (X) → may be (O)
3. 부정문 : 조동사 뒤에 not을 쓴다.	You **may not** take your pet in this shop.
4. 의문문 : 조동사를 문장 맨 앞에 쓴다.	A: **May** I have your number, please? B: Yes, you **may**. / No, you **may not**.

조동사 may의 용법

1. 허락 (~해도 좋다)	**May** I use your computer?
2. 추측 (~일지도 모른다)	The rumor **may** be true.

가사 예문

She may be the face I can't forget.
그녀는 제가 잊지 못하는 얼굴일지 모릅니다.

She may be the reason I survive.
그녀는 제가 사는 이유일지 모릅니다.

Q1 다음 밑줄 친 부분의 의미가 〈보기〉와 같은 것을 고르시오.

〈보기〉 May I come in?

① It may be her pencil. ② He may be the president.
③ She may be angry at me. ④ Tony may be late for the class.
⑤ You may use my cell phone.

Q2 다음 괄호 안의 단어를 이용하여 빈칸에 알맞은 말을 쓰시오.

Yesterday, I went to the library. There were a lot of people there and it was hard to find a seat. Finally, I found one, but there was a bag on the desk. I asked the man who was sitting on next to the bag, " ______ ______ ______ ______?" (may / sit here) He said, "I'm sorry, This seat is already taken."

Q3 다음 문장의 빈칸에 들어갈 말을 〈보기〉에서 골라 may(may not)를 이용하여 쓰시오.

〈보기〉 come be hurt go help

1. Watch out the big dog! He ______ ______ you.
2. You look tired. You ______ ______ home and take some rest.
3. Jennifer seems to be very young. She ______ ______ under twenty.
4. Christine looks very busy today. She ______ ______ ______ to the party.
5. A: ______ I ______ you?
   B: No, thank you. I am just looking around.

Fill in the Blank ① she may be ② she may not be
Question 1 ⑤
Question 2 May I sit here
Question 3 **1.** may hurt **2.** may go **3.** may be **4.** may not come **5.** May, help

27	The young ones	Cliff Richard

The young ones
Darling, we're the young ones
And young ones ①(   )(   ) afraid
to live and love while the flame is strong
Cause we may not be the young ones
very long

젊은이들,
그대여, 우리는 젊어요
젊은 사람이라면 젊음의 불꽃이 강하게
타오르는 동안은 사는 것과 사랑하는 것을
두려워해선 안 돼요
왜냐하면 우리 젊음이 그리 오래 가진 않을
테니까요

- **The young ones :** 젊은이들
- **afraid :** 두려워하는
- **while~ :** ~하는 동안은
- **flame :** 불꽃

Tomorrow, why wait till tomorrow?
Cause tomorrow sometimes never
comes
So love me
There's a song to be sung
And the best time is to sing while we're
young

내일, 왜 내일까지 기다리나요?
왜냐하면 내일은 때로는 오지 않을 수도
있으니까요
그러니 나를 사랑해주세요
불러야 할 노래가 있어요
그 노래를 부르기에 가장 좋은 때는 우리가
젊었을 때랍니다

☆ Once in every lifetime comes a love
like this
Oh, I need you and you need me
Oh, my darling, can't you see?

일생에 한 번 이런 사랑이 찾아와요
오, 난 그대가 필요하고, 그대는 내가
필요해요
오, 내 사랑, 모르시겠어요?

- **see :** ① 보다 ② 알다
  ③ 발견하다 ④ 만나다

★ Young dreams ②(   )(   ) dreamed together
And the young hearts ①(   ) (   ) afraid
And someday when the years have flown
Darling, then we'll teach the young ones of our own

젊은 꿈들은 함께 꾸어야 해요
그리고 젊은 가슴들은 두려워해선 안 돼요
그러다 언젠가 세월이 흘렀을 때
그대여, 그땐 우리가 우리의 젊은이들을 가르치게 되겠지요

- **someday** : 언젠가는
- **years fly** : 세월이 흐르다
- **fly - flew - flown**

☆ Repeat

★ Repeat

27 조동사 should

조동사 should

- 조동사 should는 동사 앞에 놓여서 '~해야 한다'(약한 의무), '~하는 게 좋겠다'(충고)의 의미를 지닌다.

조동사 should의 특징

1. 주어의 인칭과 수에 따라 형태가 변하지 않는다.	She **should** take a rest for a week. shoulds (X) → should (O)
2. 조동사 뒤에는 동사원형을 쓴다.	She **should be** back in school. should is (X) → should be (O)
3. 부정문 : should 뒤에 not을 쓰며, shouldn't로 줄일 수 있다.	Overeating is surely the main cause of obesity. You **shouldn't** eat too much. (obesity : 비만)
4. 의문문 : 조동사를 문장 맨앞에 쓴다.	**Should** we make a decision before the meeting?

조동사 should의 용법

1. 약한 의무 (~해야 한다)	You **should** be nice to the elderly.
2. 충고 (~하는 것이 좋겠다)	You **should** wear sunscreen before enjoying this weather.

가사 예문

And young ones shouldn't be afraid to live and love while the flame is strong.
젊은 사람이라면 젊음의 불꽃이 강하게 타오르는 동안은 사는 것과 사랑하는 것을 두려워해선 안 돼요.

Young dreams should be dreamed together.
젊은 꿈들은 함께 꾸어야 해요.

Q1 주어진 동사와 should(should not)를 사용하여 문장을 완성하시오.

〈보기〉 stay tell use respect look down on

1. We ______________ text messages to spread rumors or gossip.
2. You ______________ inside when yellow dust blows into Korea.
3. You ______________ a person only because he is poor.
   (look down on : 무시하다)
4. If someone bullies you, you ______________ your teachers and parents right away. (bully : 괴롭히다)
5. Even though someone is very different from you, you ______________ the person. (even though : 비록 ~할지라도)

Q2 괄호 안에 주어진 표현들과 should(should not)를 이용하여 문장을 완성하시오.

1. 너는 여기서 도로를 건너서는 안 된다. (cross the road)

→ ______________________________

2. 우리는 교실 안에 CCTV를 설치해야 할까요? (install CCTV)

→ ______________________________

3. 너는 지금 당장 진찰을 받아보는 게 좋겠다. (see a doctor)

→ ______________________________

4. 운전자들은 제한속도를 어기면 안 된다. (violate the speed limit)

→ ______________________________

Fill in the Blank ① shouldn't be ② should be

Question 1 **1.** should not use **2.** should stay **3.** should not look down on **4.** should tell **5.** should respect

Question 2 **1.** You should not cross the road here. **2.** Should we install CCTV in the classroom? **3.** You should see a doctor right now. **4.** Drivers should not violate the speed limit.

28 I believe I can fly | R. Kelly

I used to think that I could not go on
And life was nothing but an awful song
But now I know the meaning of true love
I'm leaning on the everlasting arms

난 삶을 계속할 수 없다고 생각하곤 했어요
인생은 그저 끔찍한 노래 같았죠
하지만 이제는 진실한 사랑의 의미를 알아요
영원토록 날 반겨줄 당신 두 팔에 기대어있어요

- **used to~ :** ~하곤 했다
- **go on :** 계속하다
- **nothing but :** (= only) 오직
- **awful :** 끔찍한
- **lean on :** ~에 기대다
- **everlasting :** 영원한

★ If I can see it then I can do it
If I just believe it there's nothing to it
I believe I can fly
I believe I can touch the sky
I think about it every night and day
Spread my wings and fly away
I believe I can soar
I see me running through that open door
I believe I can fly
I believe I can fly
I believe I can fly

만약 내가 그걸 볼 수 있다면 난 할 수 있는 거예요
만약 내가 그걸 믿는다면 아무것도 문제될 것이 없어요
난 날 수 있다고 믿어요
난 저 하늘에 닿을 수 있다고 믿어요
난 밤낮으로 그것에 대해 생각해요
날개를 펴고 저 멀리 날아갈 수 있다고 말이에요
난 날아오를 수 있다고 믿어요
활짝 열린 문으로 달려가는 내 모습을 봐요
난 날 수 있다고 믿어요
난 날 수 있다고 믿어요
난 날 수 있다고 믿어요

- **spread :** ① 펼치다 ② 확산
- **soar :** (허공으로) 솟구치다

See I was on the verge of breaking down
Sometimes silence it can seem so loud
There are miracles in life I (   )
(   )
But first I know it starts inside of me
Oh woo Oh woo

내가 쓰러지기 직전 이었다는 걸 알잖아요
어떤 침묵의 시간은 너무도 소란스러울 수 있어요
삶 속에는 이루어야 하는 기적들이 있어요
하지만 시작은 내 안에서 출발하는 거예요

- **on the verge of~ :** ~하기 직전에
- **break down :** 허물어지다
- **seem :** ~ 인 것처럼 보이다
- **miracle :** 기적
- **achieve :** 성취하다

★ Repeat

Cause I believe in me
Oh...

왜냐하면 내가 나 자신을 믿기 때문에
오…

★ Repeat

If I just spread my wings
I can fly I can fly I can fly
If I just spread my wings
I can fly
Hmmmmm... fly, fly, fly

만약 내가 날개를 펼칠 수만 있다면
난 날 수 있어요 난 날 수 있어요 난 날 수 있어요
만약 내가 날개를 펼칠 수만 있다면
난 날 수 있어요
흠… 날아요, 날아요, 날아요

28 조동사 must

조동사 must

- 조동사 must는 동사 앞에 놓여서 '~해야 한다'(강한 의무), '~임에 틀림없다'(강한 추측)의 의미를 지닌다.
- '~해야 한다'라는 의미로 말할 때는 have to / has to도 쓸 수 있다.

조동사 must의 특징

1. 주어의 인칭과 수에 따라 형태가 변하지 않는다.	He **must** finish his work by five. musts (X) → must (O)
2. 조동사 뒤에는 동사원형을 쓴다.	Even if she doesn't like it, she **must do** it. must does (X) → must do (O)
3. 부정문 : must 뒤에 not을 쓰며, mustn't로 줄일 수 있다.	A: **Must** I call the police? B: **Yes**, you **must**. / **No**, you **mustn't**.
4. 과거형 : had to를 쓴다.	She **had to** stay at home to take care of her mom.

조동사 must의 용법

1. 강한 의무 (~해야 한다)	You **must** hand in your assignment on time.
2. 강한 추측 (~임에 틀림없다)	There **must** be some reason for it.

가사 예문

There are miracles in life I must achieve.
삶 속에는 내가 성취해야 할 기적들이 있어요.

Attention!

강한 추측의 부정을 나타낼 때는 can't be로 표현하는 것에 유의!

A: Did you hear the news that he was arrested on a suspicion of theft?

B: That **can't be** true! I am sure of his honesty.

Q1 주어진 동사와 must(must not)를 사용하여 문장을 완성하시오.

<보기>	pay	show	tell	think

1. The government ________________ attention to the opinions of the people.
2. We ________________ about how to use our limited natural resources wisely!
3. You ________________ your passport every time you leave or enter a country.
4. Honesty is the best policy. You ________________ a lie under any circumstances.

Q2 괄호 안에 주어진 표현들과 must(must not)를 이용하여 문장을 완성하시오.

1. 모든 운전자들은 교통법규를 준수해야 한다. (keep the traffic rules)

→ ____

2. 너는 사람의 외모를 보고 그를 평가하면 안 돼. (judge a man by his appearance)

→ ____

3. 그는 골프를 치는 것에 매우 재능이 있는 것이 틀림없어! (talented at playing golf)

→ ____

4. 우리는 무슨 일이 있어도 아이들을 때려서는 안 된다. (strike children under any circumstances)

→ ____

Fill in the Blank must achieve

Question 1 **1.** must pay **2.** must think **3.** must show **4.** must not tell

Question 2 **1.** All drivers must keep the traffic rules.
2. You must not judge a man by his appearance. **3.** He must be talented at playing golf.
4. We must not strike children under any circumstances.

II
Intermediate

29 All by myself — Celine Dion

★ When I was young I never needed anyone And making love was just for fun Those days are gone	젊었을 적에는 아무도 필요치 않았어요 사랑도 그저 재미 삼아 했었죠 하지만 그런 날들은 이제 가버렸어요 • for fun : 재미 삼아
Living alone I think of all the friends I've known When I dial the telephone Nobody's home	홀로된 삶을 살며 알고 지내던 친구들을 생각하지만 아무리 전화해봐도 받는 사람이 없어요
All ( )( ), (I) don't wanna be, all ( )( ) any more	온전히 혼자죠, 혼자이고 싶지 않아요, 더 이상은
Hard to be sure Sometimes I feel so insecure And love so distant and obscure remains the cure	확신도 잃어버리고 때로는 불안이 엄습해와요 저 멀리 아련히 보이는 사랑만이 남아 날 치유해줄 수 있을 뿐 • insecure : 불안한 • distant : 먼, 떨어져 있는 • obscure : 모호한

All ( )( ),
(I) don't wanna be all ( )( )
any more
All ( )( ), don't wanna live
All ( )( ), any more

온전히 혼자죠,
더 이상 혼자이고 싶지 않아요
온전히 혼자죠, 홀로된 삶을 살고 싶지
않아요
온전히 혼자, 더 이상은

- **not ~ any more : 더 이상 ~않는**
- **wanna : want to**

★ Repeat

All ( )( ),
(I) don't wanna be all ( )( )
any more
All ( )( ), don't wanna live

Don't wanna live ( )( )
( )( ) any more
( )( ) any more

온전히 혼자죠,
혼자이고 싶지 않아요 더 이상은
온전히 혼자죠, 홀로된 삶을 살고 싶지
않아요

홀로된 삶을 살고 싶지 않아요
홀로 더 이상은
홀로 더 이상은

29 재귀대명사

재귀대명사란

- 인칭대명사의 소유격이나 목적격에 -self/-selves를 붙인 형태로 '~ 자신', '~ 자체'의 의미를 지닌다.

수 \ 인칭	1인칭	2인칭	3인칭
단수	myself	yourself	himself / herself / itself
복수	ourselves	yourselves	themselves

재귀대명사의 용법

1. 재귀용법	동사나 전치사의 목적어가 주어와 일치하는 경우로서, 재귀용법의 재귀대명사는 **생략하면 문장이 성립되지 않는다.** Megan looked at the mirror and said to **herself**, "How beautiful I am!"
2. 강조용법	주어, 목적어, 보어의 뜻을 강조하기 위해 쓰인 경우로, 강조용법의 재귀대명사는 **생략해도 문장이 성립된다.** I **myself** solved all the difficult questions.

재귀대명사의 관용적 표현

- by oneself : 혼자서(=alone)
- of itself : 저절로
- enjoy oneself : 즐거운 시간을 보내다
- for oneself : 혼자 힘으로
- kill oneself : 자살하다
- say to oneself : 중얼거리다

가사 예문

All by myself, don't wanna be all by myself any more.

온전히 혼자죠, 더 이상 혼자이고 싶지 않아요.

Q1 다음 문장의 밑줄 친 부분을 어법상 알맞은 형태로 고쳐 쓰시오.

1. She cut her on some broken glasses. → ________
2. You can't go home by you in the dark. → ________
3. As teachers us, we understand the problem. → ________
4. Did the children make the model all by them? → ________

Q2 우리말과 의미가 같도록 빈칸에 알맞은 재귀대명사의 형태를 쓰시오.

1. The door opens ________ ________. (저절로)
2. We should finish the project ________ ________. (스스로)
3. David went on a trip to New York ________ ________. (혼자서)
4. She ________ ________ ________, so I couldn't understand. (중얼거렸다)
5. They ________ ____________ at the rock festival. (즐거운 시간을 보냈다)

Q3 다음 문장에 맞는 -self 형태를 쓰시오.

1. Daniel, take care of ____________ during the trip!
2. We relaxed and enjoyed ____________ on the beach.
3. She is sitting in front of the mirror. She is looking at ____________.
4. They found a solution to the problem. They feel proud of ____________.

Fill in the Blank by myself

Question 1 1. herself 2. yourself 3. ourselves 4. themselves

Question 2 1. of itself 2. for ourselves 3. by himself 4. said to herself 5. enjoyed themselves

Question 3 1. yourself 2. ourselves 3. herself 4. themselves

30	Happy	Mocca

☆ Life is just a bowl of cherries
Sometimes it's afraid filled with worries
Don't be afraid
(   ) things go wrong, just be strong

삶은 한 그릇의 체리와 같아
가끔은 근심으로 가득 찬 인생이 두려울 때도 있지만
두려워하지 마
일이 잘 안될 땐, 그저 강해지면 돼

- bowl : 우묵한 그릇
- filled with~ : ~으로 가득 찬
- things go wrong : 일이 잘못되다

★ (   ) thing seems up in the air,
And everything is so unfair,
And you stumble and fall,
Just pick yourself up and sing

뭔가 결정되지 않은 것 같을 때,
모든 것이 불공평한 것 같을 때,
발을 헛디뎌 넘어질 것 같을 때,
기운 내고 일어나 노래해봐

- up in the air : 아직 미정인
- unfair : 불공평한
- stumble : 발을 헛디디다
- pick yourself up : 다시 일어나다

✲ If one day you lose your way,
Just remember one thing, my friend
(   ) you're under a cloud,
Just visit music and sing

언젠가 네가 길을 잃는다면,
이 한 가지만은 기억해, 친구야
네가 우울할 땐,
음악을 틀고 노래를 불러봐

- under a cloud : ① 의심을 받는 ② 우울한

If one day you lose your way,
Just remember that I'm here to stay
Don't you give up, keep your chin up,
And be happy!

언젠가 네가 길을 잃는다면
내가 여기 있다는 걸 기억해
포기하지 말고, 고개를 들어,
그리고 행복하자!

- keep your chin up : 용기를 내

☆ Repeat

★ Repeat

⁜ Repeat

If one day you lose your way,
Just remember one thing, my friend
(   ) you're under a cloud,
Just visit music and dance

언젠가 네가 길을 잃는다면
이 한 가지만은 기억해, 친구야
네가 우울할 땐,
음악을 틀고 춤을 춰봐

If one day you lose your way,
Just remember that I'm here to stay
Don't you give up, keep your chin up,
Don't you give up, keep your chin up,
Keep your chin up, and be happy!

언젠가 네가 길을 잃는다면
내가 여기 있다는 걸 기억해
포기하지 말고, 고개를 들어봐,
포기하지 말고, 고개를 들어봐,
용기를 내, 그리고 행복하자!

30 접속사 when

접속사 when

- when은 '언제'라는 의문사 외에 '~할 때'의 의미를 지니는 접속사로 쓰인다.
- 접속사 when으로 시작하는 부사절이 문장 맨 앞에 올 수도 있고, 주절 뒤에 올 수도 있다.

When **I was young**, I had many dreams for the future.

= I had many dreams for the future **when** **I was young**.

(when 절을 주절 뒤에 쓸 때는 콤마(,)를 붙이지 않는다.)

가사 예문

When things go wrong, just be strong.

일이 잘 안될 땐, 그저 강해지면 돼.

When you're under a cloud, just visit music and dance.

네가 우울할 때엔, 음악을 틀고 춤을 춰봐.

Attention!

의문사 when(언제) vs 접속사 when(~때) 구분할 것!

의문사 when

- Do you know **when** **the bus arrives**? (언제 버스가 도착하는지)
- Could you tell me **when** **the Lotte Mart opens**? (언제 롯데마트가 여는지)

접속사 when

- **When** **you come back** home from outside, wash your hands first. (집으로 돌아올 때)
- **When** **you drive a car**, you mustn't use your cell phone for your safety. (차를 운전할 때)

Q1 우리말과 의미가 같도록 빈칸에 알맞은 말을 쓰시오.

1. 나는 혼자 있을 때, 음악 듣는 것을 좋아해.

→ ____________________, I like to listen to music.

2. Ted는 그 소식을 들었을 때, 매우 놀랐다.

→ Ted was very surprised ____________________.

3. Michale은 축구할 때, 안경을 벗는다.

→ ____________________, he takes off his glasses.

4. 당신은 길을 걸을 때, 무슨 생각을 하나요?

→ What do you think about ____________________?

5. 당신은 사무실에서 일하지 않을 때, 뭐하세요?

→ What do you do ____________________?

Q2 밑줄 친 부분의 쓰임이 나머지와 다른 것은?

① Be careful when you use the scissors.

② I am not sure when I'll see her again.

③ Leonard was nine when his father died.

④ I'll call you back when I arrive at my office.

⑤ When you feel nervous, imagine your success.

Fill in the Blank When

Question 1 **1.** When I am alone **2.** when he heard the news **3.** When Michale plays soccer **4.** when you walk on the street **5.** when you are not working at the office 또는 when you do not work at the office

Question 2 ②

31	Perfect	Ed Sheeran

I found a love for me
Darling, just dive right in, and follow my lead
Well, I found a girl, beautiful and sweet
I never knew
You were the someone waiting for me
Cause we were just kids when we fell in love
Not knowing what it was,
I will not give you up this time
But darling, just kiss me slow,
Your heart is all I own
And in your eyes you're holding mine

나는 나의 사랑을 찾았어요
내 사랑, 그저 나에게 빠져들고 나를 따라와요
음, 나는 한 소녀를 찾았죠, 아름답고
사랑스러운 소녀예요
난 몰랐어요
당신이 나를 기다리고 있던 사람이었다는 걸
왜냐하면 우리가 사랑에 빠졌을 때 우린
어렸거든요
그게 무엇인지 몰랐죠,
이번에는 당신을 포기하지 않을 거예요
그대여, 나에게 천천히 입을 맞춰주세요,
나에게는 당신의 마음밖에 없죠
그리고 당신의 눈 안에는 나의 마음이 있어요

- dive in : 뛰어들다
- lead : ① 이끌다 ② 안내 ③ 납 ④ 주인공
- sweet : ① 달콤한 ② 사랑스러운 ③ 사탕류(sweets)
- give up : 포기하다
- own : ① 소유하다 ② ~자신의
- hold : ① 갖고 있다 ② 개최하다 ③ 지탱하다

Baby, I'm dancing in the dark,
with you between my arms
Barefoot on the grass,
listening to our favorite song
When you said you looked a mess,
I whispered underneath my breath
But you heard it,
"Darling, ①(　　)(　　)(　　　　)
tonight."

그대여, 난 어둠 속에서 춤을 추고 있어요,
당신을 내 품에 안고서
잔디 위에 맨발로 있죠,
우리가 가장 좋아하는 노래를 들으면서
당신의 모습이 엉망이라고 말했을 때,
나는 숨죽여 속삭이듯이 말했죠
하지만 당신은 그걸 들었어요,
"그대여, 당신은 오늘 밤 완벽해요"

- barefoot : 맨발의
- mess : ① 엉망 ② 엉망으로 만들다
- whisper : 속삭이다
- underneath one's breath : 숨죽여

Well, I found a woman,
stronger than anyone I know
She shares my dreams
I hope that someday I'll share her home
I found a love,
to carry more than just my secrets,
to carry love, to carry children of our own
We are still kids, but we're so in love,
fighting against all odds
I know we'll be alright this time
Darling, just hold my hand
Be my girl, I'll be your man
I see my future in your eyes

음, 난 한 여자를 찾았죠,
내가 아는 그 누구보다 더 강한
그녀는 내 꿈을 공유하죠
나는 언젠가 그녀와 함께 살길 희망해요
난 사랑을 찾았어요,
내 비밀보다 더 소중하게 간직하고,
우리의 사랑과 우리의 아이들을 짊어질 사랑
우린 여전히 어리죠, 하지만 우린 완전히
사랑에 빠졌어요,
모든 역경에 맞서고 있죠
난 알아요, 이번에는 괜찮을 거라는 걸
그대여, 그냥 내 손을 잡아요
내 여자가 되어줘요, 난 당신의 남자가 될게요
난 당신의 눈 속에서 나의 미래를 봐요

- **carry :** ① 나르다 ② 간직하다 ③ 짊어지다
- **against :** ~에 맞서
- **odds :** ① (어떤 일이 있을) 가능성 ② 역경

Baby, I'm dancing in the dark,
with you between my arms
Barefoot on the grass,
listening to our favorite song
When I saw you in that dress,
②(　　)ing so (　　　　　)
I don't deserve this,
"Darling, ①(　　)(　　)(　　　　)
tonight."

그대여, 난 어둠 속에서 춤을 추고 있어요,
당신을 내 품에 안고서
잔디 위에 맨발로 있죠,
우리가 가장 좋아하는 노래를 들으면서
당신이 그 드레스를 입은 걸 보았을 때,
너무나 아름다워 보였죠
난 이만한 걸 누릴 자격이 없지만,
"그대여, 당신은 오늘 밤 완벽해요"

- **deserve :** ~를 누릴 자격이 있다

Baby, I'm dancing in the dark,
with you between my arms
Barefoot on the grass,
listening to our favorite song
I have faith in what I see
Now I know I have met an angel
in person
And ③(　　)(　　　)(　　　　　),
no I don't deserve this
①(　　)(　　　)(　　　　　) tonight

난 어둠 속에서 춤을 추고 있어요,
내 품에 당신을 안고서
잔디 위에 맨발로 있죠,
우리가 가장 좋아하는 노래를 들으면서
난 내가 보는 것에 믿음이 있어요
난 이제 알죠, 내가 사람의 모습을 하고 있는
천사를 만났다는 걸
그리고 그녀는 완벽해요, 나는 이걸 누릴
자격이 없지만
당신은 오늘 밤 완벽해요

- **faith** : 믿음

31 look + 형용사

look + 형용사란

- 'look + 형용사'는 '~하게 보이다'의 의미로서, 사물의 상태 또는 특징에 대해 말할 때 look 뒤에는 형용사를 쓴다.
- look 이외에도 감각동사인 smell, taste, feel, sound 또한 형용사를 취하며, 부사는 올 수 없다.

감각동사		의미	예문
smell	+ 형용사	~한 냄새가 나다	The flower **smells sweet**. (O) The flower **smells sweetly**. (X)
look		~하게 보이다	You **look serious**. (O) You **look seriously**. (X)
feel		~하게 느껴지다	The cloth **feels soft**. (O) The cloth **feels softly**. (X)
sound		~하게 들리다	The story **sounds strange**. (O) The story **sounds strangely**. (X)
taste		~한 맛이 나다	Milk **tastes bad**. (O) Milk **tastes badly**. (X)

가사 예문

But you heard it, "Darling, you look perfect tonight."

하지만 당신은 그걸 들었어요, "그대여, 당신은 오늘 밤 완벽해요."

Q1 〈보기〉에 주어진 형용사와 괄호 안의 동사를 사용하여 문장을 완성하시오.

(필요한 경우 동사 변형)

〈보기〉 different interesting delicious dizzy bad

1. That ________ ________. Could I borrow the book? (sound)
2. The deep-sea fish looked awful but ________ ________. (taste)
3. They're twins, but they ________ ________ from one another. (look)
4. If your feet ________ ________, you need to take a shower. (smell)
5. When I stand up after sitting for a while, I ________ ________. (feel)

Q2 다음 문장을 읽고, 틀린 부분을 고쳐서 다시 쓰시오.

1. Look at the bride. She looks so happily.

→ ____________________________________

2. This pizza doesn't taste well when it is cold.

→ ____________________________________

3. I feel sadly when my friends misunderstand me.

→ ____________________________________

4. We should take away the rotten fish. It smells terribly.

→ ____________________________________

5. The singer looks excited, but the music sounds too loudly.

→ ____________________________________

Fill in the Blank ① you look perfect ② look beautiful ③ she looks perfect

Question 1 **1.** sounds interesting **2.** tasted delicious **3.** look different **4.** smell bad **5.** feel dizzy

Question 2 **1.** Look at the bride. She looks so happy. **2.** This pizza doesn't taste good when it is cold. **3.** I feel sad when my friends misunderstand me. **4.** We should take away the rotten fish. It smells terrible. **5.** The singer looks excited, but the music sounds too loud.

32 What doesn't kill you makes you stronger | Kelly Clarkson

You know the bed feels warmer sleeping here alone?
You know I dream in color
And do the things I want

혼자 누워 있는 침대는 더 따뜻한 거 알아?
그거 아니? 요즘 색깔이 있는 꿈을 꾸고
내가 하고 싶은 것들을 해

• You know : 있잖아, 너 아니?

You think you got the best of me
Think you had the last laugh
Bet you think that everything good is gone

넌 네가 이겼다고 생각할 거야
마지막에 웃는 사람은 너라고
좋은 것들은 모두 사라졌다고 생각하겠지

• get the best (of somebody) : ~를 이기다

Think you left me broken down
Think that I'll come running back
Baby, you don't know me, cause you're dead wrong

날 망가뜨렸다고 생각할 테니까
내가 다시 달려올 거라고 생각하겠지만
넌 날 몰라, 왜냐하면 그건 큰 오산이거든

• dead wrong : 말도 안 되는

☆ What doesn't kill you makes you stronger
Stand a little taller
Doesn't mean I'm lonely when I'm alone
What doesn't kill you makes a fighter
Footsteps even lighter

아픔은 너를 더 강하게 만들어
더 굳건히 설 수 있어
혼자라고 외로운 건 아니거든
아픔은 너를 강한 파이터로 만들어
발걸음은 더 가벼워지고

Doesn't mean I'm over cause you're gone

네가 떠났다고 내가 끝난 건 아니야

- What doesn't kill you : 너를 죽이지 않는 것 (이 곡에서는 감당할 수 있는 아픔)
- be over : 끝나다

★ What doesn't kill you makes you stronger,
stronger, Just me, myself and I
What doesn't kill you makes you stronger
Stand a little taller
Doesn't mean I'm lonely when I'm alone

고통은 너를 더, 더 강하게 만들어
바로 나, 내 자신을 말이지
고통은 너를 더 강하게 만들어
더 굳건히 설 수 있어
혼자라고 외로운 건 아니거든

- stronger : 더 강한(strong의 비교급)

You heard that I was starting over with
(   )(   )
They told you I was moving on, over you
You didn't think that I'd come back
I'd come back swinging
You tried to break me, but you see

내가 새로운 사람 만난다는 거 들었을 거야
사람들은 내가 너를 극복하고 앞으로 나아간다고 말했겠지
내가 다시 돌아올 줄 몰랐겠지
난 당당하게 돌아왔어
넌 날 무너뜨리려 하지만, 잘 봐

- start over : 다시 시작하다
- swing : 몸을 좌우로 흔들며 기세 좋게 걷다

☆ Repeat

★ Repeat

Thanks to you, I got a new thing started
Thanks to you, I'm not the broken-hearted
Thanks to you, I'm finally thinking about me
You know, in the end, the day you left was just my beginning in the end...

네 덕분에, 난 새롭게 시작했고
네 덕분에, 난 좌절하지 않았어
네 덕분에, 날 돌아보게 됐지
있잖아, 결국에는, 네가 떠난 그 순간이
나의 새로운 시작이 된 거야 결국에는…

- **broken hearted :** 비탄에 빠진
- **in the end :** 결국에는

☆ Repeat

★ Repeat × 2

32 -thing + 형용사

후위수식이란

- 형용사는 보통 명사 앞에서 수식하지만, -thing, -one, -where로 끝나는 명사는 형용사가 뒤에서 수식한다.

A: I'm bored. Let's do **something exciting**.

B: OK. How about going to a rock concert?

A: Who can apply that program?

B: **Anyone healthy** can do it.

A: Did you go **anywhere interesting**?

B: No, we just stayed at home.

가사 예문

You heard that I was starting over with someone new.

내가 새로운 사람 만난다는 걸 넌 들었을 거야.

Attention!

thing(s)은 형용사가 앞에서 수식한다.

I want to drink **sweet things**. 나는 단것을 마시고 싶다.

Q1 주어진 우리말과 같도록 올바른 표현을 쓰시오.

1. 우리는 조용한 어떤 곳으로 이사할 필요가 있어.

→ We need to move ________ ________.

2. 오늘 인터넷 뉴스에 흥미로운 것이 없어.

→ There is ________ ________ in today's internet news.

3. 최근에 그녀에게서 이상한 어떤 거 못 느꼈니?

→ Didn't you find ________ ________ about her recently?

4. 새로운 사람과 처음 만날 때, 꼭 공공장소에서 만나라.

→ When you are meeting ________ ________ for the first time, do it in a public place.

Q2 괄호 안의 단어를 바르게 배열하여 문장을 다시 쓰시오.

1. She saw (glittering / something / on the street).

→ ________________________________

2. He will send (concerned / further information / to anyone).

→ ________________________________

3. I want to have (spicy / when I get stressed / something).

→ ________________________________

4. There is (wrong / with giving fresh ideas / to the world / nothing).

→ ________________________________

Fill in the Blank someone new

Question 1 **1.** somewhere quiet **2.** nothing interesting **3.** anything strange **4.** someone new

Question 2 **1.** She saw something glittering on the street.
2. He will send further information to anyone concerned.
3. I want to have something spicy when I get stressed.
4. There is nothing wrong with giving fresh ideas to the world.

33 Thank you for the music | ABBA

I'm nothing special, in fact I'm a bit of a bore
If I tell a joke, you've probably heard it before
But I have ①(　)(　　　),
(　)(　　　　　)(　　　)
'Cause everyone listens when I start to sing
I'm so grateful and proud
All I want is to sing it out loud

난 전혀 특별하지 않아요, 사실 좀 따분한 사람이에요
내가 농담을 한다면, 당신이 예전에 이미 들어본 얘기일 거예요
하지만 내겐 재능이 있어요, 놀라운 것이죠
내가 노래를 시작하면 모두가 귀를 기울이니까요
너무 고맙고 자랑스러워요
내가 원하는 건 오직 큰 소리로 노래 부르는 거예요

- in fact : 사실은
- a bit of : 약간의
- bore : ① 지루하게 하다 ② 따분한 사람
- probably : 아마도
- talent : 재능
- grateful : 감사해하는

★ So I say thank you for ②(　　)(　　　),
(　　)(　　　)(　)'(　)(　　　　)
Thanks for all the joy they're bringing
Who can live without it, I ask in all honesty
What would life be?
Without a song or a dance what are we?
So I say thank you for the music
For giving it to me

그래서 나는 내가 부르는 노래인, 음악에 감사해요
노래가 가져다주는 모든 기쁨에 감사해요
어느 누가 노래 없이 살 수 있겠어요, 진심으로 물어보죠
인생이 어떻게 되겠어요?
노래나 춤이 없다면 우린 무엇인가요?
그러니 저는 음악에 감사하다고 말해요
음악을 내게 준 것에 대해서요

- in all honesty : 솔직히 말해서

Mother says I was a dancer before
I could walk
She says I began to sing long before
I could talk
And I've often wondered, how did it all start
Who found out that nothing can
capture a heart
like a melody can?
Well, whoever it was, I'm a fan

어머니는 내가 걷기도 전에 춤을 추었다고 말씀하세요
내가 말을 배우기도 전에 노래를 불렀다고 하시죠
난 종종 궁금했어요, 어떻게 그렇게 됐을까 하고
어떤 것도 멜로디만큼 심장을 사로잡을 수 없다는 것을 발견한 사람은 누구일까요?
음, 그게 누구이든, 전 그의 팬이에요

- **capture** : 사로잡다

★ Repeat

I've been so lucky
I am the girl with golden hair
I wanna sing it out to everybody
What a joy, what a life, what a chance!

난 참 운이 좋았어요
난 금발머리를 가진 소녀죠
모든 사람에게 노래하고 싶어요
얼마나 기쁜가요, 얼마나 멋진 인생인가요, 얼마나 좋은 기회인가요!

★ Repeat

So I say thank you for the music
For giving it to me

그러니 저는 음악에 감사하다고 말해요
음악을 내게 준 것에 대해서요

33 동격

동격이란

- 명사 또는 명사구를 콤마(,)로 연결하여 앞과 뒤의 말이 동격임을 나타내는데, 주로 콤마 앞의 대상을 보충 설명하기 위해 사용한다.

- **Beethoven**, **a great musician**, was deaf.
  위대한 음악가인 베토벤은 청각장애가 있었다.
- **Asiana**, **one of the greatest Korean airlines**, is well known for providing high-quality customer service.
  최고의 한국 항공사 중의 하나인 아시아나는 질 높은 고객 서비스를 제공하는 것으로 유명하다.

동격에서 수의 일치

- 동격을 나타낼 때, 수식을 받는 주어가 되는 명사의 수와 동사를 일치시키는 것에 유의한다.

- **Seoyeon**, one of my best friends, **plays** the piano very well.
  내 가장 친한 친구들 중의 한 명인 서연이는 피아노를 매우 잘 친다.
  (← Seoyeon과 plays의 수의 일치)
- **Google**, one of the world's leading companies, **is** seeking an intern.
  세계적 선도 기업들 중의 하나인 구글에서 인턴사원을 찾고 있습니다.
  (← Google과 is의 수의 일치)

가사 예문

So I say thank you for the music, the song I'm singing.
그래서 나는 내가 부르는 노래인, 음악에 감사하다고 말해요.

Q1 주어진 문장에서 밑줄 친 부분과 동격인 명사(명사구)를 찾아 빈칸에 쓰시오.

1. Paris, the largest city in France, is a very exciting place.

→ ______________________

2. Shakespeare, one of the greatest writers, wrote this book.

→ ______________________

Q2 다음 주어진 문장을 동격을 이용하여 한 문장으로 쓰시오.

1. I'm going to visit Beijing. Beijing is the capital of China.

→ ______________________

2. Zeus fell in love with a princess. Zeus is the king of the gods.

→ ______________________

3. Kathy has musical talent. Kathy is a girl with curly hair.

→ ______________________

Q3 다음 문장에서 어법상 어색한 부분을 찾아 바르게 고치시오.

1. I want to meet Elizabeth, the Queens of England.

__________ → __________

2. Daniel, one of my English teachers, were from Canada.

__________ → __________

Fill in the Blank ① a talent, a wonderful thing ② the music, the songs I'm singing

Question 1 **1.** the largest city in France **2.** one of the greatest writers

Question 2 **1.** I'm going to visit Beijing, the capital of China.
2. Zeus, the king of the gods, fell in love with a princess.
3. Kathy, a girl with curly hair, has musical talent.

Question 3 **1.** Queens, Queen **2.** were, was

34 Yesterday once more | The Carpenters

When I was young I'd listen to the radio
Waiting for my favorite songs
When they played I'd sing along
It made me smile

내가 어렸을 때 난 라디오를 듣곤 했죠
내가 좋아하는 노래들을 기다리면서
그 노래들이 나오면 나는 노래를 따라 불렀고
그것은 날 웃게 만들었죠

- I'd = I would
- would~ : ~하곤 했다(과거의 습관)
- wait for : 기다리다
- sing along : 노래를 따라 부르다

Those were ①(　　)(　　)(　　)
And not ②(　)(　　)(　　)
How I wondered where they'd gone
But they're back again just like a long lost friend
All the songs I loved ③(　)(　　)

그것들은 정말 행복한 시간들이었고
그리 오래된 일도 아닌데
그 시절이 어디로 사라져버렸는지 궁금해요
하지만 마치 오랫동안 연락이 없었던
친구처럼 기억들이 다시 돌아오네요
난 그 노래들을 정말 좋아했었죠

- just like~ : 마치 ~처럼
- lost : 잃어버린

★ Every sha-la-la-la Every wo-wo-wo still shines
Every shing-a-ling-a-ling that they're starting to sing
④(　)(　　)

매번 반복되는 샤랄라라 워워워 하는 부분은
아직도 아름다워요
노래를 시작할 때 싱어링어링 하는 부분도
정말 좋아요

When they get to the part where he's breakin' her heart
It can really make me cry just like before
It's yesterday once more

노래가사에서 남자가 여자의 마음을 아프게
하는 부분에 이르면
마치 예전으로 돌아간 것 같이 날 울게
만들어요
다시 어제로 돌아간 것처럼

Looking back on how it was in years gone by
And the good times that I had
Makes today seem rather sad
⑤(   )(   ) has changed
It was songs of love that I would sing to then
And I'd memorize each word

세월이 지나서 과거가 어땠었는지
과거 좋았던 시절을 되돌아보면
왠지 오늘을 좀 슬프게 만들어요
너무 많은 것들이 변해있네요
그때 따라 부르던 노래는 사랑노래였는데
그리고 난 모든 가사를 외우곤 했죠

- **look back on~ :** ~를 뒤돌아보다
- **go by :** 지나가다
- **rather :** 꽤

Those old melodies
Still sound ⑥(   )(   ) to me
As they melt the years away

그 오래된 멜로디는
아직도 나에겐 너무 좋게 들려요
흘러간 세월을 녹여버리듯

- **melt away :** 사라지게 하다

★ Repeat

All my best memories come back clearly to me
Some can even make me cry just like before
It's yesterday once more

나의 가장 좋은 기억들은 생생하게 내게 돌아와요
어떤 것들은 날 예전처럼 울게 만들기도 하죠
다시 어제로 돌아간 것처럼

- **clearly :** 또렷하게

★ Repeat

34 so/such

so + 형용사/부사 : 매우 ~한/~하게

- '매우'라는 의미로 형용사 또는 부사의 의미를 강조할 때 형용사와 부사 앞에 so를 쓸 수 있다.

- The answer to that question is **so easy**. (매우 쉬운)
- Don't give up **so easily**. (매우 쉽게)
- The view along the Han River is **so beautiful**. (매우 아름다운)
- She played the guitar **so beautifully**. (매우 아름답게)

such + (a/an) + 형용사 + 명사 : 매우 ~한 …

- '매우'라는 의미로 형용사+명사 앞에 such를 쓸 수 있다.

- I don't think that's **such a good idea**. (매우 좋은 생각)
- I'm very lucky to have **such good friends**. (매우 좋은 친구들)

so/such ~ that … : 매우 ~해서 …하다

- '매우 ~해서 …하다'라는 의미로 so/such 뒤에 that + 주어 + 동사를 쓸 수 있다.

- The story was **so fun that I couldn't stop reading it**.
  너무 재밌어서 읽는 것을 멈출 수 없었다.
- It was **such a lovely day that I went out for a walk**.
  너무 멋진 날이라서 산책을 나갔다.

가사 예문

Those were such happy times. 그것들은 정말 행복한 시간이었어요.

Those old melodies still sound so good to me.
그 오래된 멜로디는 아직도 나에겐 너무나 좋게 들려요.

Q1 괄호 안에 주어진 단어들과 so 또는 such를 이용하여 문장을 완성하시오.

1. I didn't realize what time it was because I was ______________________. (busy)
2. She read the novel at one go. It was ______________________. (interesting)
3. I will never go there again! It was ______________________. (horrible, experience)
4. I'm mad at you! How could you forget ______________________?
(important, thing)

Q2 〈보기〉와 같이 주어진 문장을 so/such ~ that…을 이용하여 다시 쓰시오.

〈보기〉 He fell asleep at his desk because he was so tired.
→ He was so tired that he fell asleep at his desk.

1. Nobody eats just one slice because it is so tasty.
→ ____
2. People clapped at the end because it was a touching performance.
→ ____
3. I had to keep standing all the way because the bus was so crowded.
→ ____
4. The other players looked up to her because Sanghwa Lee was a great professional in training.
→ ____

Fill in the Blank ① such happy times ② so long ago ③ so well ④ so fine ⑤ so much ⑥ so good

Question 1 **1.** so busy **2.** so interesting **3.** such a horrible experience **4.** such an important thing

Question 2
1. It is so tasty that nobody eats just one slice.
2. It was such a touching performance that people clapped at the end.
3. The bus was so crowded that I had to keep standing all the way.
4. Sanghwa Lee was such a great professional in training that the other players looked up to her.

35 History | One Direction

You gotta help me
I'm losing my mind
Keep getting the feeling you wanna
leave this all behind

넌 날 도와줘야 해
난 지금 이성을 잃을 것 같거든
계속 이런 느낌이 들어
네가 다 뒤로하고 떠나려고 한다는

- lose mind : 정신이 나가다
- leave behind : 두고 가다

☆ Thought we were going strong
I thought we were holding on,
(   )(   )?

우리는 강하다고 생각했는데
우린 잘 견뎌내고 있다고 생각했는데,
그렇지 않니?

- hold on : 계속 유지하다

No, They don't teach you this in school
Now my heart's breaking and I don't
know what to do

아니, 학교에서 네게 이런 걸 가르쳐주진 않지
이제 내 심장이 무너질 것 같고 뭘 어떻게
해야 하는지 모르겠어

☆ Repeat

★ You and me got a whole lot of history
We could be the greatest team that
the world has ever seen
You and me got a whole lot of history
So don't let it go
We can make some more
We can live forever

너와 나 함께한 시간이 얼마나 많니
우리는 세상에서 이제까지 본 것 중 가장
최고의 팀이 될 수 있어
너와 나 함께한 시간이 얼마나 많니
그러니 포기하려 하지 마
우린 더 잘할 수 있어
우린 영원히 함께할 수 있어

- get : ① 받다 ② 얻다 ③ 가지다
- let it go : 놓아주다

All of the rumors All of the fights But we always find a way to make it out alive	이상한 소문들, 숱한 싸움들이 있었지만 우린 늘 길을 잘 찾아왔잖아 • find a way : 방법을 찾다 • make out : 잘 해나가다

☆ Repeat

★ Repeat

Mini bars, Expensive cars, Hotel rooms, And new tattoos, And the good champagne, And private planes, But they don't mean anything	미니 바, 비싼 차. 호텔 룸, 새로운 문신, 좋은 샴페인, 개인 비행기, 다 내겐 의미 없어

Cause the truth is out I realize that without you here life is just a lie This is not the end, this is not the end We can make it, you know it, you know?	왜냐면 진실이 밝혀졌으니까 네가 없다면 이 삶은 하나의 거짓말에 지나지 않는다는 걸 깨달았어 이건 끝이 아니야, 이건 끝이 아니야 우린 잘 해낼 수 있어, 넌 알잖아, 그렇지? • make it : 해내다

★ Repeat x 2

So don't let me go, so don't let me go
We can live forever
Baby don't you know? Baby don't you know?
We can live forever

그러니 나를 가게 두지 마, 그러니 날 가게 두지 마
우린 영원히 함께할 거야
모르겠니? 너 모르겠니?
우린 영원히 함께할 수 있어

35 부가의문문

부가의문문이란

- 상대방에게 어떤 사실을 확인하거나 동의를 구할 때 문장 끝에 덧붙이는 의문문으로 '그렇지?'라는 의미를 나타낸다.

부가의문문 만드는 법		
형태	앞문장이 긍정이면 부정으로 앞문장이 부정이면 긍정으로	- Math is difficult, **isn't it**? - You are not angry, **are you**?
주어	앞문장의 주어를 대명사로 바꿈	- Justine is a good teacher, **isn't he**? - Jessica didn't come to the gym, **did she**?
동사	be동사나 조동사는 그대로, 일반동사는 do/does/did로	- The food was terrible, **wasn't it**? - We can dance together, **can't we**? - Your parents live in LA, **don't they**? - Bruno doesn't wear glasses, **does he**? - Jina didn't finish her project, **did she**?
축약	부정의 부가의문문은 축약형	- You are good at speaking English, **aren't you**?

가사 예문

I thought we were holding on, aren't we?

우린 잘 견뎌내고 있다고 생각했는데, 그렇지 않니?

Attention!

주의해야 할 부가의문문이 있다!

청유문은 shall we? 명령문은 will you?로 부가의문문 표현!

- Let's go to a movie this weekend, **shall we**? 우리 이번 주말에 영화 보러 가자, 그럴래?
- Turn down the volume, **will you**? 볼륨 좀 줄여줘, 그럴래?
- Don't forget to text me, **will you**? 나에게 문자하는 거 잊지 마, 알았지?

Q1 다음 문장에 알맞은 부가의문문을 쓰시오.

1. Let's go out for a walk, __________ __________?
2. Harry and Julian are friends, __________ __________?
3. Jason can play the drum well, __________ __________?
4. You didn't come to the party, __________ __________?
5. Your children don't drink soda, __________ __________?

Q2 다음 문장의 밑줄 친 부분을 어법상 알맞은 형태로 고쳐 다시 쓰시오.

1. Her babies are so cute, isn't she? → ________________
2. Don't forget to lock the door, shall we? → ________________
3. Brian loves to cook Korean food, do Brian? → ________________
4. The concert was amazing, wasn't the concert? → ________________
5. The airplane didn't arrive on time, does the airplane? → ________________

Fill in the Blank aren't we

Question 1 **1.** shall we **2.** aren't they **3.** can't he **4.** did you **5.** do they

Question 2 **1.** aren't they **2.** will you **3.** doesn't he **4.** wasn't it **5.** did it

36 Don't say you love me — M2M

Got introduced to you by a friend
You were cute and all that,
Baby, you set the trend Yes, you did oh
The next thing I know we're down
at the cinema
We're sitting there, you started kissing
me
What's that about?

친구로부터 널 소개받았지
넌 귀여웠고 꽤 괜찮았지
유행도 따를 줄 알고 말이야, 그랬었지
그 다음, 내가 기억하기로는 영화를 같이 봤어
우리가 거기 앉아 있었는데, 갑자기 넌 나에게
키스하기 시작했어
도대체 왜 그랬던 거야?

- set the trend : 유행을 따르다

You're moving too fast,
I don't understand you
I'm not ready yet,
Baby, I can't pretend, No I can't
The best I can do is tell you to talk to
me
It's possible, eventual
Love will find a way
Love will find a way

넌 너무 급해, 널 도저히 이해할 수가 없어
난 아직 준비가 안 됐어,
그런 척할 수는 없잖아, 정말 못 하겠어
내가 할 수 있는 최선은 너에게
나와 대화를 해달라고 말하는 거야
가능할 거야, 결국에는
사랑은 길을 찾아낼 테니까
사랑은 길을 찾아낼 테니까

- ready : 준비된
- pretend : ~인 척하다

★ ①(   )(   ) you love me
You don't even know me
If you really want me
Then ②(   )(   ) some time
③(   )(   ) there, baby
Not before I'm ready

날 사랑한다는 말은 하지 마
넌 날 제대로 알지도 못하잖아
네가 날 정말 원한다면
그렇다면 내게 시간을 좀 줘
앞서가지 마
내가 준비되기 전까지는

①(   )(   ) your heart's in a hurry
It's not like we're gonna get married
②(   )(   ), ②(   )(   ) some time

네 마음이 널 재촉한다는 말은 하지 마
우리가 당장 결혼할 것도 아니잖아
내게 시간을, 시간을 좀 줘

- in a hurry : 서두르는
- gonna = going to
- get married : 결혼하다

Here's how I play, here's where you stand
Here's what to prove
To get any further than where it's been
I'll make it clear, not gonna tell you twice
④(   ) it (   ), you keep pushing me
You're pushing me away
Pushing me away

여기 나의 방식이 있어, 여기에 네가 서 있고
여기 무얼 증명해야 할지가 있어
지금까지보다 앞으로 더 나아가기 위해
좀 더 정확하게 말할게, 두 번 말하지 않을 테니까
천천히 가자고, 넌 날 계속 밀어붙이고 있어
날 밀어붙이고 있지
날 밀어붙이지

- Here is~ : 여기 ~가 있다
- prove : 증명하다
- further : 더 멀리
- take it slow : 천천히 신중하게 하다
- keep ~ing : 계속 ~하다

★ Repeat

na, na, na, na, na
①(   )(   ) you love me
You don't even know me baby
Baby don't say love me, baby
②(   )(   ) some time

날 사랑한다는 말을 하지 마
넌 날 알지도 못하잖아
날 사랑한다는 말을 하지 마
내게 시간을 좀 줘

★ Repeat × 2

36 명령문 / 부정명령문

명령문 / 부정명령문이란

- 상대방에게 명령, 지시를 하는 문장을 말하며, '~해라' 또는 '~하지 마라'의 의미이다.
- 주어인 you를 생략한다.
- 명령문은 동사원형으로 시작, 부정명령문은 Don't~로 시작한다.

명령문 유형

1. be동사 명령문 : be동사를 문장 맨 앞에	**Be** quiet in the classroom.
2. 일반동사 명령문 : 일반동사의 원형을 문장 맨 앞에	**Raise** your hand if you have any questions.
3. 부정명령문 : Don't + 동사원형을 문장 맨 앞에	**Don't tell** a lie to your parents. Be honest.

가사 예문

Take it slow.
천천히 가.

Give me some time.
내게 시간을 줘.

Don't say you love me.
나를 사랑한다고 말하지 마.

Don't say your heart's in a hurry.
너의 마음이 서두른다고 말하지 마.

Attention!

부드럽게 명령할 때는 명령문과 함께 please를 붙이거나, Could you~를 사용!

- **Could you** clean up the living room?
- **Please** don't make a noise when someone is saying something.

Q1 의미가 자연스럽도록 주어진 표현을 배열하여 명령하는 문장을 만드시오.

1. The knife is dangerous. (when you use it / be / careful)

→ ______________________________

2. We have an important meeting tomorrow. (be / on time)

→ ______________________________

3. You're spending too much money. (to save / your money / try)

→ ______________________________

4. You like chocolate too much. (for your health / don't / sweets / eat / too much)

→ ______________________________

Q2 주어진 상황에 맞는 명령하는 문장을 만드시오.

1. He feels so nervous because of the exam.

→ ______________________________

2. A man is sending text messages while driving.

→ ______________________________

3. A girl is listening to music loudly late at night.

→ ______________________________

4. The children are throwing the trash in the garden.

→ ______________________________

Fill in the Blank ① Don't say ② give me ③ Don't go ④ Take, slow

Question 1 **1.** Be careful when you use it. **2.** Be on time. **3.** Try to save your money. **4.** Don't eat sweets too much for your health.

Question 2 **1.** (Please) Don't be nervous. **2.** (Please) Don't send text messages while driving. **3.** (Please) Don't listen to music loudly late at night. **4.** (Please) Don't throw the trash in the garden.

37 What a wonderful world Louis Amstrong

I see trees of green, red roses, too
I see them bloom for me and you
And I think to myself
(   )(   )(   )(   )!

난 푸른 나무들과 붉은 장미들을
바라봅니다
나와 당신을 위해 그것들이 꽃을 피우는 걸
바라보죠
그리고 나 혼자 생각해요
세상이 얼마나 아름다운가를!

- bloom : 꽃피우다

I see skies of blue and clouds of white
The bright blessed day
the dark sacred night
And I think to myself
(   )(   )(   )(   )!

난 파란 하늘과 하얀 구름을 바라봅니다
밝은 축복받은 낮
어두운 신성한 밤
그리고 나 혼자 생각해요
세상이 얼마나 아름다운가를!

- blessed : 축복받은
- sacred : 신성한

The colors of the rainbow so pretty
in the sky
Are also on the faces of people going by
I see friends shaking hands,
saying how do you do
They're really saying "I love you."

하늘에 떠 있는 무지개 일곱 색깔은
너무나 아름다워요
지나가는 사람들의 얼굴도 또한 예뻐요
난 인사를 나누며 악수를 하는 친구들을
바라보아요
그들은 "나는 당신을 사랑해요."라고
정말로 말하고 있어요

I hear babies cry
I watch them grow
They'll learn much more
than I'll never know
And I think to myself
(　　　)(　)(　　　　　　)(　　　)!
Yes, I think to myself
(　　　)(　)(　　　　　　)(　　　)!

난 아이들이 우는 소리를 들어요
그들이 자라나는 걸 바라보죠
그들은 내가 알지 못하는
아주 많은 것들을 배울 거예요
그리고 난 혼자 생각해요
세상이 얼마나 아름다운가를!
그래요, 난 혼자 생각해요
세상이 얼마나 아름다운가를!

37 감탄문

감탄문이란

- 감탄하는 감정 등을 강조하여, '정말 ~하구나!'라는 의미를 나타내며 느낌표(!)로 문장을 끝맺는다.

감탄문 유형

What 감탄문	어순	What + a(an) + 형용사 + 명사 + 주어 + 동사!
	특징	What a cute boy he is! / What good actors they are!
How 감탄문	어순	How + 형용사/부사 + 주어 + 동사!
	특징	How expensive the car is! / How fast he runs!

가사 예문

And I think to myself. What a wonderful world!

그리고 난 혼자 생각해요. 세상이 얼마나 아름다운가를!

Attention!

감탄문의 주어와 동사의 생략!

명백히 의미를 알 수 있는 경우의 주어와 동사는 생략할 수 있다.

- And I think to myself. What a wonderful world (it is)!
- What a pretty woman (she is)!
- What smart students (they are)!

Q1 다음 우리말과 의미가 같도록 괄호 안의 단어들을 바르게 배열하시오.

1. 그들은 정말 재미있구나! (humorous / how / are / they)

→ ______________________________

2. 정말 아름다운 경치구나! (is / it / a / beautiful / what / scenery)

→ ______________________________

3. 그것은 정말 슬픈 영화였어! (sad / movie / what / was / it / a)

→ ______________________________

4. 윌리스 타워는 정말 높구나! (high / is / how / the Willis Tower)

→ ______________________________

Q2 다음 주어진 문장을 〈보기〉처럼 감탄문으로 바꿔 쓰시오.

〈보기〉 You are very kind. → How kind you are!

It is an interesting game. → What an interesting game it is!

1. The idea is great. → How ____________________!
2. You have big eyes. → What ____________________!
3. The man is very brave. → How ____________________!
4. It is a lovely day. → What ____________________!
5. The cookies are yummy. → How ____________________!
6. It is a very expensive car. → What ____________________!

Fill in the Blank What a wonderful world

Question 1 **1.** How humorous they are! **2.** What a beautiful scenery it is! **3.** What a sad movie it was! **4.** How high the Willis Tower is!

Question 2 **1.** great the idea is **2.** big eyes you have **3.** brave the man is **4.** a lovely day it is **5.** yummy the cookies are **6.** an expensive car it is

38 Step by step — New Kids On The Block

Step by step, Ooh baby,
(I) gonna get to you, girl
Step by step, Ooh!

한 걸음 한 걸음씩, 오 그대여,
당신에게 다가갈 거예요
한 걸음 한 걸음씩 말이에요, 오!

- get to~ : ~에 도착하다, 닿다

☆ Step by step, Ooh baby, (I) gonna get to you, girl
Step by step, Ooh baby, (I) really want you in my world

한 걸음 한 걸음씩, 오 그대여,
당신에게 다가갈 거예요
한 걸음 한 걸음씩 말이에요,
내 삶에 정말 당신이 필요해요

(Step), Hey girl, in your eyes
I see a picture of me all the time, (Step)
And girl when you smile
You've got to know that you drive me wild

(한 걸음) 이봐요, 당신의 눈속에서
난 항상 나의 모습을 봐요, (한 걸음)
그리고 당신이 미소 지으면
나는 미칠 것만 같다는 걸 당신도 알아야 해요

- 've(have) got to~ : (구어) ~해야 한다
- drive me wild = drive me crazy

★ Step by step, Ooh baby
You're always on my mind
Step by step, Ooh girl
I really think it's just a matter of time

한 걸음 한 걸음씩, 오 그대여
당신은 항상 내 마음속에 있어요
한 걸음 한 걸음씩, 오 그대여
이건 단지 시간문제일 뿐이라고 생각해요

☆ Repeat

(Step), Hey girl, can't you see?
I've got to have you all just for me, (Step)
And girl, yes it's true
No one else will ever do

(한 걸음), 이봐요, 모르겠어요?
당신은 나만의 연인이 되어야 해요, (한 걸음)
그대여, 이건 진심이에요
아무도 당신을 차지하지 못할 걸요

★ Repeat

☆ Repeat
(Step)(Step)(Step) Step by step

(한 걸음) (한 걸음) (한 걸음) 한 걸음씩

Step one, We can have lots of fun
Step two, There's so much we can do
Step three, It's just you and me
Step four, I can give you more
Step five, ①(　　　)(　　)(　　　) that the (　　) has (　　　)?

한 걸음, 우린 즐겁게 지낼 수 있어요
두 걸음, 우리가 할 수 있는 일이 많아요
세 걸음, 오직 당신과 나만을 위한 거죠
네 걸음, 당신께 더 많은 것을 줄 수 있어요
다섯 걸음, 당신은 때가 됐다는 걸 모르나요?

• have fun : 재밌게 놀다

Step by step
②(　　　)(　　)(　　　)(　)(　　　)(　　)?
Step by step
Yes, I do, girl

한 걸음 한 걸음씩
내가 당신을 원한다는 걸 모르나요?
한 걸음 한 걸음씩
그래요, 난 알아요, 그대여

★ Repeat

☆ Repeat × 2

38 부정의문문

부정의문문이란

- 동사에 not을 결합하여 만들며, 의문문으로 상대방이 동의를 바라거나, 어떤 사실에 대한 놀라움을 나타낼 때 쓴다.

부정 의문문	Isn't / Aren't / Wasn't / Weren't...?	**Isn't that** a pretty picture? 저것 예쁜 그림 아니니?
	Don't / Doesn't / Didn't...?	**Don't you** like coffee? 커피 좋아하지 않으세요?
	Haven't / Hasn't...?	**Haven't you** been there before? 거기 이전에 가보지 않았니?
	Can't / Won't / Couldn't / Wouldn't...?	**Can't you** stay a little longer? 좀 더 머물다 가시면 안 되나요? **Won't you** go shopping with me? 나랑 쇼핑가지 않을래?

가사 예문

Don't you know that the time has arrived?

당신은 때가 되었다는 걸 모르나요?

Don't you know I need you?

내가 당신을 원하는 걸 모르나요?

Attention!

부가의문문이나 부정의문문에 답할 때, Yes와 No의 사용에 주의!

'~이다'라는 긍정의 의미로 답할 때는 Yes를, '~이 아니다'라는 부정의 의미로 답할 때는 No를 쓴다!

A: This chicken soup is too salty, **isn't it**? B: Yes, it is. (Yes, it is too salty.)

A: **Aren't you** excited about your vacation? B: Yes, I am. (Yes, I am excited.)

Q1 다음 우리말 뜻이 되도록 대화의 빈칸에 알맞은 말을 쓰시오.

1. 왜 그들은 우리를 기다리지 않았지?

→ Why ________ ________ ________ for us?

2. 네가 지불해야 한다고 생각하지 않니?

→ ________ ________ ________ you have to pay?

3. 결정을 내리기에 너무 일찍 아니에요?

→ ________ ________ ________ ________ to make a decision?

4. 너는 매일 아침 똑같은 토스트 먹는 게 지겹지 않니? (be tired of~ : ~이 지겹다)

→ ________ ________ ________ of eating the same old toast every morning?

Q2 주어진 상황을 보고 〈보기〉와 같이 부정의문문으로 표현하시오.

〈보기〉 You ask the salesperson if they have a larger jacket in a clothing shop.
→ Don't you have a larger jacket(one)?

1. You ask the clerk if he can make the pants cheaper.

→ ____

2. You ask your friend to go to a movie with you this Friday.

→ ____

3. You ask your friend why Mr. Paterson didn't participate in the program.

→ ____

4. You think Ann looks pretty on her wedding day. You want your friend to agree with you.

→ ____

Fill in the Blank ① Don't you know, time, arrived ② Don't you know I need you

Question 1 **1.** didn't they wait **2.** Don't you think **3.** Isn't it too early **4.** Aren't you tired

Question 2 **1.** Can't you make the pants cheaper? **2.** Won't you go to a movie with me this Friday?
3. Why didn't Mr. Paterson participate in the program?
4. Don't you think Ann looks(is) pretty on her wedding day? /
Doesn't Ann look pretty on her wedding day? / Isn't Ann pretty on her wedding day?

39 Longer — Dan Fogelberg

①(　　　　) than there've been fishes in the ocean
②(　　　　) than any bird ever flew
①(　　　　) than there've been stars up in the heavens
I've been in love with you

바다에 물고기들이 있었던 것보다
더 오래전부터
어떤 새가 날았던 것보다 더 높이
하늘에 별들이 있었던 것보다 더 오래전부터
난 당신을 사랑해왔어요

- **There've been~ :** ~가 존재해오다
- **flew :** fly의 과거형
- **I've been~ (=I have been~) :** ~해오다

③(　　　　) than any mountain cathedral
④(　　　　) than any tree ever grew
⑤(　　　　) than any forest primeval
I am in love with you

어떤 성당같이 웅장한 산보다도 더 강하게
어떤 나무가 자라는 것보다도 더 진실되게
어떤 오래된 숲보다 더 깊이
난 지금 당신을 사랑하고 있어요

- **cathedral :** 성당
- **grew :** grow의 과거형
- **primeval :** 태고의

I'll bring fires in the winters
You'll send showers in the springs
We'll fly through the falls and summers
with love on our wings

내가 겨울에는 불을 가져다줄게요
당신은 봄비를 가져다주세요
우린 가을과 여름에 사랑의 날개를 달고
날아갈 거예요

- **shower :** 소나기

Through the years as the fire starts to mellow
Burning lines in the book of our lives
Though the binding cracks
and the pages start to yellow
I'll be in love with you
I'll be in love with you

세월이 흘러 불길(사랑)이 누그러지고
우리 삶의 일기에서 선들이 타 없어져
희미해지고
비록 (삶의 일기의) 묶음 연결이 끊어지고
종이가 노랗게 바래도
난 당신을 영원히 사랑할 겁니다
난 당신을 영원히 사랑할 겁니다

- **Through the years :** 해를 거쳐서
- **mellow :** 누그러지다
- **Though~ :** 비록 ~하지만
- **binding :** 묶음
- **crack :** 끊어지다

①(   ) than there've been fishes in the ocean
②(   ) than any bird ever flew
①(   ) than there've been stars up in the heavens
I've been in love with you,
I am in love with you

바다에 물고기들이 있었던 것보다
더 오래전부터
어떤 새가 날았던 것보다 더 높이
하늘에 별들이 있었던 것보다
더 오래전부터
난 당신을 사랑해왔어요,
당신을 사랑합니다

39 비교급

비교급이란

- '더 ~한/하게'라는 의미로 둘 이상의 대상을 비교할 때 비교급을 사용한다.
- 형태 : 형용사/부사 끝에 -(e)r을 붙이거나, 「more + 형용사/부사」로 나타낸다.
- '~보다'라는 의미로 비교하는 대상을 말할 때에는 비교급 뒤에 than을 사용한다.

- Our new sofa is **bigger** and **more comfortable than** the old one.

규칙	**기본형태 → -er을 붙임**	The cheetah is **faster** than the cat.	fast → **faster** long → **longer**
	-e로 끝날 때 → -r을 붙임	This bag is **nicer** than that one.	late → **later** nice → **nicer**
	단모음 + 단자음 → 마지막 자음 + er	A cat is **bigger** than a rat.	big → **bigger** hot → **hotter**
	자음 + y → y를 없애고 ier	Skating is **easier** than skiing for me.	easy → **easier** happy → **happier**
	2음절 이상 → more + 형용사/부사	Happiness is **more important** than money.	important → **more important** beautiful → **more beautiful** difficult → **more difficult**
불규칙		His scores are **better** than mine.	good → **better** bad → **worse** many/much → **more** little → **less**

가사 예문

Longer than there've been fishes in the ocean,
바다에 물고기들이 있었던 것보다 더 오래전부터,

Higher than any bird ever flew, 어떤 새가 날았던 것보다 더 높이,

Longer than there've been stars up in the heavens, I've been in love with you. 하늘에 별들이 있었던 것보다 더 오래전부터, 난 당신을 사랑해왔어요.

Attention!

비교급의 의미를 강조할 때 much, a lot 사용!

Korea's history is **much** longer than Canada's.

한국의 역사는 캐나다의 역사보다 **훨씬** 더 길다.

Q1 다음 우리말과 의미가 같도록 문장을 완성하시오.

1. 백두산이 한라산보다 더 높다. → Mt.Baekdu is ______ ______ Mt.Hanla.
2. 나는 고양이가 개보다 더 귀엽다고 생각해. → I think a cat is ______ ______ a dog.
3. 이 문제는 저 문제보다 더 어렵다. → This problem is ______ ______ ______ that.
4. 샌드위치가 핫도그보다 더 비싸다. → Sandwich is ______ ______ ______ hot dog.

Q2 다음 주어진 형용사/부사를 비교급으로 사용하여 문장을 완성하시오.

〈보기〉 bad important fast beautiful early

1. The French think love is ______________ than success.
2. Of course, you look ______________ than the flowers!
3. Why does the sun rise ______________ in Seoul than in New York?
4. Take a taxi instead of the bus because it's ______________, so you can get there on time.
5. It snows heavily and the roads are becoming ______________.

Fill in the Blank ① Longer ② Higher ③ Stronger ④ Truer ⑤ Deeper

Question 1 **1.** higher than **2.** cuter than **3.** more difficult than **4.** more expensive than

Question 2 **1.** more important **2.** more beautiful **3.** earlier **4.** faster **5.** worse

40 Firework — Katy Perry

Do you ever feel like a plastic bag,
Drifting through the wind, wanting to start again?
Do you ever feel, feel so paper-thin,
Like a house of cards, one blow from caving in?

당신은 혹시 비닐봉지가 된 느낌이 든 적 있나요,
바람에 이리저리 날리며, 다시 시작하고 싶은 맘이 들면서?
종이처럼 얇아진 느낌이 든 적 혹시 있나요,
무너져서 바람에 날려버리는 카드 집처럼?

- **plastic bag :** 비닐봉지
- **drift :** ① 표류 ② 표류하다, 떠다니다
- **paper-thin :** 종잇장처럼 얇은
- **a house of cards :** 카드로 만든 구조물, 불안정한 계획
- **cave in :** 무너지다
- **blow :** ① 바람에 날리다 ② 강풍 ③ 꽃이 피다

Do you ever feel already buried deep,
Six feet under screams but no one seems to hear a thing?
Do you know that there's still a chance for you?
'Cause there's a spark in you

당신은 이미 깊이 묻혀버린 느낌이 든 적 있나요,
저 아래 땅속 깊은 곳에서 소리를 지르지만 아무도 들을 수 없는 것처럼?
당신은 여전히 당신에게 기회는 있다는 걸 아나요?
당신에게 불꽃이 있으니까요

- **bury :** 매장하다
- **scream :** 소리치다
- **spark :** 불꽃

☆ You just gotta ignite the light, and let it shine
Just own the night like the 4th of July

당신은 그냥 그 불을 붙이기만 하면 되요,
그리고 빛을 내게 해주세요
7월 4일(미국독립기념일)처럼 이 밤을 가져봐요

- **gotta :** (비격식) got to의 줄임말, = have to
- **ignite :** 불을 붙이다

★ 'Cause baby you're a firework
Come on, show 'em what you're worth
Make 'em go "Oh, oh, oh"
As you shoot across the sky-y-y
Baby, you're a firework
Come on, let your colors burst
Make 'em go "Oh, oh, oh"
You're gonna leave 'em all in "awe, awe, awe"

왜냐면 당신이 불꽃이니까요
이리 와요, 당신의 멋진 모습을 보여주세요
그들이 "오, 오, 오" 하고 놀라게 해주세요
당신이 하늘 가로질러 쏠 때
당신은 불꽃이에요
이리와요, 당신의 색깔을 터뜨려주세요
그들이 "오, 오, 오" 하고 놀라게 해주세요
사람들이 모두 경이로움을 느끼게 해주세요

- **firework :** 불꽃(놀이)
- **'em : them**의 줄임말
- **worth :** 가치 있는
- **let~ :** ~하게 하다
- **burst :** ① 터뜨리다 ② 파열
- **leave :** ① 떠나다 ② 남겨두다 ③ 휴가
- **awe :** 경외감

You don't have to feel like a waste of space
You're original, cannot be replaced
If you only knew what the future holds
After a hurricane comes a rainbow
Maybe a reason why all the doors are closed
So you could open one that leads you to the perfect road
Like a lightning bolt, your heart will glow
And when it's time, you'll know

당신은 쓸모없는 사람이라고 느낄 필요가 없어요
당신은 이 세상에 하나밖에 없는 사람이에요, 누구도 대체할 수 없어요
앞으로 어떤 일이 일어날지 당신이 알고 있다면 좋겠지만
허리케인이 지나간 뒤엔 무지개가 뜰 거예요
아마도 그 모든 문들이 닫혀 있는 이유가 있을 거예요
그래서 당신을 완벽한 길로 이끄는 문을 열 수 있을 거예요
번갯불처럼, 당신의 심장은 빛날 거예요
그리고 때가 되면, 당신은 알게 될 거예요

- **don't have to~ :** ~할 필요가 없다
- **a waste of space :** (비유) 아무짝에도 쓸모없는 사람
- **original :** ① 원래의 ② 독창적인 사람
- **replace :** 대신하다
- **lighting bolt :** 번개
- **glow :** ① 빛나다 ② 불빛

☆ Repeat

★ Repeat

Boom, boom, boom
(　　)(　　　　)(　　) the moon,
moon, moon
It's always been inside of you, you, you
And now it's time to let it through-
ough-ough

붐, 붐, 붐
달보다도 훨씬 더 밝게
그 빛은 당신 맘속에 항상 있었어요
그리고 이제 그 빛이 지나가게 할
시간이에요

- **even :** ① ~조차 ② (비교급강조) 훨씬 ③ 평평한 ④ 짝수의
- **let ~ through :** ~을 통과시키다

★ Repeat

Boom, boom, boom
(　　)(　　　　)(　　) the moon,
moon, moon
Boom, boom, boom
(　　)(　　　　)(　　) the moon,
moon, moon

붐, 붐, 붐
달보다도 훨씬 더 밝게
붐, 붐, 붐
달보다도 훨씬 더 밝게

40 다양한 비교급

비교급 강조

- '훨씬'이라는 의미로 비교급의 의미를 강조할 때 비교급 앞에 much/even/a lot/far 등을 쓸 수 있다.

- Watching TV is **a lot easier** than reading a book.
- Reading aloud is **even better** than reading to yourself!

(read to oneself : 묵독하다)

- Taking care of children is **much more difficult** than having a career.

비교급 + and + 비교급

- '점점 더 ~한/하게'라는 의미로 「비교급 + and + 비교급」을 쓸 수 있다.

- Summer is here and it's getting **hotter and hotter**!
- His music video is becoming **more and more** popular on YouTube.

the + 비교급 ~, the + 비교급 …

- '~할수록 더 …하다'라는 의미로 「the + 비교급 ~, the + 비교급 …」을 쓸 수 있다.

- **The sooner** we leave, **the earlier** we will arrive.
- **The older** we grow, **the weaker** our memory becomes.

가사 예문

Even brighter than the moon, moon, moon

달보다도 훨씬 더 밝게

Q1 다음 대화가 자연스럽도록 비교급 강조를 이용하여 표현하시오.

1. A: Which bed do you prefer?

   B: This bed is ______ ______ __________ ______ that one. I'll take this.
   (← comfortable)

2. A: How do you feel today?

   B: I feel ______ ______ ______ yesterday because I took enough rest.
   (← good)

3. A: Will you take the bus or the train?

   B: I'm going to take the train because it is __ ______ ______ ______ the bus.
   (← fast)

Q2 다음 주어진 우리말과 의미가 같도록 문장을 완성하시오.

1. 조류독감이 점점 빠르게 확산되고 있다.

→ The bird flu is spreading ______ ______ ______.

2. 더 많이 먹을수록 당신은 더 뚱뚱해진다.

→ ______ ______ you eat, ______ ______ you become.

3. 한국 음식이 전 세계에 걸쳐 점점 더 인기가 많아지고 있다.

→ Korean food is becoming ______ ______ ______ ______ around the world.

4. 네가 더 일찍 비행기 티켓을 구입할수록, 더 큰 할인을 받을 수 있다.

→ ______ ______ you buy the plane ticket, ______ ______ discount you can get.

5. 슬프게도, 우리의 지금 상황은 예전보다 훨씬 더 나쁘다.

→ Sadly, our circumstances now are ______ ______ ______ in the past.

Fill in the Blank Even brighter than

Question 1 **1.** even(much, a lot, far) more comfortable than **2.** much(even, a lot, far) better than **3.** a lot(even, much, far) faster than

Question 2 **1.** faster and faster **2.** The more, the fatter **3.** more and more popular **4.** The earlier, the more **5.** far(much, even, a lot) worse than

41	Everything at once	Lenka

As sly as a fox
①( )(   )( ) an ox
As fast as a hare
As brave as a bear
②( )(   )( ) a bird
As neat as a word
As quiet as a mouse
As big as a house

여우만큼 교활하고
소만큼 강한
토끼만큼 빠르고
곰만큼 용감한
새만큼 자유롭고
가사만큼 정돈된
쥐만큼 조용하고
집만큼 큰

- sly : 교활한
- hare : 산토끼
- neat : 정돈된

★ All I wanna be
All I wanna be oh
All I wanna be is everything

내가 원하는 것은
내가 원하는 것은 오
내가 원하는 것은 모두 다

As mean as a wolf
③( )(   )( ) a tooth
As deep as a bite
As dark as the night
④( )(   )( ) a song
As right as a wrong
As long as a road
As ugly as a toad

늑대만큼 비열하고
이빨만큼 날카로운
깨문 것만큼 깊고
밤만큼 어두운
노래만큼 달콤하고
틀린 것만큼 옳은
길만큼 멀고
두꺼비만큼 못생긴

- mean : 비열한
- bite : ① 깨물다 ② 깨묾
- toad : 두꺼비

⑤(   )(   )(   ) a picture hanging from a fixture
Strong like a family
Strong as I wanna be
Bright as day
As light as play
⑥(   )(   )(   ) nails
As grand as a whale

붙박이장에 매달려 있는 그림만큼 예쁜
가족만큼 강하고
내가 원하는 것만큼 강한
낮만큼 밝고
놀이만큼 가벼운
못만큼 단단하고
고래만큼 거대한

- **fixture** : 붙박이장
- **nail** : 못

★ Repeat

Everything at once × 3

한 번에 모두 다

⑦(   )(   )(   ) the sun
As silly as fun
⑧(   )(   )(   ) a tree
As scary as the sea
⑨(   )(   )(   ) fire
Cold as ice
Sweet as sugar
And everything nice

태양만큼 따뜻하고
장난만큼 어리석은
나무만큼 시원하고
바다만큼 무서운
불만큼 뜨겁고
얼음만큼 차가운
설탕만큼 달콤하고
멋진 모든 것

- **silly** : 어리석은

As old as time

⑩ (   )(   )(   ) a line

As royal as a queen

As buzzed as a bee

As stealth as a tiger

Smooth as a glider

Pure as a melody

Pure as I wanna be

시간만큼 오래되고
선만큼 똑바른
여왕만큼 위엄 있고
벌만큼 윙윙거리는
호랑이만큼 은밀하고
글라이더만큼 부드럽게 미끄러지는
멜로디만큼 순수하고
내가 원하는 것만큼 순수한

- **royal** : 왕실, 위엄 있는
- **(by) stealth** : 남몰래
- **glider** : 글라이더
- **pure** : 순수한

★ Repeat

Everything at once

한 번에 모두 다

41 동등비교

동등비교란

- 동등비교는 「as + 형용사/부사의 원급(…) + as 비교대상(~)」의 형태로, 정도가 동등한 두 개를 비교하며 '~만큼 …한'이라는 의미를 나타낸다.

- Today is **as hot as yesterday**. (어제만큼 더운)
- She reads books **as quickly as her brother**. (그녀의 오빠만큼 책을 빨리 읽는)

동등비교 부정

- 「not as(so) + 형용사/부사의 원급(…) + as 비교대상(~)」의 형태로, 정도가 비교 대상보다 약하다는 것을 나타내며 '~만큼 …하지 않은'의 의미를 가진다.

- He is **not as(so) strong as his father**. (그의 아버지만큼 힘이 세지 않은)
- I can**not talk as well as my sister**. (언니만큼 말을 잘하지 못하는)

가사 예문

as sly as a fox　　as strong as an ox
여우처럼 교활하고, 소처럼 강한

as fast as a hare　　as brave as a bear
토끼처럼 빠르고, 곰처럼 용감한

Attention!

동등비교의 부정문을 우등비교로 나타낼 수 있다.

A turtle can**not run as fast as** a rabbit.
= A rabbit can **run faster than** a turtle.

Q1 주어진 우리말과 같도록 올바른 표현을 쓰시오.

1. 도쿄는 서울만큼 따뜻하다.

→ Tokyo is _______ _______ _______ Seoul.

2. 그 건물은 우리 건물만큼 높다.

→ The building is _______ _______ _______ ours.

3. 말은 코끼리만큼이나 크지는 않다.

→ The horse is _______ _______ _______ _______ an elephant.

4. 그 게임은 OVERWATCH만큼 흥미롭진 않다.

→ The game is _______ _______ _______ _______ the OVERWATCH.

Q2 다음 문장에서 어법상 틀린 부분을 바르게 고쳐 문장을 다시 쓰시오.

1. Suji is as kinder as her sister.

→ ______________________________

2. This box is as heaviest as that one.

→ ______________________________

3. My shoes are as not expensive as your pants.

→ ______________________________

4. You should come back home as earlier as possible.

→ ______________________________

Fill in the Blank ① As strong as ② As free as ③ As sharp as ④ As sweet as ⑤ As pretty as ⑥ As hard as ⑦ As warm as ⑧ As cool as ⑨ As hot as ⑩ As straight as

Question 1 **1.** as warm as **2.** as tall as **3.** not as(so) big(또는 large) as **4.** not as(so) interesting as

Question 2 **1.** Suji is as kind as her sister. **2.** This box is as heavy as that one.
3. My shoes are not as expensive as your pants.
4. You should come back home as early as possible.

42 The greatest love of all — Whitney Houston

☆ I believe the children are our future
Teach them well and let them
lead the way
Show them all the beauty they
possess inside
Give them a sense of pride to make it
easier
Let the children's laughter remind us
how we used to be

나는 아이들이 우리의 미래라는 것을
믿어요
아이들을 잘 가르쳐서 길을 이끌어나가도록
해야죠
아이들 안에 잠재한 모든 아름다움을
보여주도록 하세요
아이들이 수월한 삶을 살도록 자부심을
심어주세요
아이들의 웃음을 듣고 순진했던 우리
스스로를 돌이켜 보세요

- **possess** : 소유하다
- **pride** : 긍지, 자랑
- **remind** : 생각나게 하다

Everybody is searching for a hero
People need someone to look up to
I never found anyone who
fullfilled my needs
A lonely place to be
And so I learned to depend on me

사람들은 모두 영웅을 찾고 있어요
우러러볼 누군가가 필요한 거죠
난 나의 필요를 충족시켜줄 누군가를 찾지
못했어요
(세상은) 외로운 곳이에요 그래서 난 나
자신에게 기대는 법을 배웠죠

- **search for** : ~을 찾다
- **look up to** : ~을 우러러보다
- **fulfill** : 충족시키다
- **depend on** : ~에 의지하다

★ I decided long ago never to walk in
anyone's shadow
If I fail, if I succeed,
At least I'll live as I believe
No matter what they take from me,
They can't take away my dignity

난 타인의 그늘 아래서는 절대 살지
않으리라 오래전에 결심했죠
그게 잘못되든지, 잘되든지,
적어도 난 내가 믿는 대로 살 거예요
내게서 모든 걸 앗아가더라도
내 존귀함만은 빼앗을 수 없어요

- **at least** : 적어도
- **no matter what** : 무엇을 ~한다 해도
- **dignity** : 존엄(성), 품위

✲ Because ( )( )( ) of all
is happening to me
I found ( )( )( ) of all
inside of me
( )( )( ) of all is easy
to achieve
Learning to love yourself
it is ( )( )( ) of all

왜냐면 가장 위대한 사랑이
내게 일어나고 있기 때문이죠
가장 위대한 사랑을 나 자신 안에서
발견했어요
가장 위대한 사랑은 이루기 쉬운 걸요
자기 자신을 사랑하는 것이 가장 위대한
사랑이죠

- achieve : ~을 이루다, 성취하다

☆ Repeat

★ Repeat

✲ Repeat

And if by chance that special place that you've been dreaming of, leads you to a lonely place
Find your strength in love

만약 우연히 당신이 꿈꾸어왔던 특별한
곳이 당신을 외로운 곳으로 이끌더라도
사랑 안에서 당신의 힘을 찾으세요

- by chance : 우연히
- strength : 힘

42 최상급

최상급이란

- 세 개 이상의 대상 중 어느 한쪽이 '가장 ~한'이라고 표현하는 것을 말한다.
- 「the + 형용사/부사 + est」로 표현하거나, 「the most + 형용사/부사」로 쓴다.
- 불규칙적인 최상급 표현도 있다.

\- What is **the most expensive** menu item in your restaurant?

규칙	**기본형태 → -est를 붙임**	It is **the highest** building in his town.	high → **highest** long → **longest**
	-e로 끝날 때 → -st를 붙임	New York is **the largest** city in America.	large → **largest** late → **latest**
	단모음 + 단자음 → 마지막 자음 + est	August is **the hottest** month of the year.	hot → **hottest** big → **biggest**
	자음 + y → y를 없애고 iest	The penguin is **the funniest** bird in the zoo.	funny → **funniest** happy → **happiest**
	2, 3음절 이상 → most + 형용사 /부사	What is **the most popular** model in your shop?	popular → **most popular** difficult → **most difficult** expensive → **most expensive**
불규칙		YuNa, Kim is **the best** player in figure skating.	good → **best** bad → **worst** many/much → **most** little → **least**

가사 예문

Because the greatest love of all is happening to me.
왜냐면 가장 위대한 사랑이 내게 일어나고 있기 때문이죠.

I found the greatest love of all inside of me.
가장 위대한 사랑을 나 자신 안에서 발견했어요.

Q1 다음 우리말과 의미가 같도록 표현을 완성하시오.

1. 겨울은 일 년 중 가장 추운 계절이다.

→ Winter is ________ ________ season of the year.

2. 나의 여동생이 가족 중에서 가장 키가 크다.

→ My sister is ________ ________ in my family.

3. 이 지갑이 이 가게에서 가장 작지만 가장 비싸다.

→ This wallet is the smallest but ________ ________ ________ in this shop.

4. Empire State 건물은 세상에서 가장 유명한 건물들 중 하나이다.

→ Empire State building is one of ________ ________ ________ buildings in the world.

Q2 다음 대화가 자연스럽도록 괄호 안의 말을 이용하여 공통으로 들어갈 표현을 완성하시오.

1. A: What is ______ ________ way to get there? (fast)

   B: Taking KTX is ______ ________ way to get there.

2. A: Who is ______ ______ ________ idol group in your class? (popular)

   B: BTS is ______ ______ ________ idol group in my class.

3. A: What is ______ ______ ________ thing in your life? (important)

   B: I think staying healthy is ______ ______ ________ thing in my life.

4. A: Do you know who received ______ ______ votes in the election? (many)

   B: Noah got ______ ______ votes and became the class president.

Fill in the Blank the greatest love

Question 1 **1.** the coldest **2.** the tallest **3.** the most expensive **4.** the most famous

Question 2 **1.** the fastest **2.** the most popular **3.** the most important **4.** the most

43 Top of the world — Carpenters

Such a feeling's coming over me
There is wonder in most everything I see
Not a cloud in the sky
Got the sun in my eyes
And I won't be surprised if it's a dream

그러한 느낌이 내게 다가오고 있어요
내가 보는 거의 모든 것에 경이로운 느낌이 드네요
하늘에는 구름 한 점 없고
내 눈 안에 태양이 비치네요
이것이 꿈이라고 해도 놀라지 않을 거예요

- wonder : ① 궁금해 하다 ② 경이로움

Everything I want the world to be
Is now coming true especially for me
And the reason is clear
It's because you are here
You're (   )(   )(   ) to heaven that I'(   )(   )

내가 원하는 세상의 모든 것들이
특별히 나를 위해서 실현되고 있어요
그 이유는 분명해요
그건 당신이 여기에 있기 때문이죠
당신은 내가 이제껏 보아온 것 중 천국에 가장 가까운 존재예요

- especially : 특별히
- I've seen : 이제까지 보아온

★ I'm on the top of the world, looking down on creation
And the only explanation I can find is the love that I've found ever since you've been around
Your love's put me at the top of the world

난 세상 꼭대기에서 만물들을 내려다보고 있어요
내가 찾을 수 있는 유일한 해답은 당신이 내 주위에 함께한 이후 내가 발견한 사랑이에요
당신의 사랑이 날 세상 꼭대기에 올려놓은 거죠

- explanation : 설명
- I've found ever : 내가 이제껏 발견한
- since~ : ① ~때문에 ② ~이래로

Something in the wind has learned my name
And it's telling me that things are not the same
In the leaves on the trees and the touch of the breeze
There's a pleasing sense of happiness for me

바람 속 무언가가 내 이름을 알아내고
내게 말하네요 모든 건 똑같지 않다고요
나무 위의 나뭇잎들 안에서 그리고
산들바람의 촉감에서
내게 만족스러운 행복한 느낌을 주네요

- pleasing : 만족스러운
- sense of happiness : 행복감

There is only one wish on my mind
When this day is through
I hope that I will find that tomorrow will be just the same for you and me
All I need will be mine if you are here

내 마음속에 유일한 소원이 있어요
이 시간이 지나가더라도
당신과 나에게는 변함없는 내일이 있다는
걸 알게 되기를 바라요
내가 원하는 모든 건 내 것이 될 거예요
만약 당신이 여기에 있다면요

- the day is through : 날이 지나가다

★ Repeat × 2

43 다양한 최상급

최상급 + in + 장소/집단 : ~에서 가장 …한

- What is **the most embarrassing moment in your life**?

(embarrassing : 곤혹스러운)

- The Sahara Desert is **the largest and hottest desert in the world**.

최상급 + I've (ever) + 과거분사 : 이제껏 ~한 것 중 가장 …한

- Korean BBQ is **the most delicious food I have ever tried**.
- Niagara Fall is **the most beautiful thing I've seen in my life**.

one of the + 최상급 + 복수명사 : 가장 ~한 … 중 하나

- Let me introduce **one of the most famous places** in Korea.
- Hong Kong is **one of the most populated areas** in the world.

가사 예문

You're the nearest thing to heaven that I've seen.

당신은 내가 이제껏 보아온 것 중 천국에 가장 가까운 존재예요.

Q1 다음 질문에 대한 대답을 완성하시오.

1. What's the most precious thing in your life?

→ ______________________________

2. Where is the most memorable place you've ever visited?

→ ______________________________

3. What is the most interesting movie you've ever seen recently?

→ ______________________________

4. What is the most popular activity on weekend in your family?

→ ______________________________

Q2 다음 우리말과 같도록 주어진 표현을 이용하여 문장을 완성하시오.

1. 그것은 내가 들어본 것 중 가장 뛰어난 대답이군. (outstanding, hear)

→ That is ______________________________.

2. 쌀은 한국의 음식에서 가장 중요한 부분 중 하나이다. (important, part)

→ Rice is ______________________________ of a Korean meal.

3. 맘마미아는 세계에서 가장 성공적인 뮤지컬 중 하나이다. (successful, musical)

→ Mamma Mia is ______________________________ in the world.

4. 신혼여행은 이제껏 내가 가졌던 것 중 가장 편안한 휴식이었어. (relaxing rest, have)

→ Honeymoon was ______________________________.

Fill in the Blank the nearest thing, ve seen

Question 1
1. My diary is the most precious thing in my life.
2. New York is the most memorable place I've ever visited.
3. Avengers is the most interesting movie I've ever seen recently.
4. Visiting gourmet restaurant is the most popular activity on weekend in my family. (gourmet restaurant : 맛집)

Question 2
1. the most outstanding answer that I've ever heard.
2. one of the most important parts **3.** one of the most successful musicals
4. the most relaxing rest that I've ever had.

44 Desperado — The Eagles

Desperado, ①(   )(   )(   ) come to your senses?
You've been out riding fences for so long now
Oh, you're a hard one,
But I know that you got your reasons
These things that are pleasing you can hurt you somehow

무법자여, 정신을 좀 차리는 게 어때요?
당신은 그렇게 오랫동안 담장 위를 걷듯 (방황하며) 살아왔잖아요
당신은 대하기 힘든 사람이죠,
하지만 나름 이유가 있다는 건 알아요
당신을 기쁘게 하는 일들이 당신에게 상처를 줄 수도 있답니다

- **desperado :** 무법자
- **come to senses :** 정신 차리다

Don't you draw the queen of diamonds, boy
She'll beat you if she's able
You know the queen of hearts is always your best bet
Now it seems to me, some fine things have been laid upon your table
But you only want the ones that you can't get

다이아몬드 퀸을 뽑지 마세요, 그대여
그녀는 할 수만 있다면 당신을 해칠 거예요
당신의 최선의 선택은 항상 (마음 따뜻한) '하트 퀸'이란 걸 알잖아요
당신의 테이블 위에는 좋은 패들이 놓여 있는 것처럼 보여요
하지만 당신은 가질 수 없는 것들만 원하네요

- **beat :** 치다, 때리다
- **laid :** 놓인(lay-laid-laid)

Desperado, oh, you ain't getting no younger
Your pain and your hunger, they're driving you home
And freedom, oh freedom, well, that's just some people talking

무법자여, 당신은 더 이상 젊어지진 않아요
고통과 배고픔이 당신을 집으로 데려가고 있어요
그리고 자유, 자유 말인가요,
그것은 단지 어떤 이들이 말로만 떠드는 것일 뿐

Your prison is walking through this world all alone

당신의 감옥은 홀로 세상 속을 걷고 있는 것이에요

- get younger : 젊어지다
- hunger : 배고픔

Don't your feet get cold in the winter time?
The sky won't snow and the sun won't shine
It's hard to tell the night time from the day
You're losing all your highs and lows
Ain't it funny how the feeling goes away?

겨울에 발은 시리지 않나요?
하늘에선 눈도 내리지 않고
태양도 비치지 않을 거예요
힘겨운 날(밤)과 밝은 날(낮)을 구분하는 것도 어렵죠
당신의 모든 기쁜 감정과 슬픈 감정도 무뎌져가고 있습니다
그런 감정이 어떻게 그리 사라져버리는지 우습지 않은가요?

- It's hard to~ : ~하기 힘들다
- highs and lows : 기복

Desperado, ①(　　)(　　)(　　) come to your senses?
Come down from your fences, open the gate
It may be raining, but there's a rainbow above you
You'②(　)(　　) let somebody love you
(Let somebody love you)
You'②(　)(　　) let somebody love you before it's too late...

무법자여,
정신을 좀 차리는 게 어때요?
당신의 담장에서 나와 문을 열어요
비가 내리겠지요, 하지만 무지개가
당신 머리 위에 떠 있어요
누군가가 당신을 사랑하도록 하는 게 더 좋을 거예요
(누군가 당신을 사랑하도록 하세요)
누군가가 당신을 사랑하도록 하는 게 더 좋을 거예요
너무 늦기 전에… (마음의 문을 열어요)

- come down from~ : ~로부터 내려오다
- let + A + B: A로 하여금 B하게 하다

44 Why don't you~ / You'd better~

Why don't you~ 구문

1. 용도	'~하는 게 어때?' 하고 '제안', '권유'할 때 사용
2. 특징	Why don't you 뒤에는 '동사원형'을 취함. Why don't you **stay** longer?
3. 유사구문	**How about ~ing? (What about ~ing)**과 유사 Why don't you try a new hair style? = **How about (What about) trying** a new hair style?

가사 예문

Desperado, why don't you come to your senses?
무법자여, 정신을 좀 차리는 게 어때요?

You'd better~ 구문

1. 용도	'~하는 것이 좋다'의 의미로, '충고', '조언'을 할 때 사용
2. 특징	You'd better~은 **You had better~**의 축약형. You'd better 뒤에는 '**동사원형**'을 취함. You'd better **take** the keys in case I'm out.
3. 부정형	**You'd better not~** (~하지 않는 게 낫다) You'**d better not** overdrink. You'**d better not** do that again.
4. 구문	You **had better** quit smoking for your health.

가사 예문

You'd better let somebody love you.
누군가가 당신을 사랑하도록 하는 게 좋을 거에요.

Q1 다음 우리말과 의미가 같도록 괄호 안의 단어들을 바르게 배열하시오.

1. 이 약을 복용하는 게 어때? (why don't you / take / this medicine)

→ ______________________________

2. 너는 지금 잠자리에 드는 편이 좋겠다. (go / had better / you / to bed / now)

→ ______________________________

3. 너는 그녀에게 휴대폰 번호를 주지 않는 편이 좋겠다.
   (your cell phone number / had better / her / not / you / give)

→ ______________________________

4. 밖에 나가서 가족과 함께 보름달을 찾아보는 건 어때요?
   (with your family / find a full moon / go outside / why don't you / and)

→ ______________________________

Q2 다음 문장에서 어색한 부분을 찾아 바르게 고치시오.

1. You had not better go out late when you travel alone.

______________ → ______________

2. You had better cleaning your room before your mom gets home.

______________ → ______________

3. Why don't you made some special activities with your friends?

______________ → ______________

4. Why don't you coming out and kick the ball around with us?

______________ → ______________

Fill in the Blank ① why don't you ② d better

Question 1 **1.** Why don't you take this medicine? **2.** You had better go to bed now.
3. You had better not give her your cell phone number.
4. Why don't you go outside and find a full moon with your family?

Question 2 **1.** had not better → had better not **2.** cleaning → clean **3.** made → make
4. coming → come

45	Nothing's gonna change my love for you	Westlife

If I had to live my life without you near me
The days would all be empty
The nights would seem so long
With you I see forever oh, so clearly
I might have been in love before
But it never felt this strong
Our dreams are young and we both know
They'll take us where we want to go
Hold me now, touch me now
I don't want to live without you

만약 내 곁에 있는 당신 없이 살아야 한다면
하루하루가 공허하고
밤이 너무 길게 느껴질 테죠
당신과 함께라면 영원을 선명히 볼 수 있어요
예전에도 사랑에 빠졌었지만
이렇게 강렬하진 않았죠
우리의 꿈은 기운차고 우린 둘 다 알고 있죠
우리의 꿈이 우리가 원하는 곳으로 데려다줄 거라는 걸
날 안아주세요, 날 만져보세요
당신 없이는 살고 싶지 않아요

- **without~** : ~없이는
- **empty** : 텅 빈
- **forever** : ① 영원히 ② 영원

☆ (   )'( )(   )(   ) my
love for you
You ought to know by now how much
I love you
One thing you can be sure of
I'll never ask for more than your love

아무 것도 당신에 대한 나의 사랑을 바꿀 수는 없을 거예요
당신도 지금쯤이면 내가 얼마나 당신을 사랑하는지 알아야 해요
한 가지 당신께 확신할 수 있는 것은
당신의 사랑, 그 이상은 아무 것도 더 바라지 않는다는 것이죠

- **Nothing's gonna** = Nothing is going to
- **ought to** : (기대를 나타내며) ~해야 하다

★ (   )'( )(   )(   ) my
love for you
You ought to know by now how much
I love you

아무 것도 당신에 대한 나의 사랑을 바꿀 수는 없을 거예요
당신도 지금쯤이면 내가 얼마나 당신을 사랑하는지 알아야 해요

The world may change my whole life thru but
Nothing's gonna change my love for you

세상이 내 삶을 모조리 바꿔버린다 해도
아무 것도 당신에 대한 나의 사랑을 바꿀 수는 없을 거예요

- **thru = through :** ~를 관통하여
- **by now :** 지금쯤은

If the road ahead is not so easy
Our love will lead the way for us like a guiding star
I'll be there for you If you should need me
You don't have to change a thing
I love you just the way you are
So come with me and share the view
I'll help you see forever, too
Hold me now, touch me now
I don't want to live without you

우리가 나아갈 길이 쉽지 않다 해도
길을 밝히는 별과 같은 우리의 사랑이 갈 길을 이끌어줄 거예요
만약 제가 필요하면 당신 곁에 있어줄게요
당신은 아무 것도 바꿀 필요가 없어요
난 그저 당신 그대로의 모습을 사랑해요
그러니 나와 함께 앞날을 설계해봐요
내가 당신이 영원을 볼 수 있도록 도와줄게요
날 안아주세요, 날 만져보세요
당신 없이는 살고 싶지 않아요

- **don't have to~ :** ~를 할 필요가 없다
- **just the way you are :** 지금 있는 모습 그대로

☆ Repeat

★ Repeat × 2

☆ Repeat

★ Repeat

☆ Repeat

45 be going to

be going to란

- '~할 것이다'라는 의미로 이미 하기로 결정한 미래의 일에 대해 말할 때 be going to~를 쓴다.

- 긍정문 및 부정문

I	am	(not)	going to	visit National Museum.
You/They/We	are			exercise at the gym.
He/She	is			buy a humidifier.

- 의문문

Am	**I**	going to	visit National Museum?
Are	**you/they/we**		exercise at the gym?
Is	**he/she**		buy a humidifier?

가사 예문

Nothing's gonna change my love for you.
아무것도 당신에 대한 나의 사랑을 바꿀 수는 없을 거예요.

Attention!

be going to와 will과의 차이점에 주의!

말하고 있는 시점 이전에 이미 결정해둔 일에 대해 말할 때는 am/are/is going to를 쓰고, 말하고 있는 시점인 지금 결정한 일에 대해 말할 때는 will을 쓴다!

- A: What is your plans for this weekend?
  B: I **am going to** hang out with my friends at downtown. (← 미리 결정한 일)
- A: Do you want to hang out with us tonight?
  B: Sure. I'**ll** meet you at downtown after work. (← 지금 결정한 일)

Q1 〈보기〉의 동사와 am/are/is going to를 사용하여 문장을 완성하시오.

〈보기〉	buy	have	spend	skip

1. I ____________________ time with my family on this holiday.
2. Ronaldo's wife ____________________ a baby in a week or so.
3. I had a big breakfast this morning, so I ____________________ lunch today.
4. Peter ____________________ a new car next week. He has saved $30,000 already.

Q2 다음 괄호 안에 주어진 동사와 am/are/is going to 또는 will 중 더 적절한 것을 사용하여 대화를 완성하시오.

1. A: Maybe there is someone at the door.
   B: I ____________________ who it is. (go and check)
2. A: Does she have any place to stay in London?
   B: Yes, She ____________________ in her aunt's house. (stay)
3. A: Honey, don't you think it smells bad at the kitchen?
   B: OK, I ____________________ the garbage on my way out. (take out)
4. A: Would you like to see a movie tonight?
   B: I'm sorry, I have an appointment. I ____________________ my client. (meet)

Fill in the Blank Nothing's gonna change

Question 1 **1.** am going to spend **2.** is going to have **3.** am going to skip **4.** is going to buy

Question 2 **1.** will go and check **2.** is going to stay **3.** will take out **4.** am going to meet

46 Last Christmas | Wham

★ Last Christmas

I ①( )( )( )( )

But the very next day you gave it away

This year

To save me from tears

I'll ②( )( )( )( ) special

작년 크리스마스에

난 당신에게 나의 마음을 주었죠

하지만 바로 그 다음 날 당신은 거절했어요

이번 해엔

눈물을 흘리지 않기 위해

난 특별한 누군가에게 마음을 줄 거예요

- give it away : 그만두다
- save A from B : B로부터 A를 구하다
- someone special : 특별한 누군가

★ Repeat

Once bitten and twice shy

I keep my distance

But you still catch my eye

Tell me baby

Do you recognize me?

Well, It's been a year

It doesn't surprise me

한 번 상처를 받아서 두 번째는 조심스럽네요

적당히 거리를 유지하려고요

하지만 당신은 여전히 내 눈을 사로잡네요

말해봐요

날 알아보겠어요?

글쎄요, 1년이 되었죠

놀라운 일도 아니죠

- Once bitten twice shy : (속담) 자라보고 놀란가슴 솥뚜껑보고 놀란다
- recognize : 인식하다, 알아차리다
- surprise : 놀라게 하다

Happy Christmas!
I wrapped it up and sent it
With a note saying 'I love you,'
I meant it
Now I know what a fool I've been
But if you kissed me now
I know you'd fool me again

해피 크리스마스!
선물을 포장해서 보냈었죠
'사랑해'라는 쪽지와 함께, 정말 진심이었죠
이젠 알아요 내가 얼마나 바보였는지
하지만 당신이 지금 내게 키스한다면
당신이 날 다시 바보로 만들려 한다는 걸
알아요

- wrap up : 포장하다
- I mean it : 진심입니다
- mean-meant-meant
- fool : ① 바보 ② 속이다
- I've = I have
- you'd = you would

★ Repeat × 2
Oh~ Baby

A crowded room
Friends with tired eyes
I'm hiding from you
And your soul of ice
My god, I thought you were someone
to rely on
Me?
I guess I was a shoulder to cry on

사람들이 가득한 방에
피곤한 눈의 친구들
난 얼음 같은 영혼의 당신을 피해 숨어있어요
이런, 난 생각했었죠 당신은 기댈 수 있는
누군가일 거라고
저는요?
난 기대어 울 수 있는 어깨가 될 수 있을
거라고 생각했는데

- crowded : 붐비는
- rely on : 기대다, 의지하다

A face on a lover with a fire in his heart
A man undercover
but you tore me apart
Now I've found a real love
you'll never fool me again

뜨거운 마음으로 사랑에 빠진 얼굴을
감춰왔던 남자이지만
당신은 내 마음을 완전히 찢어버렸죠
이제 난 진정한 사랑을 찾았으니
당신은 결코 날 바보로 만들지 못할 거예요

- **undercover :** 비밀의, 비밀리에 하는
- **tear apart :** 허물다, 찢어지게 하다 **(tear-tore-torn)**

★ Repeat × 2

A face on a lover with a fire in his heart
A man undercover
but you tore me apart
Maybe next year I'll ②(   )(   )(   )
(   )
I'll ②(   )(   )(   )(   ) special, special
someone...

뜨거운 마음으로 사랑에 빠진 얼굴을
감춰왔던 남자이지만
당신은 내 마음을 완전히 찢어버렸죠
아마도 내년에 난 누군가에게 내 마음을 줄 거예요
난 내 마음을 특별한, 특별한 누군가에게 줄 거예요
누군가에게…

46 수여동사

수여동사란

- '주다', '사주다' 등 수여의 의미를 지닌 동사군을 말한다.
- 「주어 + 수여동사 + 간접목적어(~에게) + 직접목적어(…를)」의 형태를 지닌다.

문장의 전환

- 2개의 목적어인 간접목적어와 직접목적어의 위치를 바꾸어 쓸 경우, 「주어 + 수여동사 + 직접목적어(…를) + 전치사 + 간접목적어(~에게)」의 순서가 되며, 이때 전치사는 수여동사에 따라 달라진다.

1. 전치사 to를 쓰는 수여동사	give, send, show, tell, lend, write, teach
	The old woman gave Snowwhite an apple. → The old woman **gave** an apple **to** Snowwhite.
2. 전치사 for를 쓰는 수여동사	buy, make, get
	My father bought me a tablet PC. → My father **bought** a tablet PC **for** me.

가사 예문

Last Christmas, I gave you my heart.
작년 크리스마스에 난 당신에게 내 마음을 주었죠.

Q1 다음 두 문장의 의미가 같도록 빈칸에 알맞은 말을 쓰시오.

1. Rebecca sent me an e-mail.

→ Rebecca sent ______________________________.

2. Will you teach me how to drive?

→ Will you teach ______________________________?

3. Andrew made his girlfriend a birthday cake.

→ Andrew made ______________________________.

Q2 다음 우리말과 의미가 같도록 괄호 안의 단어들을 바르게 배열하시오.

1. Keith는 그녀의 엄마에게 문자 메시지를 보냈다.
   (Keith / her mom / a text message / sent)

→ ____

2. Zara는 그녀의 딸을 위해 드레스를 만들어줄 것이다.
   (Zara / make / her daughter / will / a dress / for)

→ ____

3. Hunter는 노숙자들에게 일 년간 그의 집을 빌려주었다.
   (Hunter / to / lent / the homeless / his house / for a year)

→ ____

4. 의사는 그에게 담배의 위험성에 관해서 경고를 했다.
   (The doctor / him / of smoking / a warning / gave / about the dangers)

→ ____

Fill in the Blank ① gave you my heart ② give it to someone

Question 1 **1.** an e-mail to me **2.** how to drive to me **3.** a birthday cake for his girlfriend

Question 2 **1.** Keith sent her mom a text message. **2.** Zara will make a dress for her daughter.
3. Hunter lent his house to the homeless for a year.
4. The doctor gave him a warning about the dangers of smoking.

47 I saw you dancing | Yakida

★ I (　　)(　　)(　　　　)
And I'll never be the same again
for sure
I (　　)(　　)(　　　　)
Say 'Yaki-da' (my love)
I (　　)(　　)(　　　　)
And I'll never be the same again
for sure
I (　　)(　　)(　　　　)
Say 'Yaki-da'

난 네가 춤추는 걸 봤어
그리고 난 절대로 이전과 같이 될 수 없다는 걸 알아
난 네가 춤추는 걸 봤어
'야키다'라고 말해봐 (내 사랑)
난 네가 춤추는 걸 봤어
그리고 난 절대로 이전과 같이 될 수 없다는 걸 알아
난 네가 춤추는 걸 봤어
'야키다'라고 말해봐

- **Yaki-da** : 영국 웨일스 지방에서 쓰이는 cheers(환호, 갈채)의 뜻

I'm waiting for a chance
To get to know you, to ask for a dance
Just look into my eyes and I'll take you
to paradise

난 기회를 기다리고 있어
널 알게 되는, 네게 춤을 청할 기회 말이야
그냥 내 눈을 들여다봐 그러면 내가 널
낙원으로 데리고 갈게

★ Repeat

I'm falling, I'm falling
Cause life's not easy for me
Please touch me like you do
to have you near me
to go where you go
Why waste a lot of time?
My love is not a serious crime

난 절망에 빠지고 있어, 절망에 빠지고 있어
삶이란 것은 나에게 쉽지 않은 것이기 때문에
제발 네가 하는 것처럼 날 어루만져줘
널 내 곁에 두기 위해서
네가 가는 곳으로 가기 위해서
왜 시간을 낭비하는 거야?
내 사랑은 심각한 범죄가 아니야

- **waste** : 낭비하다
- **serious** : 심각한

★ Repeat

I'm falling to pieces
Who do you think you are?
Maybe I've gone too far
Maybe I'm in love with you
Don't hurt me or treat me bad
Cause I will fight for what is mine
Say 'Yaki-da'
Cause life is meant for living

난 산산이 부서지고 있어
네가 뭐라고 생각해?
아마도 난 너무 멀리 왔나봐
아마도 난 너랑 사랑에 빠졌나봐
나에게 상처를 주거나 함부로 대하지 마
난 내 것을 위해 싸울 테니까
'야키다'라고 말해봐
인생은 제대로 살아야 하는 거니까

- **treat :** ① 치료하다 ② 대우하다 ③ 처리하다

★ Repeat

47 지각동사

지각동사란

- 지각동사에는 see, watch, hear, feel 등이 있다.
- 「주어 + 지각동사 + 목적어 + 목적보어」 구문에서 목적보어 자리에 동사원형 또는 현재분사(~ing)를 취한다. (이때, 목적어와 목적보어는 능동의 관계)
- 현재분사를 취하는 경우는 목적어의 동작이 진행 중임을 강조하고 싶을 때이다.

주어		지각동사		목적어		목적보어
I		heard		the birds		sing (singing).
They	+	felt	+	the ground	+	shake (shaking).
She		watches		him		ride (riding) a bike.
We		saw		her		cross (crossing) the street.

가사 예문

I saw you dancing.
난 네가 춤추는 걸 봤어.

Attention!

지각동사 문장에서 목적어와 목적보어의 관계가 수동인 경우,
목적보어 자리에 과거분사가 위치!

- I heard **my name** called by someone. 나는 누군가에 의해 내 이름이 **불리는 것**을 들었다.
  → my name(목적어)과 call(목적보어)의 관계가 수동이므로 called를 쓴다.
- I heard **someone** calling my name. 나는 누군가가 내 이름을 **부르는 것**을 들었다.
  → someone(목적어)과 call(목적보어)의 관계가 능동이므로 calling을 쓴다.

Q1 우리말과 의미가 같도록 괄호 안의 말을 이용하여 문장을 완성하시오.

1. Josh는 그의 눈에서 눈물이 떨어지는 것을 느꼈다. (feel / tears / drop / from his eyes)

→ ______________________________

2. 우리는 가을에 나뭇잎 색깔이 변하는 것을 본다. (see / leaves / change colors / in autumn)

→ ______________________________

3. Anita는 그녀의 딸이 위층으로 올라가는 소리를 들었다. (hear / her daughter / go upstairs)

→ ______________________________

4. Rachele은 무언가가 어둠 속에서 번쩍이는 것을 보았다.
   (watch / something / spark / in the dark)

→ ______________________________

Q2 다음 문장의 빈칸에 들어갈 단어를 〈보기〉에서 골라 알맞은 형태로 바꿔 쓰시오.

〈보기〉 fall watch shout feed

1. We heard a man _________ "Help me!"
2. I see the children _________ the monkeys.
3. I felt someone at the next table _________ me.
4. They are watching the leaves _________ from the trees.

Fill in the Blank saw you dancing

Question 1
1. Josh felt tears drop (dropping) from his eyes.
2. We see leaves change (changing) colors in autumn.
3. Anita heard her daughter go (going) upstairs.
4. Rachele watched something spark (sparking) in the dark.

Question 2
1. shout (shouting) **2.** feed (feeding) **3.** watch (watching) **4.** fall (falling)

48 Honey Honey — ABBA

★ Honey honey,
How you thrill me? A-ha, honey honey
Honey honey,
Nearly kill me, ah-hah, honey honey
I'd heard about you before
I wanted to know some more
And now I know what they mean,
You're a love machine
Oh, you make me dizzy

사랑하는 사람이여,
어떻게 날 이리 전율시키나요? 아하, 그대여
사랑하는 사람이여,
죽을 것 같이 좋아요, 사랑하는 사람이여
예전에 당신에 대해 들었어요
좀 더 알기를 원했었죠
이제 그들이 말한 것을 다 알겠어요
당신이 진정 러브머신이란 걸
오, 당신은 날 어지럽게 해요

- **thrill** : 황홀감, 전율시키다
- **dizzy** : 현기증 나는

Honey honey,
(　　)(　　)(　　　)(　　), A-ha, honey honey
Honey honey,
Don't conceal it, A-ha, honey honey

사랑하는 이여,
그것을 느끼게 해줘요, 사랑하는 이여
사랑하는 이여,
그것을 숨기지 말아요, 사랑하는 이여

- **conceal** : 숨기다

The way that you kiss goodnight,
The way that you hold me tight,
I feel like I wanna sing when you do your thing

굿나잇 키스를 할 때면,
당신이 날 세게 끌어안을 때면,
당신이 그렇게 하고 있으면 나는 노래를 부르고 싶어져요

I don't wanna hurt you, baby,
I don't wanna see you cry
So stay on the ground, girl,
You'd better not get too high

당신을 다치게 하고 싶지 않아요
당신이 우는 것을 보고 싶지 않아요
그러니 그냥 있어요, 소녀여,
너무 높이까지 가지 않는 게 좋아요

- **You'd better not~** : ~하지 않는 편이 좋다

But I'm gonna stick to you, boy,
You'll never get rid of me
There's no other place in this world
where I rather would be

하지만 난 당신을 붙잡고 있을 거예요,
당신, 날 거부하지 말아요
이곳 외에 내가 있고 싶은 곳은 없어요

- stick to~ : ~에 달라붙다
- get rid of~ : ~를 제거하다

Honey honey,
Touch me, baby, A-ha, honey honey
Honey honey, hold me, baby, A-ha,
honey honey

사랑하는 이여
나에게 닿아주세요, 사랑하는 이여, 아하,
사랑하는 이여
날 잡아요, 아하, 사랑하는 이여

You look like a movie star
But I know just who you are
And, honey, to say the least,
You're a dog-gone beast

당신은 영화배우 같아요
하지만 난 당신이 누구인지 알죠
그리고 사랑하는 이여, 말 그대로,
당신은 야수 같아요

- look like~ : ~처럼 보이다
- to say the least : 조금도 과장하지 않고

So stay on the ground, girl,
You'd better not get too high
There's no other place in this world
where I rather would be

그러니 여기에 머물러요, 소녀여,
너무 높게 올라가지 않는 게 좋아요
이곳 외에 내가 있고 싶은 곳은 없어요

- You'd better not ~ :
  ~하지 않는 편이 낫다

★ Repeat

48 사역동사

사역동사란

- '~에게 …하게 하다'의 의미이며, let, make, have가 사역동사에 속한다.
- 사역동사 구문은 「주어 + 사역동사 + 목적어(~) + 목적보어(…)」 어순을 취한다.
- 사역동사 구조에서 목적어가 사람이면 능동형, 목적어가 사물이면 수동형 구조를 취한다.

능동형 사역동사 구조 : 주어는 목적어가 ~하도록 시키다

- 목적어가 사람일 때는 목적보어 자리에 동사원형을 쓴다.

		사역동사		목적어		목적보어	
주어	+	make	+	him	+	do	his homework
		have		them		repair	the car
		let		Mary		paint	the wall
				사람		동사원형	

수동형 사역동사 구조 : 주어는 목적어가 ~되도록 시키다

- 목적어가 사물일 때는 목적보어 자리에 과거분사를 쓴다.

		사역동사		목적어		목적보어	
주어	+	make	+	his homework	+	done	(by him)
		have		the car		repaired	(by them)
		let		the wall		painted	(by Mary)
				사물		과거분사	

가사 예문

Honey, let me feel it.

그대여, 그것을 느끼게 해주세요.

Q1 우리말과 의미가 같도록 괄호 안의 말을 이용하여 문장을 완성하시오.

1. 엄마는 내가 오븐을 끄도록 시키셨다. (turn)

→ Mom had me ________ off the oven.

2. 그는 그가 주문한 물건이 나의 사무실로 배달되도록 시켰다. (deliver)

→ He made his order ________ to my office.

3. 그녀는 그 컴퓨터가 수리공에 의해 수리되도록 시켰다. (fix)

→ She had the computer ________ by the mechanic.

4. 나의 영어선생님은 우리가 매일 영자신문을 읽도록 시키신다. (read)

→ My English teacher makes us ________ the English newspaper everyday.

Q2 다음 문장에서 잘못된 부분을 찾아 바르게 고치시오.

1. Please have your work do by noon. ________ → ________
2. My dad made his shoes to shine by me. ________ → ________
3. You should let I know if you change the schedule. ________ → ________
4. Mr. Lee had the students staying only in the classroom. ________ → ________

Fill in the Blank let me feel it

Question 1 **1.** turn **2.** delivered **3.** fixed **4.** read

Question 2 **1.** do → done **2.** to shine → shone **3.** I → me **4.** staying → stay

49 Goodbye — Jessica

I can see the pain living in your eyes
And I know how hard you try
You deserve to have so much more
I can feel your hurt and I sympathize
And I'll never criticize
all you ever meant to my life

당신 눈에 고인 아픔을 알 수 있어요
당신이 얼마나 노력했는지도 알아요
당신은 더 많은 사랑을 받을 만한 자격이 있어요
당신의 아픔도 느낄 수가 있고 공감해요
그리고 당신을 비난하지 않겠어요
내 삶에 커다란 존재였던 당신을

- **pain** : 고통
- **deserve** : 자격이 되다
- **sympathize** : 공감하다
- **criticize** : 비난하다

★ I don't want ①(　)(　) you (　　)
I don't want ②(　)(　) you (　)
I don't want ③(　)(　) you (　)
from where you might belong
You would never ask me why my heart is so disguised
But I just can't live a lie anymore
I would rather hurt myself than to ever make you cry
But there's nothing left to say but goodbye

당신을 실망시키고 싶지 않아요
당신을 속이고 싶지도 않아요
당신이 마땅히 있어야 할 곳으로 가지 못하도록 당신을 붙잡아두지 않겠어요
당신은 왜 저의 본심을 숨겼느냐고 묻지 않겠죠
하지만 더 이상 거짓된 삶을 살 수가 없어요
당신을 울게 하느니 차라리 제가 고통을 당하겠어요
하지만 이 말밖엔 달리 할 말이 없군요
안녕이라는 말밖에

- **let down** : 실망시키다
- **lead on** : (구어) 속이다
- **hold back from~** : ~으로부터 방해하다
- **disguise** : 위장하다
- **would rather~** : ~하는 편이 낫다

You deserve a chance at the kind of love
I'm not sure I'm worthy of
Losing you is painful for me

당신은 사랑의 기회를 얻을 자격이 있어요
내가 당신에게 가치가 있는지 모르겠군요
당신을 잃는 것은 고통스러워요

- **worthy :** 가치가 있는
- **painful :** 고통스러운

★ Repeat

You would never ask me why my heart
is so disguised
But I just can't live a lie anymore
I would rather hurt myself than to ever
make you cry
But there's nothing left to try
and though it's gonna hurt us both
There's just no other way than to say
goodbye...

당신은 왜 저의 본심을 숨겼느냐고 묻지
않겠죠
하지만 더 이상 거짓된 삶을 살 수가 없어요
당신을 울게 하느니 차라리 제가 고통을
당하겠어요
하지만 달리 할 방법이 없잖아요
우리 두 사람 모두 고통스럽겠지만
안녕이라는 말밖에 달리 어찌할 방법이
없어요

- **though :** 비록 ~하지만
- **gonna = going to**
- **than~ :** ~보다는

49 to 부정사의 명사적 용법

to 부정사의 명사적 용법이란

- to 부정사(to+동사원형) 형태가 문장에서 주어(~은/는, ~이/가), 목적어(~을/를), 보어(~것)의 역할을 하는 것을 말하다.

to 부정사의 명사적 용법 역할

1. 주어 역할	- **To walk** is good for your health. (걷는 것은) - **To keep** the promise is very important. (지키는 것은)
2. 목적어 역할	- I want **to buy** a new I-phone. (사기를) - We decided **to go** to Pusan International Film Festival. (가기를)
3. 보어 역할	- My dream is **to travel** around the world. (여행하는 것) - My hope is **to be** a doctor and (to) help sick people. (되는 것)

가사 예문

I don't want to let you down.
나는 당신을 실망시키는 것을 원하지 않아요.

I don't want to lead you on.
나는 당신을 속이는 것을 원하지 않아요.

I don't want to hold you back from where you might belong.
나는 당신이 마땅히 있어야 할 곳으로 가지 못하도록 당신을 붙잡아두지 않겠어요.

Attention!

to 부정사의 부정형 – not을 to 부정사 앞에 위치시킨다!

I decided **to meet** her again. → I decided **not to meet** her again.
(만나기를) (만나지 않기를)

Q1 다음 문장의 밑줄 친 부분이 주어, 목적어, 보어 중 어떤 역할을 하는가?

1. I hope to be a pilot when I grow up. ☐ 주어 ☐ 보어 ☐ 목적어
2. The most important thing is to do your best. ☐ 주어 ☐ 보어 ☐ 목적어
3. To keep a diary is a good way to improve your writing. ☐ 주어 ☐ 보어 ☐ 목적어

Q2 다음 문장의 빈칸에 들어갈 단어를 〈보기〉에서 골라 알맞은 형태로 바꿔 쓰시오.

〈보기〉 save go use see lose

1. You need ________ a doctor about that cough.
2. Renee decided ________ to Paris for her holidays.
3. ________ weight is one of the ways to keep away from obesity. (obesity : 비만)
4. Her new year's resolution is ________ money for buying a new car. (resolution : 결심)
5. ________ SNS wisely is helpful for building good relationship with people. (relationship : 관계)

Fill in the Blank ① to let, down ② to lead, on ③ to hold, back

Question 1 **1.** 목적어 **2.** 보어 **3.** 주어

Question 2 **1.** to see **2.** to go **3.** To lose **4.** to save **5.** To use

50 If I ain't got you — Alicia Keys

Some people live for the fortune
Some people live just for the fame
Some people live for the power
Some people live just to play the game
Some people think that the physical
things define what's within
And I've been there before
But that life's a bore
So full of the superficial

어떤 사람들은 부(富)를 위해 살고
어떤 사람들은 단지 명예를 위해 살지요
어떤 사람들은 권력을 위해 살고
어떤 사람들은 단지 경쟁하기 위해 살지요
어떤 사람들은 물질적인 것들이 내면을
규정짓는다고 생각하지요
그리고 저도 과거에는 그랬죠
하지만 그런 삶은 지루함뿐이에요
무의미할 뿐이죠

- **fortune :** 부
- **fame :** 명예
- **physical :** ① 물질적인 ② 육체적인
- **define :** 정의하다
- **bore :** 지루함
- **superficial :** 피상적인

★ Some people want it all
But I don't want nothing at all
If it ain't you, baby
If I ain't got you, baby
Some people want diamond rings
Some just want everything
But everything means nothing
If I ain't got you

어떤 사람들은 모든 걸 원하지만
저는 아무것도 원하지 않아요
당신이 아니라면, 내 사랑
제가 당신을 갖지 못한다면, 내 사랑
어떤 사람들은 다이아몬드 반지를 원하고
어떤 이들은 모든 걸 원하지만
모든 것은 무의미하지요
제가 당신을 갖지 못한다면

- **not~ at all :** 전혀 ~않는
- **ain't :** am not, is not, are not, has not, have not의 축약형 (주로 구어체에서 사용)

Some people search for a fountain that promises forever young
Some people need three dozen roses
And that's the only way ①(   )(   ) you love him
Hand me the world on a silver platter
And what good would it be?
With no one ②(   )(   )
With no one who truly cares for me

어떤 사람들은 영원한 젊음을 약속하는 샘을 찾아요
어떤 사람들은 장미 세 다발을 원하죠
그리고 그것이 당신이 그를 사랑하는 것을 입증할 오직 단 하나의 방법이죠
은쟁반 위에 곱게 담은 세상 전부를 내게 건네준다 한들 무슨 소용이 있겠어요?
함께 나눌 사람도 없고
나를 진정으로 돌보아주는 사람도 없다면요

- search for : ~을 찾는
- fountain : 분수
- a dozen of~ : ~ 한 다발
- prove : 증명하다

★ Repeat × 2

If I ain't got you with me, baby
So nothing in this whole wide world don't mean a thing
If I ain't got you with me, baby

제가 당신과 함께할 수 없다면, 내 사랑
이 세상 모든 것이 무의미해요
제가 당신과 함께할 수 없다면, 내 사랑

50 to 부정사의 형용사적 용법

to 부정사의 형용사적 용법이란

- to 부정사 형태가 앞에 있는 명사를 수식하여 형용사 역할을 한다.

- I am very thirsty. I want something **to drink**.

(마실 : 앞에 위치한 명사 something을 수식)

가사 예문

That's the only way to prove you love him.

그것이 당신이 그를 사랑하는 것을 입증할 오직 단 하나의 방법이죠.

What good would it be, with no one to share.

무슨 소용이 있겠어요, 함께 나눌 사람도 없는데.

Attention!

시적 허용

Poetic license라고 하며, 문학적 효과를 위해 비형식적이고 구어체적인 표현이 허용되는 것

- If I ain't got you (If haven't got you → O)
- I don't want nothing at all (I don't want anything at all → O)

시적 효과를 위해, 구어체적 표현을 사용한 poetic license의 예를 보여줌

Q1 다음 문장의 빈칸에 들어갈 단어를 〈보기〉에서 골라 알맞은 형태로 바꿔 쓰시오.

〈보기〉 answer show drink write live sit

1. I have a pen ____________ with.
2. He has a house ____________ in.
3. We found a chair ____________ on.
4. I have some pictures ____________ you.
5. There is no water ____________ in this room.
6. Jack was the only student ____________ the question.

Q2 다음 우리말과 의미가 같도록 괄호 안의 단어들을 배열하여 문장을 완성하시오.

1. 그녀가 잠잘 곳이 없다. (sleep / to / place / in / no)

→ She has ______________________________.

2. 따라야 할 몇 가지 중요한 규칙들이 있어. (rules / several / follow / important / to)

→ There are ______________________________.

3. 영어를 배우는 가장 좋은 방법은 무엇입니까? (learn / English / the / to / way / best)

→ What is ______________________________?

4. 나는 유럽으로 여행갈 기회가 생겼으면 좋겠다. (chance / a / to / Europe / travel / to)

→ I'd like to have ______________________________.

5. 당신은 위기에 처해 있을 때 의지할 누군가가 있나요? (to / on / someone / rely)

→ Do you have ____________________ when you're in trouble?

Fill in the Blank ① to prove ② to share

Question 1 **1.** to write **2.** to live **3.** to sit **4.** to show **5.** to drink **6.** to answer

Question 2 **1.** no place to sleep in **2.** several important rules to follow **3.** the best way to learn English **4.** a chance to travel to Europe **5.** someone to rely on

51 I just called to say I love you — Stevie Wonder

No New year's day to celebrate
No chocolate covered candy hearts to give away
No first of spring
No song to sing
In fact here's just another ordinary day

축하할 새해 첫날도 아니고
초콜릿이 발린 하트 사탕을 주려는 것도 아니에요
봄의 시작도 아니고
불러줄 노래가 있는 것도 아니에요
사실상 평범한 또 하루에 지나지 않죠

- **in fact** : 사실상
- **ordinary** : 평범한

No April rain No flowers bloom
No wedding Saturday within the month of June
But what it is something true
made up of these three words that
I must say to you
I just called ①( )( )( )( )( )
I just called ②( )( )( )( )
( )( )
I just called ①( )( )( )( )( )
And I mean it from the bottom of my heart

4월의 봄비가 내리는 것도 아니고 꽃이 피는 것도 아니죠
결혼식이 있는 6월의 토요일도 아니랍니다
하지만 내가 하는 얘기는 진실된 거죠
그대에게 꼭 전해야 할 이 세 단어로 이뤄져 있죠
그냥 당신을 사랑한다고 말하려고 전화했어요
내가 당신을 얼마나 아끼는지 말하려고 전화했어요
그냥 당신을 사랑한다고 말하려고 전화했어요
그리고 그건 내 마음 깊은 곳에서 우러난 진심이에요

- **within** : ~안에
- **made up of~** : ~로 이루어진
- **I mean it** : 진심이다

No summer's high
No warm July
No harvest moon to light one tender August night

한여름도 아니고
따뜻한 7월도 아니고
부드러운 8월 밤을 비추는 보름달이 뜬 것도 아니죠

No autumn breeze
No falling leaves
Not even time for birds to fly to southern skies

가을 산들바람이 부는 것도 아니고
낙엽이 떨어지는 것도 아니고
새들이 남쪽 하늘로 날아가는 시기는 더욱 아니죠

- **harvest moon :** 보름달
- **breeze :** 산들바람
- **southern :** 남쪽의

No Libra sun
No halloween
No giving thanks to all the christmas joy you bring
But what it is, though old so new to fill your heart like no three words could ever do

별자리 축복이 있는 것도 아니고
할로윈데이도 아니에요
크리스마스 날 당신이 가져다주는 기쁨에 감사하려는 것도 아니에요
하지만 내가 하는 얘기는, 진부하지만 아주 새로운 거죠
다른 어떤 세 마디보다 당신 가슴을 채울 만한 말이죠

- **Libra :** (별자리) 천칭자리

★ I just called ①(　)(　)(　)(　)(　)
I just called ②(　)(　)(　)(　)
(　)(　)
I just called ①(　)(　)(　)(　)(　)
And I mean it from the bottom of my heart

그냥 당신을 사랑한다고 말하려고 전화했어요
내가 당신을 얼마나 아끼는지 말하려고 전화했어요
그냥 당신을 사랑한다고 말하려고 전화했어요
그리고 그건 내 마음 깊은 곳에서 우러난 진심이에요

★ Repeat

Oh, my heart, Oh, my heart

오 나의 마음이여, 오 나의 마음이여

51 to 부정사의 부사적 용법

to 부정사의 부사적 용법이란

- 문장에서 to 부정사가 부사처럼 쓰여서 '목적(~하기 위해서)', '원인(~하다니/~해서)', '결과(~해서 결국 …하다)' 등의 의미로 쓰여 동사, 형용사, 다른 부사 등을 수식한다.

1. 목적 : ~하기 위해서	- Some people learn English **to get** a better job. (얻기 위해서) - I went to the library **to return** some books. (돌려주기 위해서)
2. 원인 : ~하게 되어서	- He was sad **to break** up with Anne. (깨져서) - I was surprised **to see** such a big man. (보게 되어서)
3. 결과 : ~해서 결국 …하다	- She grew up **to be** a pianist. (결국 되다) - He worked hard only **to fail** in the exam. (결국 실패하다)

가사 예문

I just called to say I love you.

나는 그냥 당신을 사랑한다고 말하기 위해서 전화했어요.

I just called to say how much I care.

나는 그저 당신을 얼마나 아끼는지 말하기 위해서 전화했어요.

Q1 다음 문장의 빈칸에 들어갈 단어를 〈보기〉에서 골라 알맞은 형태로 바꿔 쓰시오.

〈보기〉	stay	catch	invite	make	find

1. They left early ____________ the 7:30 train.
2. One day, she woke up ____________ herself famous.
3. We are very pleased ____________ you to our wedding.
4. He needed more money ____________ longer in London.
5. The Beatles practiced more than 8 hours a day ____________ their own style of music.

Q2 다음 우리말과 의미가 같도록 괄호 안의 단어들을 바르게 배열하시오.

1. 저는 예약을 취소하려고 전화했어요. (appointment / my / cancel / to / called / I)

→ ______________________________

2. 나는 그 소식을 듣고 매우 놀랐다. (to / hear / I / was / shocked / very / the news)

→ ______________________________

3. 에디슨은 자라서 훌륭한 과학자가 되었다. (scientist / great / grew up / Edison / a / to be)

→ ______________________________

4. 그 소방관은 사람들의 생명을 구하기 위해서 건물 안으로 돌진했다.
(people's lives / to save / the building / rushed into / The fire fighter)

→ ______________________________

Fill in the Blank ① to say I love you ② to say how much I care

Question 1 **1.** to catch **2.** to find **3.** to invite **4.** to travel **5.** to make

Question 2 **1.** I called to cancel my appointment. **2.** I was very shocked to hear the news.
3. Edison grew up to be a great scientist.
4. The fire fighter rushed into the building to save people's lives.

52 Perhaps love

John Denver & Placido Domingo

Perhaps love is like a resting place
A shelter from the storm
It exists to give you comfort
It is there to keep you warm
And in those times of trouble
When you are most alone
The memory of love will bring you home

아마도 사랑은 휴식처인 것 같아요
폭풍으로부터의 은신처이죠
사랑은 당신에게 위안을 주기 위해 존재해요
당신을 따뜻하게 지켜주는 곳이죠
그리고 어려운 시기에
당신이 가장 외로울 때
사랑에 대한 추억은 당신을 안식처로
데려다줄 거예요

- **perhaps :** 아마도
- **resting place :** 휴식처
- **shelter :** 은신처
- **comfort :** 위안

Perhaps love is like a window
Perhaps an open door
It invites you to come closer
It wants to show you more
And even if you lose yourself
And don't know (   )(   )(   )
The memory of love will see you through

아마도 사랑은 창문과 같아요
아마도 열려 있는 문이죠
사랑은 당신을 더 가깝게 다가가도록 해요
당신에게 더 많은 것을 보여주고자 하죠
그리고 당신이 길을 잃고
무엇을 해야 할지 모른다고 해도
사랑에 대한 추억은 당신이 견디도록
도와줄 거예요

- **even if~ :** 비록 ~할지라도
- **lose oneself :** 길을 잃다
- **see somebody through :** ~를 곤란을 뚫고 나가게 하다

Oh love to some is like a cloud
To some as strong as steel
For some a way of living
For some a way to feel

오, 어떤 이에겐 사랑은 구름과 같고
어떤 이에겐 강철과 같이 강해요
어떤 이에겐 살아가는 방법이고
어떤 이에겐 느끼는 방법이에요

- **as A as B :** B만큼 A한
- **steel :** 강철

★ And some say love is holding on
And some say letting go
And some say love is everything
Some say they don't know
Perhaps love is like the ocean full of conflict, full of pain
Like a fire when it's cold outside
Thunder when it rains
If I should live forever
And all my dreams come true
My memories of love will be of you

그리고 어떤 이는 말하지요 사랑은 묵묵히 견뎌내는 거라고
또한 어떤 이는 놓아주는 것이라고 하죠
어떤 이는 사랑은 모든 것이라고 하고
어떤 이는 알 수 없는 것이라고 하지요
아마도 사랑은 갈등과 고통으로 가득 차 있는 대양과도 같아요
추운 날엔 불과 같고
비가 내릴 때 천둥과도 같은 게 사랑이에요
만일 내가 영원히 살게 되어
나의 모든 꿈이 실현된다면
내 사랑의 추억은 당신일 거예요

- **hold on :** ① 견뎌내다 ② 기다리다
- **let somebody go :** ~를 보내주다
- **full of~ :** ~으로 가득 찬
- **conflict :** 갈등
- **thunder :** 천둥

★ Repeat

52 의문사 + to부정사

의문사 + to 부정사 구문이란

- to 부정사 앞에 의문사 what, how, when, where가 쓰여서 '무엇을', '어떻게', '언제', '어디서 ~할지'의 의미를 나타낸다.
- 주로 동사 know, tell, ask, show, learn, teach, decide 등의 목적어로 쓰인다.

What + to 부정사	How + to 부정사	When + to 부정사	Where + to 부정사
무엇을 ~할지	어떻게 ~할지	언제 ~할지	어디서 ~할지

가사 예문

And even if you lose yourself and don't know what to do,
그리고 당신이 길을 잃고 무엇을 해야 할지 모른다고 해도,
the memory of love will see you through.
사랑에 대한 추억은 당신이 견디도록 도와줄 거예요.

Attention!

「의문사 + to 부정사」는 「의문사 + 주어 + should + 동사원형」과 바꾸어 쓸 수 있음!

- She cannot decide **what to wear**. = She cannot decide **what she should wear**.
- Can you tell me **when to start**? = Can you tell me **when I should start**?

Q1 다음 우리말과 의미가 같도록 괄호 안의 단어를 바르게 나열하시오.

1. 무엇을 골라야 할지 내게 말해줘. (choose / what / please / me / tell / to)

→ ______________________________

2. 그녀는 그에게 중국어 읽는 법을 가르쳤다. (taught / him / how / to / she / Chinese / read)

→ ______________________________

3. 어디서 내려야 하는지 내게 알려주겠니? (me / let / can / to get off / you / know / where)

→ ______________________________

4. 그는 사회적 삶에서 어떻게 인간관계를 유지하는지 알기를 원한다.

   (wants / how / to maintain / he / to know / in social life / personal relationship)

→ ______________________________

Q2 다음 〈보기〉와 같도록 문장을 완성하시오.

〈보기〉 I don't know **what to do**. → I don't know **what I should do**.

1. Can you show me how to operate this device? (operate : 작동시키다)

→ ______________________________

2. Ethan does not know what to prepare for his job interview.

→ ______________________________

3. Mia wants to ask the doctor how to treat her high blood pressure.

   (high blood pressure : 고혈압)

→ ______________________________

Fill in the Blank what to do

Question 1 **1.** Please tell me what to choose. **2.** She taught him how to read Chinese.
3. Can you let me know where to get off?
4. He wants to know how to maintain personal relationship in social life.

Question 2 **1.** Can you show me how I should operate this device?
2. Ethan does not know what he should prepare for his job interview.
3. Mia wants to ask the doctor how she should treat her high blood pressure.

53 More than words | Extreme

(　　　) 'I love you' is not the words
I want to hear from you
It's not that I want you not to say
But if you only knew how easy it would be to show me how you feel, more than words is all you have to do to make it real
Then you wouldn't have to say that you love me
Cause I'd already know

'사랑한다'고 말하는 것은 내가 당신에게 듣고 싶은 말이 아니에요
그 말이 싫다는 건 아니지만
만약에 당신이 내게 당신의 감정을 보여주는 게 어렵지 않다는 것을 안다면,
그 사랑을 진실하게 만들기 위해서 당신은 말 이상의 것을 해야 해요
그러면 당신은 날 사랑한다고 말할 필요가 없죠
왜냐하면 난 이미 알고 있을 테니까요

- how easy it would be : 그것이 얼마나 쉬운지
- wouldn't have to say : 말할 필요가 없다
- more than~ : ~보다 그 이상의

★ What would you do if my heart was torn in two?
More than words to show you feel that your love for me is real
What would you say if I took those words away?
Then you couldn't make things new just by (　　　) 'I love you'

내 마음이 두 동강 나버리면 당신은 어떻게 할 건가요?
나에 대한 사랑이 진실하다는 걸 보여주려면 말 이상의 것이 필요해요
내가 사랑한다는 말을 없애 버리면 당신은 무슨 말을 할 건가요?
당신은 그저 '사랑한다'고 말을 하면서 상황을 바꿀 순 없어요

- tear-tore-torn : 찢다
- tear ~ in two : ~을 둘로 찢다
- take away : 제거하다

More than words

사랑한다는 말 그 이상이 필요해요

Now that I've tried to talk to you
and make you understand
All you have to do is close your eyes
and just reach out your hands
And touch me
Hold me close
Don't ever let me go

당신한테 얘기를 해서 이해시키려고
해왔어요
당신이 해야 하는 건 그저 눈을 감고 손을
내미는 거예요
그리고 날 느껴봐요
날 꼬옥 안고
절대 놓지 말아요

- **reach out ~ :** ~을 잡으려고 손을 뻗다
- **hold close :** 꽉 붙잡다
- **let somebody go :** ~를 풀어주다

More than words is all I ever needed
you to show
Then you wouldn't have to say that
you love me
Cause I already know

나는 당신이 말 그 이상을 보여주길
바라왔어요
그럼 당신은 날 사랑한다고 말할 필요가
없어요
왜냐하면 난 이미 알고 있을 테니까요

★ Repeat

53 동명사

동명사란

- 동사원형에 ing를 붙여서 만들며, 동사의 특성을 그대로 가지면서 명사의 기능을 하여 문장에서 주어, 보어, 목적어로 쓰인다.

동명사의 역할

1. 주어 (~은, ~가)	**Getting up** early is difficult for me. (일어나는 것은)
2. 목적어 (~을, ~를)	① 동사의 목적어 Finish **doing** your homework before you play computer games. (하는 것을) ② 전치사의 목적어 Jordan is not good at **speaking** in front of people because he has a stage fright. (말하는 것을)
3. 보어 (~것)	My hobby is **reading** comic books. (읽는 것)

가사 예문

Saying 'I love you' is not the words I want to hear from you.
'사랑한다'고 말하는 것은 내가 당신에게 듣고 싶은 말이 아니에요.

Then you couldn't make things new just by saying 'I love you.'
당신은 그저 '사랑한다'고 말을 하면서 상황을 바꿀 순 없어요.

Attention!

to 부정사만을 목적어로 취하는 동사 vs 동명사만을 목적어로 취하는 동사를 구분!

(want, decide, plan, expect) (finish, mind, enjoy, avoid)

I want **to watch** a movie on Friday night. vs I enjoy **watching** a movie on Friday night.

Q1 다음 밑줄 친 부분이 문장에서 어떤 역할을 하는지 표시하시오.

1. Eating carrots is good for your eyes. □ 주어 □ 보어 □ 목적어
2. My father's job is designing a humanoid robot. □ 주어 □ 보어 □ 목적어
3. How about throwing a birthday party tonight? □ 주어 □ 보어 □ 목적어
4. She enjoys watching the soap opera at home on weekends.
   (soap opera : 연속 멜로 드라마) □ 주어 □ 보어 □ 목적어

Q2 다음 문장의 빈칸에 들어갈 단어를 〈보기〉에서 골라 알맞은 형태로 바꿔 쓰시오.

〈보기〉 tell spend win protect exercise

1. Would you mind ____________ me what you're doing in here?
2. His resolution for this year is ____________ regularly for his health.
3. Britney! Congratulations on ____________ the first prize in the contest.
4. ____________ people from a danger of terrorism is a duty of the President.
5. We should avoid ____________ too much money right after we get the payment.

Fill in the Blank Saying

Question 1 **1.** 주어 **2.** 보어 **3.** 목적어 **4.** 목적어

Question 2 **1.** telling **2.** exercising **3.** winning **4.** Protecting **5.** spending

54 Mamma Mia

Mamma Mia OST

I (   ) (   ) (   ) you and I think you know when
So I made up my mind, it must come to an end
Look at me now, will I ever learn?
I don't know how but I suddenly lose control
There's a fire within my soul
Just one look and I can hear a bell ring
One more look and I forget everything, o-o-o-oh

난 당신에게 속았고 당신은 언제부터였는지 알고 있겠죠
그래서 결심했죠, 이제 끝을 내야 한다고요
지금 내 모습을 봐요, 내가 언제쯤 정신 차릴까요?
어떻게 된 건지 모르겠지만 갑자기 정신이 없어요
내 마음속에 불꽃이 있어요
당신을 한번 보면 사랑에 빠지고
한번 더 보면 모든 걸 잊게 돼요

- **cheat** : 속이다, 사기치다
- **make up one's mind** : 결심하다
- **come to an end** : 끝나다
- **learn** : ① 배우다 ② 깨닫다
- **look** : ① 보다 ② 바라봄
- **hear a bell ring** : (비유적 표현) 사랑에 빠지다

☆ Mamma mia,
Here I go again, My my
How can I resist you?
Mamma mia, does it show again?
My my, just how much I've missed you

어머나,
내가 또 그러네요, 이런
어떻게 당신을 거부하죠?
어머나, 티가 날까요?
이런, 당신을 얼마나 그리워했는데요

- **Mamma mia** : 어머나!
- **Oh, my!** : 이런! 어머나!
- **resist** : 거부하다

★ Yes, I've been brokenhearted
Blue since the day we parted
Why why did I ever let you go?

그래요, 가슴 아팠어요
우리 헤어진 후로 우울했어요
왜 왜 난 당신을 떠나보냈을까요?

- **brokenhearted :** 상심한
- **blue :** ① 푸른 ② 낙담한
- **part :** ① 일부, 부분 ② 헤어지다

⁂ Mamma mia, now I really know
My my, I should not have let you go

어머나, 이제는 알겠어요
이런, 당신을 떠나보내지 말았어야 했는데

I was angry and sad when I knew we were through
I can't count all the times I cry over you
Look at me now, will I ever learn?
I don't know how but I suddenly lose control
There's a fire within my soul
Just one look and I can hear a bell ring
One more look and I forget everything, o-o-o-oh

나는 우리가 헤어졌을 때 화가 나고 슬펐죠
당신을 향해 울었던 때가 셀 수 없이 많았죠
지금 내 모습을 봐요, 내가 언제쯤 정신 차릴까요?
어떻게 된 건지 모르겠지만 갑자기 정신이 없어요
내 마음속에 불꽃이 있어요
당신을 한 번 보면 사랑에 빠지고
한 번 더 보면 모든 걸 잊게 돼요

- **be through :** 관계를 끝내다

☆ Repeat

★ Repeat

⁂ Repeat

54 수동태

능동태와 수동태란

• 능동태는 주어가 동작을 가하는 것을, 수동태는 주어가 동작을 받는 것을 말한다.

수동태 만드는 법

He ③ broke ② the window. ① (능동태) 그가 창문을 깼다.

The window was broken by him. (수동태) 창문은 그에 의해 깨졌다.

① 능동태 목적어(the window)를 찾아 **주어**(The window)로 보내기!

② 능동태 동사(broke)는 **be동사 + 과거분사**(was broken)로 바꾸기!

③ 능동태 주어(He)는 **by + 목적격**(him)으로 변신!

가사 예문

I was cheated by you and I think you know when.

나는 당신에게 속았고 당신은 언제부터였는지 알고 있겠죠.

Attention!

수동태의 부정은 be동사 뒤에 not을 쓴다!

The telephone was invented by Edison. → The telephone was **not** invented by Edison.

수동태의 의문문은 주어와 **be**동사 위치를 바꾼다!

The Pandora's box was opened by her. → **Was** the Pandora's box opened by her?

조동사가 있는 수동태는 조동사 다음에 「**be** + 과거분사」를 쓴다!

We should keep the secret. → The secret **should be kept** by us.

행위자가 일반인(we, they, people)이거나 중요하지 않을 때, 「**by** + 목적격」은 생략 가능!

He was killed in the Korean War (**by someone**).

Q1 다음 문장을 수동태로 바꾸어 쓸 때, 빈칸에 알맞은 표현을 쓰시오.

1. He caught the two thieves last night.

→ The two thieves ________ ________ last night by ________.

2. We should not take a picture here.

→ A picture ________ ________ ________ ________ here (by us).

3. King Sejong invented Korean Alphabet.

→ Korean Alphabet ________ ________ ________ King Sejong.

4. Shakespeare wrote the play, 'Romio and Juliet'.

→ The play, 'Romio and Juliet' ________ ________ ________ Shakespeare.

Q2 다음 문장에서 밑줄 친 부분을 바르게 고치시오.

1. The house was building by my father. → ________
2. This work should is finished until tomorrow. → ________
3. The picture were painted by Vincent Van Gogh. → ________
4. The robbers not were found by the police officer. → ________

Fill in the Blank was cheated by

Question 1 **1.** were caught, him **2.** should not be taken **3.** was invented by **4.** was written by

Question 2 **1.** built **2.** be **3.** was **4.** were not

55 The best thing

Mocca

☆ I've got the best thing in the world
Coz' I got you in my heart
in this cruel little world
Let's hold hands together
We can share forever
Maybe someday the sky (   ) (   )
(   ) with our love

나는 세상에서 가장 근사한 것을 가졌어
왜냐하면 이 험한 작은 세상 속에서 난 너를 가졌으니까
우리 함께 손을 잡자
우리는 영원히 함께할 수 있어
아마 언젠가 우리의 사랑으로 저 하늘이 물들 날이 올 거야

- **have got** : (구어) 가지고 있다, 소유하다
- **Coz** : (약어) because
- **cruel** : 잔혹한
- **color(colour)** : ① 색 ② 색칠하다

I wake up in the morning
Feeling emptiness in my heart
This pain is just too real
I dream about you with someone else

아침에 일어나서
내 마음이 너무 공허해
이 고통이 너무 생생해
다른 누군가와 있는 너에 관한 꿈을 꾼 거야

- **feeling emptiness** : 공허감
- **someone else** : 다른 어떤 사람

Please say that you love me
that we'll never be apart

제발 나를 사랑한다고 말해줘
그래서 우리가 절대 헤어지지 않을 거라고

- **apart** : 떨어져, 헤어져

★ You have to promise that you will be faithful
And there will be lots and lots of love
It is the thing that really matters
in this world

제발 약속해줘 너를 믿어도 된다고
그리고 우리의 사랑은 더욱더 깊어질 거라고
바로 그게 이 세상에서 정말 중요한 일인 걸

- **faithful :** 믿을 수 있는
- **matter :** ① 사안 ② 중요하다

☆ Repeat

★ Repeat

55 다양한 수동태

조동사 수동태 / 진행형 수동태 / 완료형 수동태

- 조동사 수동태 : 「조동사 + be + 과거분사」

  We should take care of sick people.

  → Sick people **should be taken** care of by us.

- 진행형 수동태 : 「be동사 + being + 과거분사」

  Birds are building the nests. → The nests **are being built** by birds.

- 완료형 수동태 : 「have(has) + been + 과거분사」

  He has just reported the news. → The news **has just been reported** by him.

가사 예문

Maybe someday the sky will be colored with our love.

아마 언젠가 우리의 사랑으로 저 하늘이 물들 날이 올 거야.

Attention!

by 이외의 전치사를 쓰는 수동태에 유의!

- be covered with : ~로 덮여 있다
- be interested in : ~에 흥미가 있다
- be surprised at : ~에 놀라다
- be pleased with : ~에 기뻐하다
- be made of : ~로 만들어지다
- be disappointed with : ~에 실망하다
- be filled with : ~로 가득 차다
- be known to : ~에게 알려지다
- be satisfied with : ~에 만족하다
- be tired of : ~에 싫증나다
- be worried about : ~에 대해 걱정하다
- be ashamed of : ~을 부끄러워하다

Q1 다음 문장을 수동태로 바꾸어 쓸 때, 빈칸에 알맞은 표현을 쓰시오.

1. We should finish this project by tomorrow.

→ This project ________ ________ ________ by tomorrow by us.

2. People must not bring their pets in the restaurant.

→ Pets ________ ________ ________ ________ in the restaurant.

3. Mom was preparing dinner when I got home.

→ Dinner ________ ________ ________ by mom when I got home.

4. The mechanic has just repaired Mark's car.

→ Mark's car ________ ________ ________ ________ by the mechanic.

Q2 괄호 안에 주어진 동사를 사용하여 수동태 문장을 완성하시오.

1. A: Why is it so cold in here?

   B: I'm sorry. Our heater ________ ________ ________ at the moment.

   (fix) (at the moment = now)

2. A: Is it ok if I give them our information?

   B: I'm afraid you can't. The information ________ ________ ________ secret.

   (must keep)

3. A: There was a big accident on the highway last Friday.

   B: The road ________ ________ ________ since then because of safety concerns.

   (has close)

4. A: Did you hear the news about infectious pneumonia?

   (infectious pneumonia : 전염성 폐렴)

   B: The situation is serious. Something ________ ________ ________ before it is too late."

   (should do)

Fill in the Blank will be colored(coloured)

Question 1 **1.** should be finished **2.** must not be brought **3.** was being prepared **4.** has just been repaired

Question 2 **1.** is being fixed **2.** must be kept **3.** has been closed **4.** should be done

56 Seasons in the sun | Westlife

Goodbye to you, my trusted friend
We'①(   )(   ) each other since we were nine or ten
Together we'②(   )(   ) hills and trees,
(we've) ③(   ) of love and ABCs,
(we've) ④(   ) our hearts, and
④(   ) our knees

잘 있어, 나의 믿음직스런 친구여
아홉 살, 열 살 때부터 우린 서로 알고 지내왔지
우린 함께 언덕과 나무를 오르고,
사랑과 글을 배우고,
마음의 상처를 입기도 하고,
넘어져 무릎이 벗겨지기도 했지

- **season :** 계절, 인생의 한창 때
- **skin :** 상처를 입히다

Goodbye, my friend, It's hard to die
when all the birds are singing in the sky
Now that the spring is in the air
Pretty girls are everywhere
Think of me and I'll be there

잘 있어, 나의 친구여, 난 이 세상을 떠나고 싶지 않아
새들이 하늘을 날며 지저귀는 때에 말이지
이제 봄이 완연하고
아리따운 아가씨들은 어디에나 있지만
날 생각해봐
그러면 내가 바로 그곳에 있을 테니까

- **Now that :** 이제

☆ We had joy, We had fun
We had seasons in the sun
But the hills that we climbed
were just seasons out of time

우린 즐거움과, 기쁨과
태양 아래 모든 계절을 누렸는데
하지만 우리가 오르던 언덕에는
계절이 지나버렸어

- **In the sun :** 양지에, 걱정 없이
- **out of time :** 때늦은, 철 지난

Goodbye Papa, please pray for me
I was the black sheep of the family
You tried to teach me right from wrong
Too much wine and too much song
Wonder how I got along

안녕히 계세요, 아버지, 저를 위해서
기도해주세요
저는 집안의 말썽꾸러기였죠
아버지께서는 제게 옳고 그름을 가르치려
애쓰셨지만 저는 술과 노래로만 지냈어요
제가 어떻게 살아왔는지 모르겠어요

- **pray** : 기도하다
- **black sheep of the family** : (비유) 가문의 수치
- **get along** : 살아가다, 꾸려나가다

Goodbye, papa, it's hard to die
when all the birds are singing in the sky
Now that the spring is in the air
Little children everywhere
When you see them I'll be there

안녕히 계세요, 아버지, 난 죽고 싶지 않아요
새들이 창공에서 노래하는 걸 보니
이제 봄이 완연하고
어린 아이들이 뛰어다니죠
당신께서 그 아이들을 보실 때면
제가 그곳에 머물겠어요

★ We had joy, We had fun
We had seasons in the sun
But the wine and the song
like the seasons ⑤(　　　) all (　　　)

우린 즐거움과 기쁨과
태양 아래 모든 계절을 누렸는데
하지만 계절이 지나가버리듯
술과 노래도 모두 사라져버렸지

★ Repeat

Goodbye, Michelle, my little one
You gave me love and helped me
find the sun
And every time that I was down
You would always come around
And get my feet back on the ground

잘 있어, 미셸, 내 사랑
당신은 내게 사랑을 베풀어주고
내가 양지를 찾을 수 있도록 도와주었어
내가 우울할 때마다 다가와서
용기를 북돋워주었지

- **be down** : 우울하다
- **get one's feet back on the ground** : 다시 설 수 있게 하다 (용기를 주다)

Goodbye Michelle, it's hard to die
when all the birds are singing in the sky
Now that the spring is in the air
With the flowers everywhere
I wish that we could both be there

잘 있어, 미셸, 이 세상을 떠나고 싶지 않아
새들이 하늘을 날며 지저귀는 때에 말이지
이제 봄이 완연하군
사방에 꽃들과 함께
우리 둘이 같이 이 봄을 즐기면 좋을 텐데

- **It's hard to~** : ~하기 힘들다

☆ Repeat

★ Repeat × 3

56 현재완료

현재완료란

- 과거의 일이 현재까지 영향을 미치거나, 과거부터 현재까지의 계속되는 상황을 표현할 때, 「have/has + 과거분사」의 현재완료 시제를 쓴다.

현재완료 형태

긍정문	have [has] + 과거분사	I **have been** sick for three days. (아파오고 있다)
부정문	haven't [hasn't] + 과거분사	She **hasn't traveled** to abroad. (여행해본 적 없다)
의문문	Have [has] + 주어 + 과거분사	**Have** you **finished** your work? (끝냈니?)

현재완료 용법

용법	의미	함께 쓰이는 부사	예문
1. 계속	**~해오고 있다**	for, since	I **have studied** English **for** 10 years.
2. 경험	**~한 적 있다**	ever, never, before, once, twice	**Have** you **ever heard** about it **before**?
3. 완료	**막 ~하였다**	just, already, yet	She **has just arrived** at the Incheon International Airport.
4. 결과	**~결과 지금 …이다**		He **has gone** to France, so he is not here.

가사 예문

We've known each other since we were nine or ten.
아홉, 열 살 때부터 우린 서로 알고 지내왔지.

We've climbed hills and trees, (we've) learned of love and ABCs,
우린 함께 언덕과 나무를 오르고, 사랑과 글을 배우고,

(We've) skinned our hearts, and (we've) skinned our knees.
마음의 상처를 입기도 하고, 넘어져 무릎이 벗겨지기도 했었어.

Attention!

현재완료와 과거시제의 차이

현재완료	We **have lived** in Busan **since** 1990. 우리는 1990년 이후로 부산에 계속 살고 있다. (살아오고 있다) (이래로)
과거	We **lived** in Busan **in** 1990. 우리는 1990년에 부산에 살았다. (지금은 모름) (살았다) (~에)

Q1 주어진 우리말과 같도록 빈칸에 알맞은 표현을 쓰시오.

1. Dr. Ha는 그의 프로젝트를 막 끝냈다.

→ Dr. Ha ________ just ________ his project.

2. 당신은 그의 노래를 들어본 적 있나요?

→ ________ you ever ________ of his song?

3. Taylor와 나는 10년간 서로를 알아오고 있다.

→ Taylor and I ________ ________ each other for ten years.

4. 그는 지갑을 잃어버렸다. 그래서 티켓을 살 돈이 없다.

→ He ________ ________ his wallet. So he doesn't have money to buy the ticket.

Q2 다음 두 문장을 〈보기〉와 같이 현재완료를 이용하여 한 문장으로 연결하시오.

〈보기〉 It began to rain yesterday. It still rains.
→ **It has rained since yesterday.**

1. I lost my puppy. I can't find it now.

→ ______________________________

2. I first met Jonathan six months ago. I still date with him.

→ ______________________________

3. Sue went to Los Angeles for her business. She is not here now.

→ ______________________________

4. My family started to live in Ulsan in 2000. My family still lives in Ulsan.

→ ______________________________

5. Mark started to work at Samsung three years ago. He still works at Samsung.

→ ______________________________

Q3 괄호 안에 주어진 동사를 사용하여 현재완료 시제 문장을 완성하시오.

(필요한 경우 부정문 또는 의문문으로)

1. I am very hungry. I ______________ breakfast. (eat)
2. ______________ our new manager? I wonder who he or she is. (meet)
3. Eric ______________ computer games for a few days. He has been busy with his final exams. (play)
4. I forgot to visit my parents today, so I ______________ the restaurant reservation for our meeting. (cancel)

Fill in the Blank ① ve known ② ve climbed ③ learned ④ skinned ⑤ have, gone

Question 1 **1.** has, finished **2.** Have, heard **3.** have known **4.** has lost

Question 2 **1.** I have lost my puppy. **2.** I have dated with Jonathan for six months.
3. Sue has gone to Los Angeles for her business. **4.** My family has lived in Ulsan since 2000.
5. Mark has worked at Samsung for three years.

Question 3 **1.** haven't eaten **2.** Have you (ever) met **3.** hasn't played
4. have canceled (또는 have cancelled)

57	Way back into love	Hugh Grant & Haley Bennett

I'①(　)(　　)(　　) with a shadow overhead
I'②(　)(　　)(　　) with a cloud above my bed
I've been lonely for so long
Trapped in the past, I just can't seem to move on

난 내 머리 위로 그림자가 드리워진 채로 살아오고 있어요
난 내 침대 위로 구름이 드리워진 채로 잠을 자곤 했죠
난 너무나 오랫동안 외로웠어요
과거에 갇힌 채, 난 도저히 나아갈 수가 없었죠

- **above** : ~위로
- **trapped** : 갇힌 채
- **seem to~** : ~인 것 같다
- **move on** : 나아가다

I'③(　)(　　)(　　) all my hopes and dreams away
Just in case I ever need them again someday
I'④(　)(　　)(　　) aside time
To clear a little space in the corners of my mind

난 내 꿈과 희망을 숨겨오고 있었죠
혹시라도 언젠가 그것들이 필요할 때를 대비해서
난 시간을 따로 떼어놓았었죠
내 마음 한구석의 작은 공간을 비우기 위해

- **hide** : 숨기다
- **Just in case** : 만약의 경우에 대비해서
- **set aside** : 떼어놓다

★ All I want to do is find a way back into love
I can't make it through without a way back into love

내가 원하는 것은 사랑 안으로 돌아갈 수 있는 길을 찾는 것뿐이죠
나는 사랑으로 돌아가지 않고는 이대로 견뎌낼 수 없는 걸요

- **way** : 방법
- **make it through** : 이겨내다

I'⑤(　)(　　)(　　　　) but the stars refuse to shine I'⑥(　)(　　)(　　　　) but I just don't see the signs I know that it's out there There's got to be something for my soul somewhere	오랫동안 쳐다봐왔지만 별들은 반짝이길 거부해요 오랫동안 찾아봐왔지만 아무런 흔적도 찾을 수 없어요 나는 알아요, 저 어딘가에 그것이 존재한다는 것을 저기 어딘가에 내 영혼을 위한 무언가가 분명이 있을 것이란 것을 • **refuse** : 거절하다 • **shine** : 반짝이다 • **There's got to be** : 거기 있을 거야 • **soul** : 영혼 • **somewhere** : 어딘가에
I'⑦(　)(　　)(　　　　) for someone to shed some light Not somebody just to get me through the night I could use some direction And I'm open to your suggestions	나는 빛을 비춰줄 누군가를 찾고 있었죠 나와 밤을 함께 지새울 아무나가 아닌 난 누군가의 도움을 받아들일 수 있어요 그리고 난 당신의 제안도 받아들일 수 있어요 • **look for~** : ~를 찾다 • **shed** : 비추다 • **suggestion** : 제안

★ Repeat

And if I open my heart again I'm guess I'm hoping you'll be there for me in the end	그리고 만약 내가 마음을 다시 연다면 결국에는 당신이 내 곁에 있어 줄 거라고 생각해요 • **in the end** : 결국에는

There are moments when I don't know
if It's real
or if anybody feels the way I feel
I need inspiration not just another
negotiation

진실인지 아닌지 헷갈리는 순간들이 있어요
혹은 내가 느끼는 이 감정을 누군가도
느끼고 있을까 하는
난 또 다른 협상이 아닌 영감이 필요해요

- **inspiration :** 영감
- **negotiation :** 협상

★ Repeat

And if I open my heart to you
I'm hoping you'll show me what to do
And if you help me to start again
You know that I'll be there for you
in the end

만약 내가 당신에게 마음을 연다면 당신이
내게 뭘 해야 하는지 보여주길 바라요
당신이 내가 새로 시작하게 도와준다면
결국에는 내가 당신의 곁에 있어 줄 거라는
걸 알잖아요

57 현재완료 진행형

현재완료 진행형이란

- '~해오고 있는 중이다'의 의미로 과거의 어떤 시점부터 현재까지 계속 이어지는 동작이나 사건을 나타낸다는 점에서 현재완료의 계속적 용법과 비슷하다.
- 형태는 「have(has) been + 동사원형-ing」이다.

현재완료 vs 현재완료 진행형

현재완료	현재완료 진행형
I **have watched** TV for two hours. 2시간 동안 TV를 보고 있다.	I have **been watching** TV for two hours. 2시간 동안 TV를 보고 있는 중이다.
We **have lived** in Busan since 2010. 우리는 부산에 2010년도 이래로 살고 있다.	We **have been living** in Busan since 2010. 우리는 부산에 2010년도 이래로 살고 있는 중이다.

가사 예문

I've been living with a shadow overhead.
난 내 머리 위로 그림자가 드리워진 채로 살아오고 있어.

I've been looking for someone to shed some light.
난 빛을 비춰줄 누군가를 찾아오고 있어.

Q1 다음 괄호 안에서 알맞은 것을 고르시오.

1. Sophia (have / has) been sleeping on the sofa for 5 hours.
2. Eva has been running around the town (for / since) an hour.
3. The students (have / has) been playing soccer since this morning.
4. Emma has been managing the internet cafe (for / since) her graduation.
5. Mr. Carter (has been worked / has been working) in this bank for ten years.

Q2 다음 글을 읽고, 빈칸에 알맞은 말을 쓰시오.

1. Fred started studying French two months ago. He is still studying it.

   = Fred ______ ______ __________ French for two months.

2. Sunny began reading the book 30 minutes ago. She is still reading the book.

   = Sunny ______ ______ __________ the book for 30 minutes.

3. A: It's raining again. I'm sick and tired of this raining season.

   B: Me. too. It ______ ______ __________ for more than two weeks.

   (sick and tired of~ : 진절머리나는)

4. A: Chad is a great tennis player. I ______ ______ __________ his play for an hour.

   B: Yes, he is very talented. I have never seen such a good player before.

Q3 다음 우리말과 의미가 같도록 문장을 완성하시오.

1. 그 아기는 몇 시간째 울고 있다.

→ The baby ______ ______ __________ for hours.

2. Daniel은 한 시간째 그녀를 기다리고 있는 중이다.

→ Daniel ______ ______ __________ for her for an hour.

3. Olivia는 40분째 전화통화를 하고 있는 중이다.

→ Olivia ______ ______ __________ on the phone for forty minutes.

4. Mr. Cooper는 25년 넘게 학생들을 가르쳐오고 있다.

→ Mr. Cooper ______ ______ __________ students for over twenty five years.

Fill in the Blank ① ve been living ② ve been sleeping ③ ve been hiding ④ ve been setting ⑤ ve been watching ⑥ ve been searching ⑦ ve been looking

Question 1 **1.** has **2.** for **3.** have **4.** since **5.** has been working

Question 2 **1.** has been studying **2.** has been reading **3.** has been raining **4.** have been watching

Question 3 **1.** has been crying **2.** has been waiting **3.** has been talking **4.** has been teaching

III
Advanced

58 Count on me — Bruno Mars

①( ) you ever find yourself stuck in the middle of the sea,
I'll sail the world to find you
①( ) you ever find yourself lost in the dark and you can't see,
I'll be the light to guide you
Find out what we're made of ②(   ) we are called to help our friends in need

만약 네가 바다 한가운데에서 곤경에 처해있다면,
난 너를 찾아 세상을 항해할 거야
만약 네가 어둠 속에 갇혀 앞을 볼 수 없다면,
난 너를 이끌어주는 빛이 될 거야
어려움에 처한 친구를 도와줘야 할 때,
우리가 어떤 사이인지 생각해 봐

- stuck : 갇힌
- sail : 항해하다
- lost : 길을 잃은
- guide : 인도하다
- be made of~ : ~로 구성되다
- what we are made of : 우리가 어떤 사이인지
- help a friend in need : 어려움에 처한 친구를 돕다

★ You can count on me like 1, 2, 3,
I'll be there
And I know ②(   ) I need it I can count on you like 4, 3, 2,
③(   ) you'll be there
④(   ) that's what friends are supposed to do
Oh, yeah,
Woooooh, Woooooh
Yeah, Yeah

네가 나를 향해 1, 2, 3을 세면,
내가 거기 있을 거야
또한 내가 필요할 때 너를 향해 4, 3, 2를 세면,
너도 거기에 있을 테니까
친구라면 그렇게 해야 하니까

- count : 수를 세다
- count on ~ : ① ~를 향해 수를 세다
  ② ~를 의지하다
  (중의적 의미로 쓰임)
- cause : ① 원인 ② 초래하다
  ③ because의 구어적 표현
- be supposed to~ : ~하기로 되어있다

①(　) you're tossing and you're turning ③(　　) you just can't fall asleep, I'll sing a song beside you And ①(　) you ever forget how much you really mean to me, Everyday I will remind you, oh Find out what we're made of ②(　　) we are called to help our friends in need	만약 네가 이리저리 뒤척이며 잠에 들 수 없다면, 내가 네 옆에서 노래를 불러 줄게 만약 네가 나에게 얼마나 소중한지 잊게 된다면, 매일매일 내가 생각나게 해줄게 어려움에 처한 친구를 도와줘야 할 때, 우리가 어떤 사이인지 생각해 봐 • toss and turn : 몸을 뒤척이다 • fall asleep : 잠들다 • mean : 의미하다 • remind : 상기시키다

★ Repeat

You'll always have my shoulder ②(　　) you cry I'll never let go, never say goodbye	네가 울 때는 내 어깨를 빌려도 돼 난 결코 떠나보내지도, 떠나지도 않을 거니까

★ Repeat

You can count on me ④(　　) I can count on you	너는 나에게 기댈 수 있어 왜냐하면 내가 너에게 기댈 수 있으니까

58 접속사

접속사란

- 문장 안에서 단어, 구, 절 등을 연결해주는 말이다.

접속사의 종류

- 접속사는 문법적으로 대등한 표현을 연결하는 등위접속사와, 주가 되는 문장과 그에 속해 있는 문장을 연결해주는 종속접속사가 있다.

등위 접속사		**and**	그리고	She fell downstairs **and** broke her leg.
		but	그러나	We went to the library, **but** it was closed.
		or	또는	Would you like coffee **or** tea?
종속접속사	때	**when**	~할 때	**When** I was young, I had many dreams for the future.
		while	~하는 동안	**While** I was there, I stayed in a nice hotel.
		after	~한 후에	**After** I graduate, I'll work at the computer company.
		before	~하기 전에	Let's have dinner **before** we go to the concert.
		until	~할 때까지	I played on-line games **until** my parents arrived.
		since	~이래로	I have known him **since** he was a child.
		as	~하자	**As** time went by, his health got worse.
	이유 · 결과	**because**	~때문에	**Because** the traffic was terrible, we were late.
		as		**As** I was so tired, I fell asleep on the sofa.
		since		**Since** he had a bad cold, he was absent for school.
		so	그래서	He studied very hard, **so** he passed the test.
	조건 · 양보	**if**	만약 ~라면	You can't learn **if** you are afraid of making mistakes.
		unless = if ~ not	만약 ~하지 않으면	**Unless** you have a ticket, you cannot go in. = **If** you **don't** have a ticket, you cannot go in.
		though	비록 ~하지만	**Though** she is quite small, she is very strong.
		although		**Although** it was rainy, the baseball game was not cancelled.
		even though		**Even though** he didn't go to the university, he succeeded as a businessman.

가사 예문

If you ever find yourself stuck in the middle of the sea,
I'll sail the world to find you.
만약 네가 바다 한가운데에서 곤경에 처해있다면, 난 너를 찾아 세상을 항해할 거야.

Q1 다음 빈칸에 접속사 and, but, so, or 중에서 알맞은 것을 쓰시오.

1. It's an old car, ________ it's very reliable. (reliable : 믿을 만한)
2. There are no buses, ________ you'll have to walk.
3. She picked up the kitten ________ put it in the box.
4. Shall we go out to the cinema ________ stay at home?

Q2 다음 두 문장을 접속사 and나 but을 이용하여 한 문장으로 쓰시오.

1. I missed lunch. / I'm starving! → ________________________
2. He fell down the stairs. / He didn't get hurt. → ________________________
3. Jack knocked on the door. / He went in. → ________________________
4. She invited her neighbors. / They did not come to her house.

→ ____

Q3 다음 우리말과 의미가 같도록 괄호 안의 단어들을 배열하여 문장을 완성하시오.

1. 어두워지기 전에 돌아와야 한다. (it / dark / before / gets)

→ You should come back ________________________.

2. Jenny가 그를 처음 보았을 때, 그녀는 사랑에 빠졌다. (Jenny / when / saw / him / at first)

→ ________________________, she fell in love with him.

3. Brendon은 그의 보스가 말하기를 마칠 때까지 기다렸다.
(speaking / finished / his boss / until)

→ Brendon waited ________________________.

4. 그녀가 잠들어 있는 동안, 도둑들이 방에 몰래 들어와서 그녀의 보석을 훔쳤다.
(was / she / asleep / while)

→ ______________________, thieves sneaked into the room and stole her jewelry.

5. Betty는 그것이 잘못인 줄 알았지만, 진실을 말할 수 없었다.
(wrong / although / Betty / knew / was / it)

→ ______________________________, she could not tell the truth.

6. 그는 배가 고팠다, 그래서 스스로 샌드위치를 만들었다.
(so / a sandwich / made / he / for himself)

→ He felt hungry, ______________________________.

7. 웃는 법을 모르면 가게를 열지 마라. (속담)
(smile / unless / how / you / know / to)

→ Don't open a shop ______________________________.

Q4 다음 빈칸에 공통으로 들어갈 알맞은 접속사를 쓰시오.

1. (a) ________ his mom got out of the room, the baby cried.
   (b) ________ she didn't know English, she could not read the sign.

2. (a) ________ it rained heavily, we stayed at home.
   (b) We've been friends ________ we were at high school students.

Fill in the Blank ① If ② when ③ and ④ Cause(cause)

Question 1 **1.** but **2.** so **3.** and **4.** or

Question 2 **1.** I missed lunch and I'm starving! **2.** He fell down the stairs, but he didn't get hurt.
3. Jack knocked on the door and he went in.
4. She invited her neighbors, but they did not come to her house.

Question 3 **1.** before it gets dark **2.** When Jenny saw him at first
3. until his boss finished speaking **4.** While she was asleep
5. Although Betty knew it was wrong **6.** so he made a sandwich for himself
7. unless you know how to smile

Question 4 **1.** As **2.** Since

59 Lovefool

Cardigans

Dear, I fear we're facing a problem
You love me no longer, I know
And maybe there is nothing that I can do to make you do

그대여, 나는 우리 사이에 문제가 생긴 것 같아 두려워요
당신은 나를 더 이상 사랑하지 않죠, 알아요
그리고 아마도 당신이 나를 다시 사랑하게 만들 수는 없겠죠

- face : 직면하다
- no longer : 더 이상 ~않는

Mama tells me I shouldn't bother
That I ought to stick to another man, a man that surely deserves me
But I think you do!
So I cry, I pray, and I beg

엄마는 내가 당신을 귀찮게 하면 안 된대요
나에게 정말로 어울리는 다른 남자를 만나야 한대요
나에게 정말로 어울리는 남자
하지만 나는 그게 당신이라고 생각해요!
그래서 나는 울고, 기도하고, 빌지요

- bother : 괴롭히다
- ought to~ : ~해야 하다
- stick to~ : ~에 달라붙다
- deserve : ~할 가치가 있다

★ Love me love me,
①(　　)(　　)(　　)(　　)(　)
Fool me fool me, Go on and fool me
Love me love me,
②(　　　)(　　)(　　)(　　)(　)
Lead me lead me, Just
③(　　)(　　)(　　)(　　)(　)
So I cry, and I beg for you to
Love me love me,
①(　　)(　　)(　　)(　　)(　)

사랑해줘요 나를 사랑해줘요,
나를 사랑한다고 말해줘요
나를 속이는 것도 괜찮으니, 어서 속여보세요
사랑해줘요 나를 사랑해줘요,
나를 사랑하는 척이라도 해주세요
이끌어줘요 나를 이끌어줘요,
내가 필요하다고 말해봐요
그래서 나는 울고 당신에게 빌죠
사랑해줘요 나를 사랑해줘요,
나를 사랑한다고 말해줘요

Lead me lead me, Just

③(　　)(　　)(　　)(　　)(　　)

I can't care about anything but you

이끌어줘요 나를 이끌어줘요,
내가 필요하다고 말해봐요
나는 당신 말고 다른 것들에는 관심이 없어요

- pretend : ~인 척하다
- beg : 애원하다
- but~ : ① 하지만 ② ~를 제외하고(=except)

Lately I have desperately pondered,
Spent my nights awake and I wonder
What I could have done in another way
to make you stay
Reason will not lead to solution
I will end up lost in confusion
I don't care, if you really care, as long as
you don't go
So I cry, I pray, and I beg

최근에 나는 절실하게 고민했어요,
밤을 새워가며 궁금해했죠
당신을 내 곁에 머무르게 하려면 내가
무엇을 했어야 하는지
이성적으로 생각할 수가 없어요
나는 혼란 속에 빠져 끝나버리고 말죠
나는 상관없어요, 만약 당신이 정말
걱정한다 해도, 당신이 떠나지 않는 한
그래서 나는 울고, 기도하고, 빌어요

- desperately : 절실하게
- ponder : 깊이 생각하다
- could have done : (과거에 대한 후회) 할 수 있었을 텐데
- reason : 이성
- lead : 이끌다
- solution : 해결책
- confusion : 혼란
- care : 신경쓰다
- as long as~ : ~하는 한

★ Repeat

anything but you
Love me love me, (Say that you love me)
Fool me fool me, (Go on and fool me)
Love me love me, (I know that
you need me)
I can't care about anything but you

당신 외에 어떤 것도
사랑해줘요 나를 사랑해줘요,
(나를 사랑한다고 말해줘요)
속여봐요 속여봐요,
(나를 속이는 것도 괜찮으니, 어서 속여보세요)
사랑해줘요 나를 사랑해줘요,
(나는 당신이 나를 원한다는 걸 알아요)
나는 당신 말고 다른 것에는 관심이 없어요

59 접속사 that

접속사 that이란

- 접속사 that이 이끄는 절은 '~하는 것을'의 의미로, think, know, believe, say, pretend, hope, show 등과 같은 동사의 목적어의 역할을 한다.
- 이때 that은 생략할 수 있다.

that의 여러 가지 용법

1. 지시대명사 → '저것'	- **That** is the book I have been looking for.
2. 주격, 목적격 관계대명사 (who, which, whom) 대체	- It is the best movie **that** (←which) I have ever seen. - Look at the man **that** (←who) is standing on the top. - She is the girl **that** (←whom) my boss introduced to me at the meeting.
3. 목적어를 이끄는 접속사 → '~것을'	- I can't believe **that** she's only 17.

가사 예문

Love me love me, Say that you love me.
나를 사랑해줘요 나를 사랑해줘요, 나를 사랑한다고 말해줘요.

Love me love me, Pretend that you love me.
나를 사랑해줘요 나를 사랑해줘요, 당신이 나를 사랑하는 척이라도 해주세요.

Q1 다음 밑줄 친 that의 쓰임이 〈보기〉와 같은 것은? (답 2개)

〈보기〉 Jennifer thought that everything was fine.

① That's my favorite restaurant.

② I don't like that type of movie.

③ You are the only friend that I depend on.

④ This picture shows that we live in a wonderful city.

⑤ She said that she would be back before the meeting.

Q2 다음 두 문장을 that을 이용하여 〈보기〉와 같이 한 문장으로 쓰시오.

〈보기〉 We all know + The earth is round.
→ **We all know that the earth is round.**

1. I don't believe + she lied about her age.

→ ____

2. We hope + more students will join the course.

→ ____

3. I can't pretend + I understand these technical problems.

→ ____

4. I always said + I would buy a motorbike if I had enough money.

→ ____

Fill in the Blank ① say that you love me ② pretend that you love me ③ say that you need me

Question 1 ④, ⑤

Question 2
1. I don't believe that she lied about her age.
2. We hope that more students will join the course.
3. I can't pretend that I understand these technical problems.
4. I always said that I would buy a motorbike if I had enough money.

60 We are the champions | Queen

I've paid my dues
Time after time
I've done my sentence
But committed no crime
And bad mistakes
I've made ( )(   )
I've had my share of sand kicked in my face
But I've come through
And I need to go on and on

난 책임을 다했어요
시간이 흐르고 흘러 결국
내게 주어진 형기도 모두 마쳤어요
하지만 사실 난 아무 죄도 저지르지 않았어요
그저 나쁜 실수를
몇 가지 저질렀을 뿐
난 내게 떨어지는 비난과 시련에 맞서야 했죠
하지만 난 그 어려움을 모두 견뎌냈어요
그리고 나는 계속 앞으로 나가야 해요

- **pay dues :** 마땅한 대가를 지불하다
- **sentence :** ① 문장 ② 형벌 ③ (형을) 선고하다
- **commit :** (범죄를) 저지르다
- **come through :** 살아남다, 견디다

★ We are the champions, my friends
And we'll keep on fighting till the end
We are the champions
We are the champions
No time for losers
'Cause we are the champions of the world

우리는 챔피언이에요, 친구들이여
그리고 우리는 끝까지 싸워나갈 거예요
우리는 챔피언
우리는 챔피언
패배자에게 따르는 고통의 시간 따위는 없어요
왜냐하면 우리는 이 세상 챔피언이니까요

- **keep on ~ing :** ~를 계속하다

I've taken my bows
And my curtain calls
You brought me fame and fortune and
every thing that goes with it
I thank you all
But it's been no bed of roses
No pleasure cruise
I consider it a challenge before the
whole human race
And I ain't gonna lose
And I need to go on and on

나는 환호에 인사하며
앵콜을 받았죠
여러분이 내게 명예와 부 그리고 거기에
따르는 모든 걸 가져다 주었어요
그 모든 걸 여러분에게 감사해요
하지만 결코 안락한 생활만은 아니었어요
즐겁기만 했던 항해는 아니었죠
하지만 난 그걸 모든 인간에게 놓인 하나의
도전이라고 생각해요
그러니까 난 더 이상 패배하지는 않을 거예요
그리고 나는 계속 앞으로 나가야 해요

- **take one's bow** : (환호하는 청중에게) 절하다
- **fame** : 명예
- **fortune** : 부
- **go with~** : ~와 어울리다
- **bed of roses** : (비유) 근심 없는 안락한 생활
- **go on** : 계속하다

★ Repeat × 2

60 a few/a little과 few/little

a few / a little : 몇몇의(약간의)

- '몇몇의(약간의)'라는 의미를 표현할 때 a few 또는 a little을 쓸 수 있다.
- 단, a few 뒤에는 셀 수 있는 명사의 복수형을 쓰고, a little 뒤에는 셀 수 없는 명사를 쓴다.

- Can I talk to you for **a few minutes**? 몇 분간 얘기할 수 있나요?
- **A little knowledge** is a dangerous thing. (속담) 약간의 지식은 오히려 위험하다.

few / little : ~이 거의 없는

- '~이 거의 없는'이라는 의미를 표현할 때 few 또는 little을 쓸 수 있다.
- 단, few 뒤에는 셀 수 있는 명사의 복수형을 쓰고, little 뒤에는 셀 수 없는 명사를 쓴다.

- **Few people** know about her private life. 그녀의 사생활에 대해 아는 사람은 거의 없다.
- There is **little oxygen** under water. 물 밑에는 산소가 거의 없다.

용법	몇몇의(약간의)	~이 거의 없는
셀 수 있는 명사와 함께	a few	few
셀 수 없는 명사와 함께	a little	little

가사 예문

I've made a few bad mistakes.

나는 약간의 나쁜 실수를 저질렀어.

Attention!

앞서 언급된 명사를 생략하고 a few / a little과 few / little만 쓸 수도 있다!

- "How many countries have you visited?" "**A few**." (A few = a few countries)
- "Would you like some coffee?" "Yes, just **a little**." (a little = a little coffee)

Q1 다음 문장의 빈칸에 a few / few 또는 a little / little을 써 넣으시오.

1. I have ________ questions about my surgery today.
2. Gambling attracts desperate people who have ________ money.
3. I found ________ mistakes on your essay. You did a great job!
4. I cannot move this box for myself. Can you give me ________ help?

Q2 〈보기〉의 명사와 a few / few 또는 a little / little을 사용하여 문장을 완성하시오.

〈보기〉 minutes friends break rain

1. Sera just moved to this school, so she has ________________.
2. I had to work overtime yesterday, so I need ________________.
3. I have something to tell you. Would you stop by my office for ________________?
4. Because we had ________________ and it was dry this summer, the price of crops has jumped.

Fill in the Blank a few

Question 1 **1.** a few **2.** little **3.** few **4.** a little

Question 2 **1.** few friends **2.** a little break **3.** a few minutes **4.** little rain

61 Because of you — Kelly Clarkson

I will not make the same mistakes that you did
I will not let myself cause my heart so much misery
I will not break the way you did
You fell so hard
I've learned the hard way, to never let it get that far

난 당신이 저지른 실수를 똑같이 되풀이하지 않을 거야
난 스스로 내 마음이 비참하도록 내버려 두지 않을 거야
네가 그랬던 것처럼 그렇게 무너지지 않을 거야
당신은 참혹하게 무너졌지
난 뼈저리게 배웠지, 절대 그 지경에 이르도록 내버려 두어서는 안 되겠다고

- make mistakes : 실수를 저지르다
- let~ : ~하게 하다
- cause A B : A에게 B를 야기하다
- misery : 고통, 불행

★ (　　　　)(　)(　　),
I'll never stray too far from the sidewalk
(　　　　)(　)(　　),
I learned to play on the safe side
So I don't get hurt
(　　　　)(　)(　　),
I find it hard to trust
Not only me, but everyone around me
(　　　　)(　)(　　),
I am afraid

너 때문에,
난 절대 안전한 길에서 멀리 벗어나지 않을 거야
너 때문에,
안전한 데서 놀아야 한다는 걸 배웠어
그래야 내가 상처받지 않을 테니까
너 때문에,
난 사람을 신뢰하기가 힘들어
나뿐만 아니라, 내 주위 모든 이들을 신뢰하기가
너 때문에,
난 두려워

- stray : ① 옆길로 벗어나다 ② 길을 잃은 ③ 부랑자
- sidewalk : 보도, 인도
- get hurt : 다치다
- Not only A, but (also) B : A뿐만 아니라 B도

I lose my way
And it's not too long before you point it out
I cannot cry
Because you know that's weakness in your eyes
I'm forced to fake a smile, a laugh
Every day of my life, my heart can't possibly break
When it wasn't even whole to start with

난 방향을 잃었어
그리고 넌 얼마 가지 않아 그걸 지적하지
난 울 수 없어
왜냐하면 네 눈에 비친 내 약점을 눈치챌 테니까
난 가짜 웃음을 지을 수밖에 없어
매일 내 심장은 이제 더 이상 무너질 수가 없어
시작부터 온전하지 못했으니까

- **be forced to~** : ~하도록 강요당하다
- **fake** : ① 위조하다 ② 가짜의 ③ 모조품

★ Repeat

I watched you die
I heard you cry every night in your sleep
I was so young
You should have known better than to lean on me
You never thought of anyone else
You just saw your pain
And now I cry in the middle of the night
For the same damn thing

난 너의 최후를 지켜보았지
매일 밤 너의 잠자리에서 네가 우는 걸 들었어
난 매우 어렸어
넌 나한테 기대는 것보다 더 현명했어야 했어
넌 절대로 너 아닌 누군가를 생각해본 적이 없지
넌 그냥 너의 아픔만 볼 줄 알았지
난 이 한밤중에 울고 있어
똑같은 몹쓸 고통 때문에

- **should have known** : 알았어야 했다
- **lean on** : 기대다

( )( )( ),
I'll never stray too far from the sidewalk
( )( )( ),
I learned to play on the safe side
So I don't get hurt
( )( )( ),
I tried my hardest just to forget everything
( )( )( ),
I don't know how to let anyone else in
( )( )( ),
I'm ashamed of my life, because it's empty
( )( )( ),
I am afraid

너 때문에,
난 절대 안전한 길에서 멀리 벗어나지 않을 거야
너 때문에,
안전한 곳에서 지내야 한다는 걸 알았지
그래야 상처받지 않을 테니까
너 때문에,
난 그 모든 것들을 잊기 위해 안간힘을 쓰고 있어
너 때문에,
난 다른 사람들을 내 마음 속으로 들이는 방법을 몰라
너 때문에,
난 공허함만 남은 내 삶이 부끄러워
너 때문에,
난 두려워

- try hardest : 최선을 다하다
- be shamed of~ : ~를 부끄러워하다

( )( )( )
( )( )( )

너 때문에
너 때문에

61 두 단어 이상으로 이루어진 전치사

두 단어 이상으로 이루어진 전치사란

- 대부분의 전치사는 한 개의 단어로 이루어져 있으나, 두 개 이상의 단어로 이루어져 구(phrase)를 이루는 경우의 전치사이다.

두 단어로 이루어진 전치사

because of	~ 때문에	He didn't go out **because of** the bad weather.
due to		The accident was **due to** the carelessness of the driver.
owing to		The game was cancelled **owing to** heavy rain.
instead of	~ 대신에	I'll have tea **instead of** coffee, please.
thanks to	~ 덕분에	**Thanks to** your help, I was able to do it.
along with	~와 함께	Please come **along with** me. I need your help.
according to	~에 따르면	**According to** the newspaper, he has awarded a Novel Peace Prize.
contrary to	~와 반대로	**Contrary to** my expectations, she showed up for the meeting.
regardless of	~에 상관없이	Our club welcomes all new members **regardless of** age.
prior to	~ 이전에	All the reservations should be made **prior to** your departure.

세 단어로 이루어진 전치사

in front of	~ 앞에	Who parked the trucks **in front of** my house?
on behalf of	~을 대표하여	I'm here **on behalf of** my company.
by means of	~의 도움으로	The piano was lifted **by means of** a crane.
in addition to	~에 추가하여	**In addition to** discounts, they offer a free gift.
in spite of	~에도 불구하고	**In spite of** their efforts, they failed to win the prize.

in place of	~에 대신하여	I came here to see you **in place of** the president.
in relation to	~에 관하여	I have some comments to make **in relation to** this matter.
in accordance with	~에 부합하여	The teams played the game **in accordance with** the rules.
for the sake of	~을 위하여	He saved money **for the sake of** his family.
for the purpose of	~을 위하여	We were given the loan **for the purpose of** buying a car.
with reference to	~에 관련하여	I have a question **with reference to** your lecture.
in line with	~에 따라	She became a teacher, **in line with** her aptitude.
in charge of	~를 책임지고 있는	Are you the person **in charge of** the film advertising?
on account of	~때문에	Our flight will be delayed **on account of** the bad weather.

가사 예문

Because of you, I'll never stray too far from the sidewalk.

너 때문에, 난 절대 안전한 길에서 멀리 벗어나지 않을 거야.

Attention!

접속사 Because vs 전치사 Because of의 차이점에 유의!

- Because <u>**the weather was so bad**</u>, we stayed home all day long.

  (Because + 주어 + 동사)

- Because of <u>**the bad weather**</u>, we stayed home all day long.

  (Because of + 명사 또는 대명사)

Q1 다음 문장이 자연스럽도록 because of 또는 thanks to를 넣어 완성하시오. (대소문자 유의)

1. He was absent from work ______________ his illness.
2. The accident happened ______________ her carelessness.
3. ______________ her invention, many people enjoy better lives.
4. Mark could finish the project ______________ his team's great effort.

Q2 다음 빈칸에 들어갈 표현을 〈보기〉에서 고르시오. (대소문자 유의)

〈보기〉 due to　　instead of　　in addition to　　contrary to

1. ______________ complaining all the time, do something about it.
2. ______________ the monthly pay, he earns $500 by his second job.
3. The building work was not completed on time ______________ our expectations.
4. That night, my father ended up going to the emergency room ______________ his high blood pressure.

Q3 우리말과 의미가 같도록 전치사와 괄호 안의 표현을 이용하여 문장을 완성하시오.

1. 남녀노소 상관없이 모두가 이 게임을 즐길 수 있다. (age or gender)
→ This game can be enjoyed by anyone ______________________________.
2. 오늘 부로 당신은 영업부를 담당하게 될 겁니다. (Sales Department)
→ Starting from today, you will be ______________________________.
3. 그 지문에 의하면 우리는 에너지 절약을 위해 무엇을 해야 하지? (article)
→ ______________________________, what should we do for saving energy?
4. 그들은 그들의 언어장벽에도 불구하고 사랑에 빠졌다. (language barrier)
→ They fell in love ______________________________.

Fill in the Blank Because of you

Question 1 1. because of 2. because of 3. Thanks to 4. thanks to

Question 2 1. Instead of 2. In addition to 3. contrary to 4. due to

Question 3 1. regardless of age or gender 2. in charge of Sales Department 3. According to the article 4. in spite of their language barrier

62 Baby — Justin Bieber

You know you love me, I know you care
You shout whenever, and I'll be there
You are my love, you are my heart
And we will never ever ever be apart
Are we an item? Girl, ①(   )(   )
We're just friends, what are you saying?
Said "There's another, look right in my eyes"
My first love broke my heart for the first time
And I was like...

네가 날 사랑하는 걸 너도 알잖아,
나는 알아 너도 신경 쓰고 있다는 걸
언제든 외쳐, 그러면 내가 갈게
넌 내 사랑이야, 내 심장이야
그리고 우린 절대, 절대 떨어지지 않아
우리 사귄 거 맞아? 날 가지고 놀지 마
우린 그냥 친구라구? 무슨 말 하는 거야?
"뭔가 있어. 내 눈을 제대로 쳐다봐."라고 말했잖아
내 첫사랑이 처음으로 내 맘을 아프게 했어
그리고 나는…

- **whenever** : ~할 때면 언제나
- **be apart** : 떨어지다
- **be an item** : 사귀다(속어)
- **break one's heart** : 상처 주다

★ Baby, baby, baby, Oooooh
Baby, baby, baby, Nooooh
Baby, baby, baby, Oooooh
(I) Thought you'd always be mine

Baby, baby, baby, Oooooh~
Baby, baby, baby, Nooooh~
Baby, baby, baby, Oooooh~
넌 언제나 내 것일 줄 알았어

★ Repeat

For you I would have done whatever
And I just can't believe we ain't together
And I ②(　　　)(　)(　　　) it cool, But
I'm losing you
I'd buy you anything
I'd buy you any ring
And now please say "Baby, fix me"
And you shake me
Til you wake me from this bad dream
I'm going down, down, down
And I just can't believe my first love
won't be around
And I'm like...

너를 위해서라면 난 무엇이든 했을 텐데
그런데 우리가 함께가 아니라니 믿을 수 없어
난 침착해지고 싶어, 하지만 난 너를 잃고 있는 걸
내가 너에게 어떤 것이든 사줄 텐데,
내가 너에게 어떤 반지라도 사줄 텐데
그리고 이제 말해주겠니
"날 바로잡아줘"라고
그리고 넌 날 흔들지
이 악몽에서 날 깨울 때까지
난 점점 우울해지고 있어
난 믿을 수가 없어
내 첫사랑이 더 이상 곁에 없어서
그래서 난…

- whatever : 무엇이든
- ain't : am not / is not / are not의 축약형
- play it cool : 냉정하게 대처하다
- til = until
- go down : 우울해지다

★ Repeat × 2

Luda! When I was 13, I had my first love
There was nobody compared to my baby
And nobody came between us,
No-one could ever come above
She had me going crazy
Oh, I was star-struck
She woke me up daily,
don't need no Starbucks

루다! 내가 13살 때, 첫사랑을 했지
그녀는 그 누구와도 비교할 수 없었지
그리고 누구도 우리 사이에 끼어들 수 없었지
누구도 들어올 수 없었지
그녀는 날 미치게 만들었지
난 완전히 빠졌지
그녀는 매일 날 깨워줬어,
스타벅스 커피 같은 건 필요 없었어

She made my heart pound
I skip a beat when I see her in the street
and at school on the playground
But I really ③(   )(   )(   ) her on the weekend
She knows she's got me dazing,
cause she was so amazing
And now my heart is breaking,
but I just keep on saying

그녀는 내 심장을 뛰게 만들었지
난 심장이 멎어 내가 그녀를 길에서
그리고 학교 운동장에서 볼 때마다
하지만 난 그녀를 주말에 꼭 보고 싶어
그녀는 알아 그녀가 날 멍하게 만든다는 걸
그녀는 아주 환상적이었으니까
그리고 지금 내 심장은 아파와
하지만 난 계속 말을 할래

- **be compared to~** : ~와 비교되다
- **stuck** : (속어) 반한
- **make heart pound** : 심장을 뛰게 하다
- **daze** : 현혹시키다, 멍하게 하다
- **keep on ~ing** : 계속해서 ~하다

★ Repeat × 2

Now I'm gone
Yeah, Yeah, Yeah, Yeah, Yeah
Now I'm all gone
Now I'm all gone
Now I'm all gone
Gone, gone, gone, I'm gone

이제 나 떠나
Yeah, Yeah, Yeah, Yeah, Yeah
이제 정말 떠나
이제 정말 떠나
이제 정말 떠나
떠나, 떠나, 떠나, 나 떠나

62 '동명사' 또는 'to 부정사'를 취하는 동사 1

동사 + '동명사'

• 다음과 같은 동사 뒤에는 '동사 + ing'를 쓴다.

동사 + 동명사	enjoy, keep, finish, mind, quit, avoid, practice, suggest, give up
	- Are you trying to quit **smoking**? - Would you mind **opening** the window? - I enjoy **watching** movies at home on Friday nights.

동사 + 'to 부정사'

• 다음과 같은 동사 뒤에는 'to + 동사원형'을 쓴다.

동사 + to 부정사	want, need, hope, plan, ask, expect, decide, intend, learn, promise
	- We hope **to hear** from you soon. - What do you want **to be** in the future? - I decided **to join** the broadcasting club at school.

가사 예문

Are we an item? Girl, quit playing.

우리 사귄 거 맞아? 날 가지고 놀지 마.

I want to play it cool, but I'm losing you.

난 침착해지고 싶어, 하지만 난 너를 잃고 있는 걸.

Q1 다음 주어진 동사를 이용하여 문장을 완성하시오. (~ing 또는 to~로 변형할 것)

〈보기〉 dance　send　read　open　tell

1. Stop trying to avoid __________ the truth.
2. You need __________ me the file until tomorrow.
3. They plan __________ a new office near the downtown area.
4. We should practice __________ to win a prize in the talent show.
5. My goal is to finish __________ this book by the end of the month.

Q2 다음 우리말에 해당하도록 괄호 안의 표현을 이용하여 문장을 완성하시오.

1. 나는 올해 호주를 방문할 작정이야. (intend / visit Australia)

→ ______________________________

2. 왜 너는 기타 치는 것을 포기했니? (give up / play the guitar)

→ ______________________________

3. 너는 어디서 중국어를 말하는 것을 배웠니? (learn / speak Chinese)

→ ______________________________

4. 만약 당신이 저 방향으로 계속 걸어가면, 당신의 왼편에 지하철역을 볼 수 있을 거예요.
(keep walk in that direction / find the subway station)

→ ______________________________

Fill in the Blank ① quit playing ② want to play ③ want to see

Question 1 **1.** telling **2.** to send **3.** to open **4.** dancing **5.** reading

Question 2 **1.** I intend to visit Australia this year. **2.** Why did you give up playing the guitar?
3. Where did you learn to speak Chinese?
4. If you keep walking in that direction, you will find the subway station on your left.

63 Try to remember — The Brothers Four

(　)(　)(　　　　) the kind of September
When life was slow and oh, so mellow
(　)(　)(　　　　) the kind of September
When grass was green and grain was yellow
(　)(　)(　　　　) the kind of September
When you were a tender and callow fellow
(　)(　)(　　　　) and if you remember
Then follow, follow

9월쯤 그날의 기억을 떠올려 보세요
삶은 여유롭고 너무나 달콤했던 그때를
9월쯤 그날의 기억을 떠올려 보세요
초원은 푸르고 곡식은 노랬던 그때를
9월쯤 그날의 기억을 떠올려 보세요
당신이 부드럽고 풋풋한 청년이었던 그때를
기억을 떠올려 보세요 그리고 만약 기억이 난다면 그 추억을 따라가 봐요, 따라가 봐요

- kind of~ : ~같은, ~류의
- mellow : ① 부드러운 ② 달콤한 ③ 부드럽게 하다
- tender : ① 부드러운 ② 입찰하다 ③ 제출하다
- callow : 미숙한, 풋내기인
- fellow : ① 동료 ② 사람
- follow : 따라가다

(　)(　)(　　　　) when life was so tender
That no one wept except the willow
(　)(　)(　　　　) the kind of September
When love was an ember about to billow
(　)(　)(　　　　) and if you remember
Then follow, follow

삶이 그렇게 부드러웠던 때를 떠올려 보세요
버드나무 외에는 누구도 눈물짓지 않았죠
9월쯤 그날의 기억을 떠올려 보세요
사랑이 바람에 타오르려는 숯불이었을 때
기억을 떠올려 봐요 그리고 만약 그대가 기억한다면
그 추억을 따라가요, 따라가요

- wept : 울다 (weep-wept-wept)
- except~ : ~을 제외하고
- willow : 버드나무
- ember : 잔열이 남아있는 불
- be about to~ : 막 ~하려던 참이다
- billow : ① 바람에 부풀어 오르다 ② 큰 파도

Deep in December it's nice to remember
Although you know the snow will follow
Deep in December it's nice to remember
The fire of September that made us mellow
Deep in December our hearts should remember
Then follow, follow, follow

깊어가는 12월에는 기억하기에 좋죠
비록 눈이 내린다고 하더라도
깊어가는 12월에는 기억하기에 좋죠
우리를 감미롭게 만드는 9월의 불꽃
깊어가는 12월에 우리의 마음은 기억해야만 해요
그렇다면 따라가 봐요, 따라가 봐요, 따라가 봐요

- **Although** : 비록 ~하지만

63 '동명사' 또는 'to 부정사'를 취하는 동사 2

'동명사' 또는 'to 부정사' 모두 취할 수 있는 동사 (의미 차이 없음)

• 다음과 같은 동사 뒤에는 '동사 + ing' 또는 'to + 동사원형' 모두 쓸 수 있고, 의미 차이가 없다.

like, love, prefer, hate, bother, start, begin, propose	- I **like eating** a big brunch on weekend. 또는 I **like to eat** a big brunch on weekend. - When does the new person **start working**? 또는 When does the new person **start to work**? - Many people **hate waiting** in lines at grocery stores. 또는 Many people **hate to wait** in lines at grocery stores. - Which program do you **prefer watching**? 또는 Which program do you **prefer to watch**?

'동명사' 또는 'to 부정사' 모두 취할 수 있는 동사 (의미 차이 있음)

• 다음과 같은 동사 뒤에는 '동사 + ing' 또는 'to + 동사원형' 모두 쓸 수 있으나, 의미에 차이가 있다.

remember/ forget	~ing : ~한 것을 기억하다 / 잊다
	- I **remember hearing** about it on the radio. 나는 라디오에서 그것에 관한 이야기를 들었던 것을 기억해. - I will never **forget meeting** the President last year. 나는 작년에 대통령을 만났던 것을 결코 잊지 않을 거야.
	to~ : ~할 것을 기억하다 / 잊다
	- I always **remember to bring** a bottle of water when I go out. 나는 외출할 때 물을 한 병 가져가는 것을 항상 기억해둔다. - Don't **forget to buy** some milk on your way home. 집에 오는 길에 우유 좀 사오는 것 잊지 마.

try	**~ing : 시험 삼아 ~해보다**	
	- Most teenage girls want to **try putting** some makeup on. 대부분의 10대 여자아이들은 화장을 시도해보고 싶어 한다.	
	to~ : ~하려고 노력하다	
	- I **try to read** books every day before going to bed. 나는 매일 잠들기 전에 책을 읽으려고 노력한다.	

stop	**~ing : ~하는 것을 멈추다**
	- Please **stop interrupting** me while I am talking. 부탁인데 내가 말하는 도중에 끼어들지 마.
	to~ : ~하기 위해 (하던 일을) 멈추다
	- A traveler **stopped to take** pictures of the wonderful view. 여행객은 멋진 광경의 사진을 찍기 위해서 가던 길을 멈추었다.

가사 예문

Try to remember, the kind of September.
9월쯤 그날의 기억을 떠올려 보세요.

Q1 다음 괄호 안에 주어진 동사들을 적절히 변형하여 문장을 완성하시오.

1. I would ____________________ the meeting. (prefer / postpone)
2. I ____________________ his name somewhere. (remember / hear)
3. ____________________ me while I'm trying to study! (stop / bother)
4. Don't ____________________ the light when you go to bed. (forget / turn off)
5. From now on, I will ____________________ early and study harder. (try / wake up)

Q2 다음 우리말에 해당하도록 괄호 안의 표현을 이용하여 문장을 완성하시오.

1. 외출할 때 문 잠그는 것 잊지 마. (forget / lock the door / go out)

→ ____

2. 나는 가족을 위해서 요리하는 것을 좋아해요. (like / cook / for my family)

→ ____

3. 그는 타이어를 교체하기 위해서 갓길에 멈추어야 했다.

(stop / change tires / on the shoulder of the road)

→ ____

4. 우리는 더 좋은 관계를 위해서 서로서로 이해하도록 노력해야 해.

(try / understand each other / for the better relationship)

→ ____

5. 나는 카메라를 찾을 수 없어요, 하지만 나는 오늘 아침에 카메라를 챙긴 것을 기억해요.

(remember / pack the camera / this morning)

→ ____

Fill in the Blank Try to remember

Question 1 **1.** prefer to postpone / prefer postponing **2.** remember hearing **3.** Stop bothering
4. forget to turn off **5.** try to wake up

Question 2 **1.** Don't forget to lock the door when you go out.
2. I like to cook for my family. / I like cooking for my family.
3. He had to stop to change tires on the shoulder of the road.
4. We should try to understand each other for the better relationship.
5. I cannot find my camera, but I remember packing the camera this morning.

64	Thinking out loud	Ed Sheeran

When your legs don't work like they used to before
And I can't sweep you off of your feet
Will your mouth still remember the taste of my love?
Will your eyes still smile from your cheeks?

너의 두 다리로 예전처럼 걸을 수 없을 때
내가 너의 마음을 사로잡을 수 없어도
너의 입은 여전히 내 사랑의 그 맛을 기억할까?
너의 두 눈은 여전히 활짝 미소를 지어줄까?

- used to~ : (과거에 ~했는데) 지금은 하지 않는다
- sweep off one's feet : ~의 마음을 사로잡다
- cheek : 볼, 뺨

And, darling, I (   )(   )(   ) you till we're 70
And, baby, my heart could still fall as hard at 23
And I'm thinking about how people fall in love in mysterious ways
Maybe just the touch of a hand
Well, me? I fall in love with you every single day
And I just wanna tell you I am

그대여, 난 우리가 70살이 되어도 널 사랑하고 있을 거야
그리고 그대여, 나의 사랑은 여전히 23살 때처럼 강렬할 거야
난 어떻게 사람들이 신비로운 방식으로 사랑에 빠지는지에 대해서 생각하고 있어
아마도 살짝 스치는 손길 때문인가
글쎄, 난 매일 너와 사랑에 빠지지
정말 그렇다는 걸 알려주고 싶어

- mysterious : 이해하기 힘든, 신비로운

So, honey, now take me into your loving arms
Kiss me under the light of a thousand stars
Place your head on my beating heart
I'm thinking out loud
Maybe we found love right where we are

그러니, 그대여, 이제 날 너의 사랑스러운 품으로 데려가
천 개의 별빛 아래서 내게 입맞춤해줘
너의 머리를 뛰고 있는 내 심장에 대어봐
난 크게 생각을 외칠 테니까
아마도 지금 이 순간 우리는 서로의 사랑을 찾은 것 같다고

When my hair's all but gone and my memory fades
And the crowds don't remember my name
When my hands don't play the strings the same way (mmm...)
I know you will still love me the same

내 머리카락이 전부 빠지고 나의 기억이 희미해지고
사람들이 내 이름을 기억하지 못하고
내 손이 예전처럼 기타를 치지 못해도
난 알아 그래도 넌 여전히 날 변함없이 사랑해줄 거라는 걸

- be gone : 없어지다
- fade : 희미해지다
- string : 현악기 줄

Cause, honey, your soul could never grow old, it's evergreen
And, baby, your smile's forever in my mind and memory
I'm thinking about how people
fall in love in mysterious ways

왜냐하면, 그대여, 너의 영혼은 절대 늙지 않고, 언제나 푸를 거거든
그리고 그대여, 너의 미소는 영원히 내 마음과 기억 속에 있을 거야
난 어떻게 사람들이 신비로운 방식으로 사랑에 빠지는지에 대해서 생각하고 있어

- evergreen : ① 상록수 ② 늘 푸른

Maybe it's all part of a plan Well, I'll just keep on making the same mistakes hoping that you'll understand	아마 그건 이미 정해진 일일 수도 있어 글쎄, 난 같은 실수를 계속 하게 되겠지 네가 이해해주길 바라면서
★ So, baby, now take me into your loving arms Kiss me under the light of a thousand stars Place your head on my beating heart I'm thinking out loud Maybe we found love right where we are	그러니, 그대여, 이제 날 너의 사랑스러운 품으로 데려가 천 개의 별빛 아래서 내게 입맞춤해줘 너의 머리를 뛰고 있는 내 심장에 대어봐 난 크게 생각을 외칠 테니까 아마도 지금 이 순간 우리는 서로의 사랑을 찾은 것 같다고

★ Repeat

Maybe we found love right where we are And we found love right where we are	아마도 지금 이 순간 우리는 서로의 사랑을 찾은 것 같아 그리고 지금 이 순간 우리는 서로의 사랑을 찾은 것 같아

64 will be + ~ing

will be + ~ing란

- will be + ~ing는 미래진행 시제로서 '~하고 있을 것이다'라는 의미로 미래의 특정한 시점에 진행되고 있을 일을 표현할 때 쓴다.
- I **will be taking** a driving test at 9 a.m. tomorrow.
  나는 내일 오전 9시에 운전면허시험을 치르고 있을 거야.

- 긍정문 및 부정문

I	**will**	be	exercising then.
You/They/We			working at 9 p.m. tomorrow.
He/She	**will not(won't)**		meeting her at 4 o'clock this Sunday.

- 의문문

Will	I	be	exercising then?
	you/they/we		working at 9 p.m. tomorrow?
	he/she		meeting her at 4 o'clock this Sunday?

가사 예문

Daring, I will be loving you till we're 70.
그대여, 난 우리가 70살이 되어도 당신을 사랑하고 있을 거예요.

Attention!

will~ vs will be ~ing 차이점!

- He **will perform** at the concert at 5 p.m. (5시에 콘서트 공연을 시작할 것임.)
- He **will be performing** at the concert at 5 p.m. (5시에 콘서트 공연을 하고 있을 것임.)

Q1 다음 괄호 안에 주어진 동사를 사용하여 자연스러운 문장을 완성하시오.

1. I ________________ for my kids at the bus stop at 4 o'clock tomorrow. (wait)
2. I'm leaving on a vacation this Friday.
   This time next week, I ________________ on Haeundae beach. (lie)
3. Jennifer can't go camping with us on Saturday because she ________________ in the seminar held in London then. (participate)

Q2 문맥에 어울리도록 괄호 안에 주어진 표현들을 배열하여 문장을 완성하시오. (첫 대문자 유의)

1. (Paris / flying / be / will / to / this Sunday / I /.) I'm so excited.
   → ________________________________
2. I won't call her this evening. (will / she / be / then / a blind date / having /.)
   → ________________________________
3. (be / staying / you / your business trip / during / where / will /?) At a hotel?
   → ________________________________
4. (be / won't / my friends / this week / me / visiting /.) Maybe I'll meet them next week.
   → ________________________________

Fill in the Blank will be loving

Question 1 **1.** will be waiting **2.** will be lying **3.** will be participating

Question 2 **1.** I will be flying to Paris this Sunday. **2.** She will be having a blind date then.
3. Where will you be staying during your business trip?
4. My friends won't be visiting me this week.

65 Anyone of us

Gareth Gates

I've been letting you down, down
Girl, I know I've been such a fool,
giving in to temptation
I ①(   )(   )(   ) it cool...
The situation got out of hand
I hope you understand

난 지금까지 널 실망만 시켜왔어
내가 지금까지 얼마나 바보였는지 알아,
유혹에 넘어가는 그런 바보
내가 냉정하게 행동했어야 했는데...
어쩔 수 없는 상황이 돼버렸어
네가 부디 이해해주길 바라

- have been ~ing : ~해오고 있다 (현재완료진행)
- let down : 실망시키다
- give in to : ① 항복하다 ② (유혹에) 넘어가다
- temptation : 유혹
- play it cool : 냉정하게 행동하다

☆ It can happen to anyone of us
Anyone you think of
Anyone can fall
Anyone can hurt someone they love
Hearts will break
Coz I made a stupid mistake

우리 중 누구에게나 일어날 수 있는 일이야
네가 생각할 수 있는 아무나 말이야
누구나 빠질 수 있는 있는 거야
누구나 사랑하는 사람에게 상처 줄 수 있지
가슴이 무너질 거야
내가 바보 같은 실수를 했으니까

- Coz = Because
- stupid : 멍청한
- make a mistake : 실수하다

★ It can happen to anyone of us
Say you will forgive me
Anyone can fail
Say you will believe me
I can't take, my heart will break
Coz I made a stupid mistake
A stupid mistake

우리 중 누구에게나 일어날 수 있는 일이야
날 용서한다고 말해줘
누구든지 실패할 수 있어
날 믿는다고 말해줘
난 감당할 수가 없어, 내 가슴이 무너질 거야
내가 바보 같은 실수를 했으니까
바보 같은 실수를

- happen to~ : ~에게 일어나다
- forgive : 용서하다

She was kind of exciting
A little crazy, I ②(   )(   )
(   )...
She ③(   )(   )(   ) my senses
Coz I offered to walk her home
The situation got out of hand
I hope you understand

그녀는 다소 흥미로웠지
조금은 제정신이 아니었지, 미리 알았어야 했는데…
그녀가 내 감각을 바꿔놓은 게 틀림없어
내가 그녀의 집까지 바래다준다고 했으니까
어쩔 수 없는 상황이 됐어
네가 부디 이해해주기 바라

- kind of : 다소
- should've = should have
- alter : 변화시키다
- offer : 제의하다

☆ Repeat

★ Repeat

Stupid mistake

바보 같은 실수

She means nothing to me
Nothing to me
I swear every word is true
(I) Don't wanna lose you

그녀는 나에게 아무런 의미가 없어
아무 의미도 없어
정말 진실임을 맹세해
널 놓치고 싶지 않아

- swear : 맹세하다

The situation got out of hand
I hope you understand

내가 어찌할 수 없는 상황이었어
네가 부디 이해해주길 바라

- get out of hand : 감당할 수 없는 상황이 되다

☆ Repeat

★ Repeat

Anyone can fall
Anyone can hurt someone they love
Hearts will break
Coz I made a stupid mistake
A stupid mistake

누구나 빠질 수 있는 거야
누구나 사랑하는 사람에게 상처 줄 수 있지
가슴이 무너질 거야
내가 바보 같은 실수를 했으니까
바보 같은 실수를

65 should have + p.p / must have + p.p

should have + p.p(과거분사)

- '~했어야 했다'의 의미를 지니며, 과거에 하지 못한 일에 대한 후회를 나타낸다.

- I had an appointment with the doctor, but I didn't go. I'm very sick now. I **should have gone** to see a doctor.
(갔어야 했다)

가사 예문

I should have played it cool...
내가 냉정하게 행동했어야 했는데….

A little crazy, I should have known...
조금 제정신이 아니었지, 내가 그걸 알았어야 했는데….

must have + p.p(과거분사)

- '~했음에 틀림없다'의 의미를 지니며, 과거 사실에 대한 강한 추측을 나타낸다.

- She looks so tired! She **must have worked** overtime yesterday.
(일했음에 틀림없다)

가사 예문

She must have altered my senses.
그녀가 내 감각을 바꿔놓은 게 틀림없어.

Q1 우리말과 의미가 같도록 대화의 빈칸에 알맞은 표현을 쓰시오.

A: Aiden came to school late today.

B: I'm very surprised to hear that. He is never late for school!

A: I know. He ________ ________ ________. (그는 늦잠을 잤음에 틀림없어.)

B: He practices hard until midnight for the speaking contest these days.

A: Right, He must have been tired.

He ________ ________ ________ the alarm in 5 minutes interval.

(그는 5분 간격으로 알람을 맞춰놓았어야 했어.)

(oversleep : 늦잠자다 / set the alarm : 알람 맞추다)

Q2 다음 괄호 안의 말을 이용하여 문장을 완성하시오.

1. A: I have a stomachache and diarrhea now. (diarrhea : 설사)

   B: You ________ not ________ ________ too much pizza and chicken last night. (eat)

2. A: Did you hear the news? The stock prices went up by 20% today!

   B: Oh, No! I ________ not ________ ________ mine yesterday to make a profit. (sell)

3. A: I got a perfect score on the driving test.

   B: Awesome! You ________ ________ ________ a lot for the driving test. (practice)

Fill in the Blank ① should have played ② should have known ③ must have altered

Question 1 1. must have overslept 2. should have set

Question 2 1. should, have eaten 2. should, have sold 3. must have practiced

66 Rolling in the deep — Adele

There's a fire starting in my heart
Reaching a fever pitch
It's bringing me out the dark
Finally I can see you crystal clear
Go ahead and sell me out
and I'll lay your ship bare
See how I'll leave with every
piece of you
Don't underestimate the things
that I will do

내 마음속에는 불꽃이 타오르기 시작했어
분함은 극도로 다다랐고
격한 흥분은 어둠으로부터 날 꺼내주었지
결국에 난 널 유리처럼 깨끗하게 볼 수 있게
되었어
어서 가서 나에 대해 다 떠벌려봐
나도 너에 대한 걸 다 말할 거니까
내가 어떻게 너의 모든 것을 가지고
떠나는지 지켜봐
내가 하려고 하는 것들을 우습게 보지 마

- **fever pitch** : 흥분상태
- **sell~ out** : ~를 배신하다
- **underestimate** : 과소평가하다
- **bare** : 벌거벗은
- **lay bare** : 음모를 까발리다

There's a fire starting in my heart
Reaching a fever pitch
And it's bringing me out the dark

내 마음속에는 불꽃이 타오르기 시작했어
분함은 극도로 다다랐고 활활 타올라서
날 어둠에서 꺼내주었어

The scars of your love remind me of us
They keep me thinking that we almost
had it all
The scars of your love,
They leave me breathless
I can't help feeling

너로 인한 사랑의 상처는 우리를
돌이켜보게 하지
그 상처는 우리가 모든 것을 가질 수도
있었다는 것을 계속 생각하게 해
사랑이 만든 상처,
그것들이 나를 숨 쉴 수 없게 만들어
그렇게밖에 느껴지지 않아

- **scar** : 상처
- **keep ~ing** : 계속 ~하다
- **breathless** : 숨 쉴 수 없는
- **cannot help ~ing** : ~하지 않을 수 없다

★ We (   )(   )(   ) it all
Rolling in the deep
You had my heart inside of your hand
And you played it to the beat
(But you played it with a beating)

우리는 모든 것을 가질 수도 있었는데
깊이 사랑하면서
너는 내 심장을 손에 넣고는
박자에 맞춰 좋을 대로 가지고 놀았지
(하지만 너는 내 맘을 심하게 가지고 놀았어)

- beating : 구타, 때리기

Baby, I have no story to be told
But I've heard one on you
And I'm gonna make your head burn
Think of me in the depths of your despair
Make a home down there
As mine sure won't be shared

아봐, 난 들을 얘기는 없지만
너에 대한 얘기는 하나 있지
그리고 난 널 아주 열 받게 만들 거야
넌 깊은 절망 속에서 나에 대한 생각을 하게 되겠지
그 절망 아래에다가 새로운 집을 만들어봐
내 집은 더 이상 같이 쓰는 공간이 아니니깐

- despair : 절망
- won't (will not) be shared : 공유되지 않을 것이다

The scars of your love remind me of us
They keep me thinking that we almost had it all

너로 인한 사랑의 상처는 우리를 돌이켜보게 하지
그것들은 우리가 모든 것을 가질 수도 있었다는 것을 계속 생각하게 해

- remind A of B: A로 하여금 B를 생각나게 하다

The scars of your love,
They leave me breathless
I can't help feeling

너로 인한 사랑의 상처,
그것들은 날 숨도 쉬지 못하게 만들어
그렇게밖에 느껴지지 않아

★ Repeat × 2

Throw your soul through every open door
Count your blessings to find what you look for
Turn my sorrow into treasured gold
You'll pay me back in kind and reap just what you sow

그래 너의 영혼을 열린 모든 문으로 던져봐
네가 구하는 것을 찾기 위해 네게 내려진 축복에 기대봐
내 슬픔을 전부 값진 금으로 바꿔놔
넌 나에게 동등하게 갚아야 하니까
그리고 넌 뿌린 대로 거둘 거야

- **count :** 세다
- **blessing :** 축복
- **reap what you sow :** 뿌린 대로 거두다

We (　　　)(　　　)(　　) it all,
We (　　　)(　　　)(　　) it all,
It all, it all, it all, it all

우리가 모든 것을 가질 수도 있었는데,
우리가 모든 것을 가질 수도 있었는데,
그것 모두를, 그것 모두를, 그것 모두를

★ Repeat

We (　　　)(　　　)(　　) it all
Rolling in the deep
You had my heart inside your hand

우리는 모든 것을 가질 수도 있었는데
깊이 사랑하면서
너는 내 심장을 손에 넣고는

But you played it
You played it
You played it
You played it to the beat

넌 가지고 놀았어
내 맘을 갖고 놀았어
넌 가지고 놀았어
넌 내 맘을 가지고 놀았어

66 could have + p.p

could have + p.p(과거분사)

- '~했을 수도 있었다'라는 과거의 능력에 대한 추측 및 후회를 나타낸다.

could have + p.p / may have + p.p / must have + p.p / should have + p.p

표현	뜻	용도
could + have + p.p	~했을 수도 있었다	과거의 능력에 대한 추측 및 후회
may + have + p.p	~이었을지도 모른다	과거에 대한 약한 추측
must + have + p.p	~했음에 틀림없다	과거에 대한 강한 추측
should + have + p.p	~했어야 했다	과거에 하지 못한 일에 대한 후회

가사 예문

We could have had it all.

우리가 모든 것을 가질 수도 있었는데.

Q1 우리말과 같은 뜻이 되도록 주어진 표현을 빈칸에 알맞게 고쳐 쓰시오.

1. 중국에 머물렀을 때, 우리는 만리장성을 방문할 수 있었는데.
   (could have / visit / the Great Wall)

→ When we stayed in China, we ______________________________.

2. Brian은 모든 과목에서 A를 받았다. 그는 열심히 공부했음에 틀림없다.
   (must have / study hard)

→ Brian got 'A' in all subjects. He ______________________________.

3. 우리는 어두워지기 전에 산에서 내려왔었어야 했다. (should have / go down)

→ We ______________________ the mountain before it got dark.

4. 분실물 센터에 전화해봐. 네가 지갑을 지하철 안에 두고 왔을지도 몰라.
(may have / leave your wallet)

→ You'd better call Lost and Found center. You ______________________ behind the subway.

Q2 다음 빈칸에 들어갈 알맞은 말을 〈보기〉에서 골라 쓰시오.

〈보기〉	must have been	shouldn't have told
	may have been bullied (bullied : 괴롭힘을 당하는)	could have stayed

1. A: You were very rude to Emily. She feels so frustrated. (frustrated : 낙담한)
   B: I know. I ______________ her that way. I think I should apologize to her.
2. A: Jack mumbled in his speech. I could not understand what he said because his words were unclear. (mumble : 중얼거리다)
   B: Yes, same with me. He ______________ very nervous in public.
3. A: Hey, Chris! We had a party yesterday, and I sent you a message. Why didn't you call me ? You ______________ with us.
   B: Oh, no! My battery was dead yesterday. I should have charged it.
   (charge : 충전하다)
4. A: Why do teenagers struggle with depression? (depression : 우울증)
   B: They ______________ at school or have faced conflict at home.
   (conflict : 갈등)

Fill in the Blank could have had

Question 1 **1.** could have visited the Great Wall **2.** must have studied hard **3.** should have gone down **4.** may have left your wallet

Question 2 **1.** shouldn't have told **2.** must have been **3.** could have stayed **4.** may have been bullied

67	You belong with me	Taylor Swift

You're on the phone with your girlfriend, she's upset
She's going off about ①(　　　　　)(　　) you said
'Cause she doesn't get your humor like I do
I'm in the room, It's a typical Tuesday night
I'm listening to the kind of music she doesn't like
And she'll never know your story like I do

너는 너의 여자 친구와 통화 중이고,
그녀는 화나 있어
그녀는 네가 말한 뭔가에 화가 났어
그녀는 네 농담을 나처럼 이해하지 못해
평범한 화요일 밤에 난 방에 있어
난 그녀가 싫어하는 스타일의 노래를 들어
그녀는 나처럼 너의 이야기를 이해하지
못할 거야

- go off : ~에 버럭 화를 내다
- like~ : ~처럼
- typical : 평범한

☆ But she wears short skirts (high heels), I wear T-shirts (sneakers)
She's cheer captain and I'm on the bleachers, dreaming about the day when you wake up and find that what you're looking for has been here the whole time
If you could see that I'm the ②(　　)(　　) understands you,
(I've) Been here all along, so why can't you see?
You, You belong with me,
You belong with me

그녀는 짧은 치마(하이힐)를 입고(신고),
나는 티셔츠(스니커즈)를 입어(신어)
그녀는 치어리더 캡틴이고 난 관람석에 있어,
네가 찾던 사람이 너의 옆에 항상 있었던
나였다는 걸 네가 어느 날 깨어나
알아차리기를 꿈꾸면서 말이야
만약 네가 오직 나만이 널 이해할 수 있다는
것을 안다면,
내가 항상 곁에 있어왔는데, 너는 왜 모르니?
넌 내 거야, 넌 내 거야

- bleacher : (야구장의) 관람석
- belong~ : ~에 속하다
- look for : 찾다
- has(have) been~ : ~에 있어오다

Walking the streets with you and your worn-out jeans, I can't help thinking this is how it ought to be
Laughing on a park bench, thinking to myself
Hey, isn't this easy?
And you've got a ③(   )(   ) could light up this whole town
I haven't seen it in a while since she brought you down
You say you're fine,
I know you better than that
Hey, what ya doing with a girl like that?

다 낡은 청바지를 입은 너랑 이 거리를 걸으면서, 난 이게 옳다는 생각을 하지 않을 수 없어
공원 벤치에 앉아 웃으며 혼자 생각해
야, 이게 훨씬 편하지 않아?
그리고 너는 마을 전체를 빛낼 수 있는 미소를 가졌어
그녀가 너를 실망시킨 이후로
한동안 나는 그걸(미소를) 보지 못했어
넌 네가 괜찮다고 해,
난 그전의 네가 더 나았다는 걸 알아
야, 너 왜 그런 여자애랑 사귀는 거야?

- **worn-out :** 닳은
- **can't help ~ing :** ~하지 않을 수 없다
- **haven't seen :** 본 적이 없다
- **since~ :** ~이래로
- **bring down :** 실망시키다

☆ Repeat

★ Standing by and waiting at your back door
All this time how could you not know?
Baby, you belong with me,
you belong with me

너의 뒷문에 서서 기다려
어떻게 넌 지금까지 모를 수 있니?
너는 내 거야, 너는 내 거라고

- **You belong with me :** 넌 내 거야

Oh, I remember you driving to my house in the middle of the night
I'm the ②(　　)(　　) makes you laugh when you know you're 'bout to cry
And I know your favorite songs and you tell me about your dreams
Think I know where you belong, think I know it's with me
Can't you see that I'm the ②(　　)(　　) understands you?
(I've) Been here all along, so why can't you see?
You belong with me

네가 한밤중에 나를 집까지 바래다주던 게 기억이 나
난 네가 울려고 할 때 웃게 만드는 사람이야
난 네가 가장 좋아하는 노래도 알고
너는 내게 너의 꿈에 대해서도 말해주지
난 이제 네가 누구 것인지 알겠어,
넌 내 안에 있다고 생각해
내가 너를 이해해주는 바로 그 사람이라는 걸 모르겠어?
난 네 곁에 계속 있어왔는데, 너는 왜 모르니?
넌 내 거야

★ Repeat

Have you ever thought just maybe you belong with me?
You belong with me

혹시라도 네가 내 거라고 생각한 적 있니?
넌 내 거야

- **Have you ever thought~?** : (현재완료로서) ~ 생각해본 적 있니?

67 관계대명사

관계대명사란

- 관계대명사란 접속사와 대명사 역할을 동시에 하는 것으로 주격, 소유격, 목적격이 있다.
- 관계대명사절은 형용사처럼 앞에 나오는 명사인 선행사를 수식한다.

관계대명사의 종류

선행사 \ 격	주격(~은, 는)	소유격(~의)	목적격(~을, 를)
사람	who (that)	whose	whom (that)
사물 / 동물	which (that)	whose / of which	which (that)

주격 · 소유격 · 목적격 관계대명사의 쓰임

1. 주격 관계대명사	He married a woman + ~~She~~ was from Canada. (선행사 : 사람) → He married a woman **who** was from Canada. This is a book + ~~It~~ is good for children. (선행사 : 사물) → This is a book **which** is good for children.
2. 소유격 관계대명사	I know a man + ~~His~~ father is a famous musician. (선행사 : 사람) → I know a man **whose** father is a famous musician. She has a dog + ~~Its~~ hair is very long. (선행사 : 동물) → She has a dog **whose** hair is very long.
3. 목적격 관계대명사	Did I tell you about the girl? + I met ~~her~~ during the trip. (선행사 : 사람) → Did I tell you about the girl **whom** I met during the trip? I can't find the book + I borrowed ~~it~~ from the library. (선행사 : 사물) → I can't find the book **which** I borrowed from the library.

가사 예문

I'm the one who understands you.

나는 너를 이해할 수 있는 한 사람이야.

You've got a smile that could light up this whole town.

너는 이 마을 전체를 밝힐 수 있는 미소를 가졌어.

Attention!

관계대명사 that은 주격 혹은 목적격 관계대명사로 쓸 수 있음!

- Do you know the shop **that** sells delicious bread in this town?

(주격 which 대신 that)

- Fried chicken and beer is the food **that** many foreigners like so much.

(목적격 which 대신 that)

Q1 다음 두 문장을 한 문장으로 바꿔 쓸 때 괄호 안에서 알맞은 것을 고르시오.

1. Will you give me the book? + The book's cover is green.

→ Will you give me the book (which / whose) cover is green?

2. Christine lost the ring. + Her fiance bought the ring for her.

→ Christine lost the ring (whose / which) her fiance bought for her.

3. That man is the police officer. + The police officer caught the thief yesterday.

→ That man is the police officer (who / which) caught the thief yesterday.

Q2 다음 두 문장을 관계대명사로 연결하여 한 문장으로 쓰시오.

1. Look at the girl. Her hair is red.

→ ______________________________

2. I have a friend. She is from Australia.

→ ______________________________

3. May I lie on this couch? This couch looks so comfortable.

→ ______________________________

4. He was reading a book. The book's writer was J.K.Rowling.

→ ______________________________

5. I am looking for a friend. I want to travel with the friend.

→ ______________________________

6. The blouse is too small for me. I bought the blouse yesterday.

→ ______________________________

Q3 다음 빈칸에 들어갈 말을 〈보기〉에서 골라 쓰시오. (중복사용 가능)

〈보기〉 who whose whom which

1. That's the man __________ house has burned down.
2. Where is my ice cream __________ was on the table?
3. The new camera __________ I bought last week has broken.
4. She is the student __________ I taught English two years ago.
5. Please quit the smoking __________ is very harmful to your body.
6. I want to climb up the mountain __________ top is covered with snow.

Fill in the Blank ① something that ② one who ③ smile that

Question 1 **1.** whose **2.** which **3.** who

Question 2 **1.** Look at the girl whose hair is red. **2.** I have a friend who (that) is from Australia.
3. May I lie on this couch which (that) looks so comfortable?
4. He was reading a book whose writer was J.K.Rowling.
5. I am looking for a friend whom (that) I want to travel with.
6. The blouse which (that) I bought yesterday is too small for me.

Question 3 **1.** whose **2.** which **3.** which **4.** whom **5.** which **6.** whose

68 Do what you wanna do — Mocca

Take it easy, my friend
Grab the chance what you can
It's time for us to move on
Let the world sing you a song

마음을 편하게 가져, 친구야
할 수 있을 때 기회를 잡아
이제 앞으로 나아갈 시간이야
세상이 너에게 노래를 불러주게 해

- Take it easy : 진정해, 마음을 편히 가져

★ Take it easy, my friend
Wipe the tears from your eyes
There's a magic in the air tonight
High in the lavender sky

마음을 편하게 가져, 친구야
네 눈에서 흐르는 눈물을 닦아
오늘 밤, 라벤더 빛으로 물든 높은 하늘에
마법 같은 분위기가 감돌아

- wipe ~ from ... : ...로부터 ~를 지우다

You've gotta ①(   ) (   ) (   ) (   )
(   ) (Do what you wanna do)
②(   ) (   ) (   ) (   ) (   ) (Say
what you wanna say)
①(   ) (   ) (   ) (   ) (   ) and
don't be afraid
As long as everybody's happy
(Everybody's happy)
And everybody's feeling okay
You've gotta ①(   ) (   ) (   ) (   )
(   )
②(   ) (   ) (   ) (   ) (   ) now

네가 하고 싶은 것을 해야 해
네가 말하고 싶은 것을 말해
네가 하고 싶은 것을 하고 두려워하지 마
모두가 행복해한다면
그리고 모두가 기분이 좋다면
네가 하고 싶은 것을 해야 해
이제 네가 말하고 싶은 것을 말해

- You've gotta(You've got to~) : 너는 해야 해(=You have to~)
- wanna = want to
- As long as~ : ~하는 한

Make it easy, my friend
Cause the storm will calm down
Just be true to yourself
Everything will be alright

마음을 편하게 가져, 친구야
폭풍은 잠잠해질 테니까
그저 너에게 솔직해져
모든 게 다 잘될 거야

- **Make it easy :** 마음을 편하게 가져
- **storm :** 폭풍우
- **calm down :** ① 가라앉다 ② 진정시키다

★ Repeat

Do what you wanna do (Do what you wanna do)
Say what you wanna say (Say what you wanna say)
Do what you wanna do And don't be afraid
As long as everybody's happy (Everybody's happy)
And everybody's feeling okay
You've gotta do what you wanna do
Say what you wanna say now

네가 하고 싶은 것을 해
네가 말하고 싶은 것을 말해
네가 하고 싶은 것을 하고 두려워하지 마
모두가 행복해한다면
그리고 모두가 기분이 좋다면
네가 하고 싶은 것을 해야 해
이제 네가 말하고 싶은 것을 말해

You've gotta do what you wanna do
Say what you wanna say now
You've gotta do what you wanna do
Say what you wanna say now

네가 하고 싶은 것을 해야 해
네가 말하고 싶은 것을 말해
네가 하고 싶은 것을 해야 해
네가 말하고 싶은 것을 말해

68 관계대명사 what

관계대명사 what이란

- 선행사를 포함하는 관계대명사로 '~하는 것'의 의미를 나타낸다.
- 쓰임이 the thing which와 같다.

I will give you **the thing** + You want **the thing**

(~~the thing~~ → 목적격 관계대명사 which로)

→ I will give you **the thing which** you want.

(~~the thing which~~ → 관계대명사 what으로)

= I will give you **what** you want.

가사 예문

You've gotta do what you wanna do.

네가 하고 싶은 것을 해야 해.

Say what you wanna say.

네가 말하고 싶은 것을 말해야 해.

Attention!

의문사 what(무엇) vs 관계대명사 what(~것) 구분!

- I don't know **what** his name is. (what이 '무엇'이라는 의문사로 쓰임)
- This is **what** makes me upset. (what이 '~것'이라는 **관계대명사**로 쓰임)

Q1 밑줄 친 부분을 바르게 해석하시오.

1. What I need is your help.

→ ____________________ 은 너의 도움이야.

2. This is what I want to buy you.

→ 이것이 너에게 ____________________ 이야.

3. I don't understand what he said.

→ 나는 ____________________ 을 이해할 수 없어.

4. What those kids need is real love and affection.

→ ____________________ 은 진정한 사랑과 애정이야.

5. What makes my life happy is the joy of teaching.

→ ____________________ 은 가르치는 것의 즐거움이야.

Q2 다음 우리말과 의미가 같도록 괄호 안의 단어들을 배열하여 문장을 완성하시오.

1. 오늘 할 수 있는 것을 내일로 미루지 마라. (today / can / you / what / do)

→ Never put off till tomorrow ____________________.

2. 나는 그녀가 방금 한 말을 믿을 수 없어. (said / has / what / she / just)

→ I can't believe ____________________.

3. 네가 벼룩시장에서 산 것을 보여줘. (at the flea market / you / what / bought)

→ Show me ____________________.

4. 내가 가장 필요로 하는 것은 그 문제에 대한 너의 조언이야. (most / what / need / I)

→ ____________________ is your advice on that matter.

5. 내가 알고 싶은 것은 그곳까지 가는 데 얼마나 걸리는가야. (to / I / what / want / know)

→ ____________________ is how long it takes to get there.

Fill in the Blank ① Do(do) what you wanna do ② Say what you wanna say

Question 1 **1.** 내가 원하는 것 **2.** 사주고 싶은 것 **3.** 그가 말한 것 **4.** 저 아이들이 필요로 하는 것 **5.** 나의 삶을 행복하게 만드는 것

Question 2 **1.** what you can do today **2.** what she has just said **3.** what you bought at the flea market **4.** What I need most **5.** What I want to know

69 One summer night — Jinchua & Abi

☆ One summer night,
The stars were ①(   ) bright
One summer dream ②(   ) with fancy whims
That summer night,
My whole world tumbled down,
I could have ③(   ) if not for you

어느 여름 밤,
별들은 밝게 빛나고 있었어요
복잡한 기분으로 가득 차 있던 어느 여름날의 꿈
그 여름 밤,
내 모든 세상이 무너져 내렸을 때,
만약 당신이 아니었더라면 난
죽어버렸을지도 몰라요

- fancy : ① 화려한 ② 복잡한 ③ 상상
- whim : 기분
- tumble down : 굴러 떨어지다
- could have p.p(~) : ~했을 수도 있었다

★ Each night I pray for you
My heart would cry for you
The sun won't shine again since you have ④(   )
Each time I think of you
My heart would beat for you
You are the one for me

매일 밤 난 당신을 위해 기도할 때마다
내 가슴은 당신을 향해 울부짖어요
당신이 떠난 후로부터는 태양은 다시 떠오르지 않아요
매번 당신을 생각할 때마다
내 가슴은 당신을 향해 두근거려요
당신은 저에게 유일한 존재거든요

- pray : 기도하다
- since : ① ~때문에 ① ~이래로
- beat : ① 이기다 ② 때리다 ③ 고동치다 ④ 맥박 ⑤ 박자

Set me free
Like the sparrows up the tree
Give a sign so I would ease my mind
Just say a word and I'll come running wild
Give me a chance to live again

날 자유롭게 해주세요
나무 위 새들처럼
내 마음이 편안해지도록 한 가닥의 표시라도 해주세요
한마디만 해주세요 그러면 거침없이 바로 달려가겠어요
다시 새 삶을 살 수 있는 기회를 주세요

- set free : 자유의 몸이 되게 하다
- sparrow : 참새
- ease : ① 쉬움 ② 편안함 ③ 수월하게 하다

★ Repeat

☆ Repeat

★ Repeat

69 현재분사 및 과거분사

분사란

- 동사에 -ing나 -ed를 붙인 형태로 현재분사와 과거분사가 있다.

종류	형태	쓰임	의미	예시
현재분사	동사 + ing	능동 또는 진행	~하는, ~하고 있는	crying, playing, writing, making
과거분사	동사 + ed	수동 또는 완료	~된, ~해진	cried, played, written, made

분사의 쓰임

역할	형태	쓰임
형용사 역할	명사의 앞이나 뒤에서 명사를 수식	Be careful! The **barking** dog is running after you! (barking이 dog 앞에서 수식) He repaired the door **broken** by a strong wind. (broken이 door 뒤에서 수식)
보어 역할	주격보어나 목적격보어로 주어나 목적어의 상태를 보충 설명	They are **taking** a picture in front of the Statue of Liberty. (taking이 주어 They의 상태를 설명)
		I had the window **cleaned** by my students. (cleaned가 목적어 window의 상태를 설명)
진행형	be + 현재분사	All of my family are **watching** TV in the living room.
완료형	have(has, had) + 과거분사	The weather has **been** cold since last week.
수동태	be + 과거분사	Harry Potter was **written** by J.K. Rowling.

가사 예문

One summer night, the stars were shining bright.

어느 여름 밤, 별들은 밝게 빛나고 있었어요.

One summer dream made with fancy whims

복잡한 기분으로 가득 차 있던 어느 여름날의 꿈

Q1 다음 괄호 안에서 알맞은 것을 고르시오.

1. He bought a (using / used) car at a good price.
2. She picked up some (falling / fallen) leaves to make the bookmark.
3. Can you see the boy (crying / cried) over there? We should help him.
4. Many people were (shocking / shocked) by the sudden death of Whitney Huston.

Q2 다음 우리말과 뜻이 같도록 빈칸에 알맞은 말을 쓰시오.

1. 저 뛰는 소년을 봐! 그는 매우 빨라.

→ Look at the _________ boy! He runs very fast!

2. Bella는 영어로 쓰인 편지를 한 통 받았다.

→ Bella received a letter _________ in English.

3. Tom은 부서진 자전거를 혼자 수리했다.

→ Tom repaired the _________ bicycle by himself.

4. 셀카봉으로 셀카를 찍고 있는 여자 아이들은 내 여동생들이야.

→ The girls _________ some selfies with the stick are my sisters.

Fill in the Blank ① shining ② made ③ died ④ gone

Question 1 **1.** used **2.** fallen **3.** crying **4.** shocked

Question 2 **1.** running **2.** written **3.** broken **4.** taking

70 Do Re Mi

The Sound of Music OST

Let's start at the very beginning
A very good place to start
When you read you begin with (ABC)
When you sing you begin with Do Re Mi
(Do Re Mi) Do Re Mi
The first three notes just happen to be
Do Re Mi (Do Re Mi)
Do Re Mi Fa So La Ti
Oh, let's see if I can make it easier

그럼 처음부터 시작해보자
아주 좋은 출발점이지
우리가 처음 글을 읽을 땐 ABC로 시작하듯이
노래를 하려면 도레미부터 시작해야 한단다
(도 레 미) 도 레 미
첫 세 음에게 우연히 붙여진 이름이
도 레 미 (도 레 미)
도 레 미 파 솔 라 시
더 쉽게 배울 방법이 있을까 생각해보자

- **note :** 음표
- **begin with~ :** ~부터 시작하다
- **happen to~ :** 우연히 ~하다
- **if :** ① 만약에 ~라면 ② ~인지 아닌지

Doe, a deer, a female deer
Ray, a drop of golden sun
Me, a name I call myself
Far, a long, long way to run
Sew, a ( )( )( )
La, a note to follow Sew
Tea, a drink with jam and bread
That will bring us back to Do (oh oh oh)

'도'는 사슴의 암사슴
'레'는 황금빛 태양 한 방울
'미'는 내가 나 자신을 부르는 이름
'파'는 달려가야 할 멀고도 먼 길
'솔'은 실을 잡아당기는 바늘
'라'는 솔 다음에 나오는 음
'시'는 잼 바른 빵과 함께 마시는 음료
그런 다음 다시 우린 '도'로 돌아가지

- **doe :** 암사슴
- **deer :** 사슴
- **female :** 여성
- **ray :** 광선

Doe, a deer, a female deer
Ray, a drop of golden sun
Me, a name I call myself
Far, a long, long way to run
Sew, a (   )(   )(   )
La, a note to follow Sew
Tea, a drink with jam and bread
That will bring us back to Do (oh oh oh)

'도'는 사슴의 암사슴
'레'는 황금빛 태양 한 방울
'미'는 내가 나 자신을 부르는 이름
'파'는 달려가야 할 멀고도 먼 길
'솔'은 실을 잡아당기는 바늘
'라'는 솔 다음에 나오는 음
'시'는 잼 바른 빵과 함께 마시는 음료
그런 다음 다시 우린 '도'로 돌아가지

- **drop :** 물방울
- **far :** 먼, 멀리
- **sew :** 바느질하다
- **needle :** 바늘

Doe, a deer, a female deer
Ray, a drop of golden sun
Me, a name I call myself
Far, a long, long way to run
Sew, a (   )(   )(   )
La, a note to follow Sew
Tea, a drink with jam and bread
That will bring us back to Do
Do Re Mi Fa So La Ti Do, So Do!

'도'는 사슴의 암사슴
'레'는 황금빛 태양 한 방울
'미'는 내가 나 자신을 부르는 이름
'파'는 달려가야 할 멀고도 먼 길
'솔'은 실을 잡아당기는 바늘
'라'는 솔 다음에 나오는 음
'시'는 잼 바른 빵과 함께 마시는 음료
그런 다음 다시 우린 '도'로 돌아가지
도 레 미 파 솔 라 시 도, 솔 도!

- **pull :** 잡아당기다
- **thread :** 실

70 명사를 수식하는 분사

명사를 수식하는 분사란

- 현재분사 및 과거분사는 명사 뒤에 와서 명사를 수식할 수 있는데, 이때 분사 앞에는 「주격관계대명사 + be동사」가 생략되었다고 볼 수 있다.

현재분사의 명사 수식	**The girl** (who is) **dancing** on the stage is my sister. → The girl과 dancing 사이에 「주격관계대명사 + be동사」인 '**who is**'가 생략되었다고 볼 수 있음.
과거분사의 명사 수식	**The spaghetti** (which was) **cooked** by my dad was delicious. → The spaghetti와 cooked 사이에 「주격관계대명사 + be동사」인 '**which was**'가 생략되었다고 볼 수 있음.

가사 예문

a needle pulling thread

실을 잡아당기는 바늘

Q1 다음 괄호 안에 알맞은 표현을 고르시오.

1. Do you know those girls (singing / sung) on the stage?
2. What is the name of the river (flowing / flown) through Seoul?
3. The dress (displaying / displayed) in that shop is very gorgeous.
4. Southeast Asians are crazy about the goods (making / made) in Korea.
5. A man (talking / talked) on the phone got hit by the ball during a baseball game.

Q2 다음 괄호 안의 말을 바르게 배열하여 문장을 다시 쓰시오. **(첫 대문자 유의)**

1. (the library / studying / in / the children) are my cousins.

→ ______________________________

2. Your present is (tied / yellow ribbons / the package / with).

→ ______________________________

3. Did you check (the web site / provided / on / the information)?

→ ______________________________

4. The award ceremony began (by Maroon 5 / a song / performed / with).

→ ______________________________

5. (this novel / described / in / the characters) are very unique and dynamic.

→ ______________________________

Fill in the Blank needle pulling thread

Question 1 **1.** singing **2.** flowing **3.** displayed **4.** made **5.** talking

Question 2
1. The children studying in the library are my cousins.
2. Your present is the package tied with yellow ribbons.
3. Did you check the information provided on the web site?
4. The award ceremony began with a song performed by Maroon 5.
5. The characters described in this novel are very unique and dynamic.

71 Haven't met you yet — Michael Buble

I'm not ①(   ), not everything lasts
I've broken my heart so many times
I stopped keeping track
Talk myself in, I talk myself out
I get all worked up then I let myself down
I tried so very hard not to lose it
I came up with a million excuses
I thought, I thought of every possibility
And I know someday that it'll all turn out
You'll make me work, so we can work to work it out
And I promise you, kid, that I'll give so much more than I get
I just haven't met you yet

난 놀랍진 않아요, 모든 것이 영원하진 않으니까요
난 가슴 아파본 게 한두 번이 아니거든요
세는 것도 포기했죠
속으로 달래기도 했다가, 내 모든 걸 다 끄집어도 보여줬다가
정말 속상해하고 그러고 나선 또 내 자신을 실망시키죠
내 사랑을 잃지 않으려고 정말 열심히 노력했어요
만 개도 넘는 이유를 찾아냈어요
정말 모든 가능성은 다 생각해봤어요
그리고 난 언젠가는 다 괜찮아진다는 걸 알아요
당신은 내가 노력하게 만들 것이고,
우린 이 모든 걸 잘할 수 있을 거예요
당신께 약속해요, 난 내가 받는 것보다 훨씬 더 많이 당신께 드리겠다고
난 그저 당신을 만나지 못했을 뿐이에요

- surprised : 깜짝 놀란
- last : ① 마지막의 ② 마지막 ③ 계속되다
- keep track : 파악하다, 기록하다
- get worked up : 속상해하다
- let down : 실망시키다
- come up with~ : ~를 생각하다
- excuse : 변명
- possibility : 가능성

I might have to wait, I'll never give up
I guess it's half timing, and the other half's luck
Wherever you are, whenever it's right

아마 난 기다려야 할 거예요, 하지만 포기는 안 해요
반은 타이밍이에요, 그리고 반은 행운이죠
당신이 어디 있든, 때가 되거든

You'll come out of nowhere and into my life
And I know that we can be so
②(　　　　　　)
And baby, your love is gonna change me

당신은 갑자기 나타나서 내 인생에 들어오겠죠
그리고 난 우리가 정말 멋진 커플이 될 거란 것도 알아요
그리고 당신의 사랑은 날 변화시킬 거예요

- timing : 타이밍, 시기
- wherever : 어디에나
- whenever : 언제든지
- out of nowhere : 갑자기, 난데없이
- amazing : 놀라운

And now I can see every possibility
And somehow I know that it'll all turn out
You'll make me work, so we can work to work it out
And I promise you, kid, that I'll give so much more than I get
I just haven't met you yet

이제 난 모든 가능성이 보여요
그리고 난 어떻게든 다 괜찮아진다는 걸 알아요
당신은 나를 움직일 것이고,
우린 이 모든 걸 잘할 수 있을 거예요
당신께 약속해요, 난 내가 받는 것보다 훨씬 더 많이 당신께 드리겠다고
난 그저 당신을 만나지 못했을 뿐이에요

- somehow : 어떻게든
- turn out : ~인 것으로 드러나다
- work out : (일이) 잘 풀리다

They say 'All's fair in love and war.'
But I won't need to fight it
We'll get it right and we'll be united

사람들은 '사랑과 전쟁에 있어서는 모든 게 정당화된다.'라고 말을 해요
하지만 난 싸울 필요가 없어요
우리는 괜찮을 거거든요 그리고 우리는 언젠가 만날 거니까요

- fair : ① 정당한 ② 공평한 ③ 제법 큰 ④ 예쁜
- All is fair in love and war : (속담) 사랑과 전쟁에 있어서는 모든 게 정당화된다
- get right : 바르게 되다
- unite : ① 연합하다 ② 통합시키다

And I know that we can be so ②(　　　　　) And being in your life is gonna change me And now I can see every single possibility And someday I know that it'll all turn out And I'll work to work it out I promise you, kid, I'll give more than I get, than I get, than I get, than I get	그리고 난 우리가 정말 멋진 커플이 될 거란 것을 알아요 그리고 당신의 삶 속에 사는 것은 날 변화시킬 거예요 난 이제 모든 가능성이 보여요 그리고 언젠가는 다 괜찮아진다는 걸 알아요 난 모든 걸 잘할 수 있도록 노력할 거예요 당신께 약속해요, 난 내가 받는 것보다 훨씬 더 많이 당신께 드리겠다고, 내가 받는 것보다, 내가 받는 것보다, 내가 받는 것보다
Oh, you know it'll all turn out And you'll make me work, so we can work to work it out And I promise you, kid, to give so much more than I get Yeah, I just haven't met you yet I just haven't met you yet Oh, promise you, kid, to give so much more than I get I said love love love love love love love I just haven't met you yet I just haven't met you yet	당신도 알다시피 모든 게 현실이 될 거예요 그리고 당신은 내가 노력하게 만들 것이고, 그래서 우린 이 모든 걸 잘할 수 있을 거예요 그리고 난 당신께 약속해요, 난 내가 받는 것보다 훨씬 더 많이 당신께 드리겠다고 그래요, 난 그저 당신을 아직 못 만났을 뿐이에요 난 그저 당신을 아직 못 만났을 뿐이에요 오, 당신께 약속해요, 내가 받는 것보다 훨씬 더 많이 드릴 것을 난 사랑 사랑 사랑 사랑 사랑 사랑 사랑이라고 말했어요 난 당신을 아직 만나지 못했을 뿐이에요 난 당신을 아직 만나지 못했을 뿐이에요

71 감정을 나타내는 분사

감정을 나타내는 현재분사 및 과거분사

- 감정이나 느낌에 대해 말할 때 현재분사 ~ing 및 과거분사 ~ed를 쓸 수 있다. 이때 ~ing와 ~ed는 다음과 같은 의미 차이가 있다.

현재분사 ~ing	과거분사 ~ed
(사람 또는 사물이) ~한 감정을 일으키는	(사람이) ~한 감정을 느끼게 되는
• surprising : 놀라게 하는 • amazing : 감탄하게 하는 • exciting : 신이 나게 하는, 흥분시키는 • interesting : 흥미를 일으키는 • pleasing : 기쁨을 주는 • satisfying : 만족스러운 • relaxing : 마음을 편하게 해주는	• surprised : 놀란 • amazed : 감탄한 • excited : 신이 난, 흥분한 • interested : 흥미를 느끼는 • pleased : 기쁜 • satisfied : 만족한 • relaxed : 마음이 편안한
• tiring : 피곤하게 하는 • boring : 지루하게 만드는 • annoying : 짜증나게 하는 • depressing : 우울하게 하는 • disappointing : 실망시키는 • frustrating : 좌절감을 주는	• tired : 피곤한 • bored : 지루함을 느끼는 • annoyed : 짜증난 • depressed : 우울한 • disappointed : 실망한 • frustrated : 좌절한
• frightening : 무섭게 하는 • shocking : 충격을 주는 • confusing : 혼란스럽게 하는 • puzzling : 어리둥절하게 하는 • embarrassing : 당황하게 하는	• frightened : 무서워하는 • shocked : 충격 받은 • confused : 혼란스러워하는 • puzzled : 어리둥절해 하는 • embarrassed : 당황한

A : Did you watch speed-skating competition yesterday?

B : Of course I did. Choi was really **amazing**. Choi powered her way to a gold medal in women's short-track 1500 meters.

A : I was very **surprised** by her concentration and agility. (agility : 민첩성)

가사 예문

I'm not surprised, not everything lasts.

난 놀랍지 않아요, 모든 것이 영원하진 않으니까요.

Q1 다음 괄호 안에서 알맞은 것을 고르시오.

1. Most of men think that shopping is (tiring / tired).
2. I like to have a (relaxing / relaxed) time in sauna.
3. Are you (satisfying / satisfied) with the customer service?
4. These days, I am very (confusing / confused) and worried about my future.

Q2 괄호 안에 주어진 단어를 적절한 형태로 사용하여 대화를 완성하시오.

1. A: Are you __________ about studying abroad? (excite)

   B: Yes! I have been __________ in experiencing foreign cultures. (interest)

2. A: You look __________, what's the matter? (frustrate)

   B: He turned down my proposal. It was a very __________ moment. (embarrass)

3. A: Did you hear the __________ news about K's sexual harrassment? (shock)

   B: Yes. I was very __________ with him. He should resign from his post. (disappoint)

   (sexual harrassment : 성추행, resign from one's post : 자리에서 물러나다)

Fill in the Blank ① surprised ② amazing

Question 1 **1.** tiring **2.** relaxing **3.** satisfied **4.** confused

Question 2 **1.** excited, interested **2.** frustrated, embarrassing **3.** shocking, disappointed

72 Sk8er boy — Avril Lavigne

He was a boy, she was a girl
Can I make it anymore obvious?
He was a punk, she did ballet
What more can I say?
He wanted her, she'd never tell
Secretly she wanted him as well
But all of her friends stuck up their nose
They had a problem with his baggy cloth

그는 소년이었고, 그녀는 소녀였어요
더 분명하게 말해야 할까요?
그는 노는 아이였고, 그녀는 발레를 했죠
더 이상 무엇을 말할까요?
그는 그녀를 원했고,
그녀는 결코 말하지 않았지만
비밀스럽게 그녀도 그를 원했었죠
하지만 그녀의 친구들 모두는 코를 삐죽이
내밀고서는 그의 헐렁한 옷을 문제 삼았죠

- **obvious :** 명백한
- **secretly :** 비밀스럽게
- **as well :** 또한, 게다가
- **problem :** 문제
- **baggy clothes :** 헐렁한 옷

He was a skater boy, she said see you later, boy
He wasn't good enough for her
She had a pretty face
But her head was up in space
She needed to come back down to earth

그는 스케이터 보이였어요
잘 가, 다음에 또 만나라고 그녀가 말했죠
그는 그녀만큼 잘나지 않았죠
그녀의 얼굴은 예쁘장했지만
그녀의 머리는 우주 꼭대기까지
올라가 있을 정도로 눈이 높았죠
그녀는 현실을 직시할 필요가 있었죠

- **later :** 나중에
- **enough :** 충분히

Five years from now,
she sits at home, ①(　　　　) the baby,
she's all alone
She turns on TV, guess who she sees

5년이 흐른 뒤,
그녀는 아기에게 밥을 먹이면서, 집에 앉아 있네요
그녀는 종일 혼자 있죠
TV를 켜고는, 그녀가 누굴 보는지 맞혀 보세요

Skater boy rockin' up MTV
She calls up her friends,
They already know
and they've all got tickets
to see his show
She tags along and stands in the crowd
Looks up at the man that she turned down

MTV를 뒤흔들고 있는 스케이터 보이죠
그녀는 친구들에게 전화했죠,
그들은 이미 알고 있네요
이미 모두들 그의 쇼를 보기 위해 티켓을 샀고요
그녀는 따라가서는 군중 속에 서 있어요
그녀가 거절했던 그 남자를 올려다보네요

- feed : 음식을 먹이다
- turn on : 켜다
- rock : 흔들다
- already : 이미, 벌써
- tag along : 따라붙다
- turn down : 거절하다

☆ He was a skater boy, she said see you later boy
He wasn't good enough for her
Now he's a super star slamming on his guitar
Does your pretty face see what he's worth?

그는 스케이터 보이였어요,
잘 가, 담에 또 만나라고 그녀가 말했었죠
그는 그녀만큼 잘나지 않았었죠
이제 그는 기타를 세게 치는 슈퍼스타이지요
너의 예쁜 얼굴은 그의 주가가 얼마나 올라 있는지 알아보겠니?

- slam on guitar : 기타를 세게 치다
- worth : 가치가 있는

☆ Repeat

Sorry girl, but you missed out
Well, tough luck that boy's mine now
We are more than just good friends
This is how the story ends
Too bad that you couldn't see
See the man that boy could be

미안하지만 넌 놓쳐버렸지
불운인 셈이지, 그는 이제 나의 것이니까
우린 좋은 친구 이상이지
이것이 이 이야기의 결말이지
네가 예견할 수 없었던 건 정말 안됐어
그가 될 수 있었던 가능성을 말이지

There is more than meets the eye
I see the soul that is inside

눈으로 보는 것 그 이상이 존재해
난 그 내면의 영혼까지 보고 있어

- miss out : 놓치다
- tough luck : 불운
- This is how~ : 이렇게 해서 ~하게 되다
- soul : 영혼

He's just a boy, and I'm just a girl
Can I make it anymore obvious?
We are in love, haven't you heard?
How we rock each other's world

그는 그냥 남자애고, 난 그저 여자애지
내가 더 이상 확실히 이야기해줄까?
우린 사랑하고 있어, 너 못 들었니?
어떻게 우리가 서로의 세계를 흔들고
있는지를

- make it obvious : 확실하게 하다

★ I'm with the skater boy,
I said see you later boy
I'll be back stage after the show
I'll be at a studio, ②(   ) the song
we wrote about a girl you used to
know

난 스케이터 보이와 함께 있어,
난 말했지 곧 만나자고
쇼가 끝난 뒤 무대 뒤로 갈게
난 우리가 썼던 그 노래를 부르면서
스튜디오에 있을게,
네가 예전에 알던 한 여자애에 관한 노래
말이야

- used to~ : ~하곤 했다 (과거에는 했으나, 지금은 하지 않는 상태를 표현)

★ Repeat

72 분사구문

분사구문이란

- 「접속사 + 주어 + 동사~」의 부사절을 분사의 형태로 간단하게 나타내며, 시간, 이유, 조건, 동시상황을 나타낸다.

분사구문 만드는 법

① 부사절의 접속사를 생략 → ② 부사절의 주어를 생략 (단, 부사절의 주어가 주절의 주어와 같은 경우만) → ③ 부사절의 동사를 현재분사인 「동사원형-ing」 형태로 변경 (단, 부사절의 동사가 주절의 동사와 시제가 같은 경우만)

~~As~~ ~~he~~ ~~watches~~ the movie, he eats popcorn and soda.
① ② ③

→ **Watching** the movie, he eats popcorn and soda.

분사구문의 쓰임

1. 시간 : **Seeing** the policeman, he ran away. (← When he saw the policeman, ~)
2. 이유 : **Feeling** tired, I went to bed early. (← Because I felt tired, ~)
3. 조건 : **Turning** right, you'll find the Starbucks. (← If you turn right, ~)
4. 동시상황 : **Listening** to music, he reads the book. (← As he listens to music, ~)

Attention!

분사구문의 부정문에서는 not을 맨 앞에 가져온다!

He seems to be a workaholic. When he doesn't have work to do, he feels nervous.
= He seems to be a workaholic. **Not having** work to do, he feels nervous.

(workaholic : 일 중독자)

가사 예문

She sits at home, feeding the baby.

그녀는 아기에게 밥을 먹이며, 집에 앉아 있지.

I'll be at a studio, singing the song we wrote.

나는 우리가 썼던 그 노래를 부르면서, 스튜디오에 있을게.

Q1 다음 문장을 분사구문으로 바꿔 쓰시오.

1. As she watches TV, she always eats something.

→ ____________________

2. If you buy a T-shirt today, you will get another one for free.

→ ____________________

3. While she stayed in Canada, she took lots of beautiful pictures.

→ ____________________

4. After she won the prize, Victoria donated the prize money to the society.

→ ____________________

5. Because she was deeply moved, the singer expressed her thanks to the audiences.

→ ____________________

Q2 다음 분사구문을 부사절로 바꿔 쓰시오.

1. Feeling tired, you'd better take some rest.

→ ____________________, you'd better take some rest.

2. Talking on the phone, Mason played a video game.

→ ____________________, Mason played a video game.

3. Turning to the right, you will find the subway station.

→ ____________________, you will find the subway station.

4. Taking a test, you should read the questions on the exam sheet carefully.

→ ______________________, you should read the questions on the exam sheet carefully.

5. Not having enough money, he bought a used car instead of a new one.

→ ______________________, he bought a used car instead of a new one.

Q3 다음 문장에서 밑줄 친 부분을 어법상 알맞은 형태로 고치시오.

1. Cooking not well, I often eat fast food. → ______________
2. Heard the news, William was very shocked. → ______________
3. Being was busy, I could not attend the ceremony. → ______________
4. After eat lunch, Luke always drinks a cup of coffee. → ______________
5. Listen to the lectures, Natalie takes notes on her iPad. → ______________
6. Being injuring, she could not join in the ice-skating competitions in the Olympics. → ______________
7. Not know where to stay, we searched the internet for the information about a hotel. → ______________

Fill in the Blank ① feeding ② singing

Question 1 **1.** Watching TV, she always eats something. **2.** Buying a T-shirt today, you will get another one for free. **3.** Staying in Canada, she took lots of beautiful pictures. **4.** Winning the prize, Victoria donated the prize money to the society. **5.** Being deeply moved, the singer expressed her thanks to the audiences.

Question 2 **1.** If you feel tired **2.** As he talked on the phone **3.** If you turn to the right **4.** When you take a test **5.** Because he didn't have enough money

Question 3 **1.** Not cooking **2.** Hearing **3.** Being **4.** (After) Eating **5.** Listening **6.** Being injured **7.** Not knowing

73 Call me maybe — Carly Rae Japsen

I threw a wish in the well
Don't ask me, I'll never tell
I looked to you as it fell
and now you're in my way
I trade my soul for a wish,
pennies and dimes for a kiss
I wasn't looking for this,
but now you're in my way
Your stare was holding,
Ripped jeans, skin was showing,
Hot night, wind was blowing,
Where do you think you're going, baby?

난 우물에 소원을 던졌어
(그 소원이 뭔지) 묻지 마, 절대 얘기 안 할 거야
동전이 떨어졌을 때 난 널 봤어
그리고 넌 이제 내 삶에 들어왔어
내 영혼과 바꿔서라도 그 소원을 이루고 싶어,
페니와 다임을 단 한 번의 입맞춤을 위해서
내가 이런 걸 바란 건 아니었는데,
넌 내 삶에 들어왔어
너의 시선은 멈춰있었어,
찢어진 청바지, 그 사이로 살갗이 보였어,
뜨거운 밤, 바람은 불었지,
넌 어디로 가고 있는 거니?

- threw : 던졌다 (throw-threw-thrown)
- trade A for B: A를 B로 교환하다
- 1 penny = 1 cent
- 1 dime = 10 cent
- stare : 시선
- hold : ① 쥐다, 잡다 ② 유지하다 ③ 가지다 ④ 개최하다
- ripped : 찢어진
- blow : 불다

★ Hey, I just met you, and this is crazy,
but here's my number,
so call me maybe
(   )'s (   )(   )(   ) right at you,
baby, but here's my number,
so call me maybe
Hey, I just met you, and this is crazy,
but here's my number,
so call me maybe

난 방금 너를 만났고, 이건 말도 안 되는데,
여기 내 번호 있어, 그러니 전화해줄래
널 똑바로 쳐다보는 것은 정말 힘들어,
하지만 여기 내 번호가 있어,
그러니 전화해줄래
헤이, 난 방금 너를 만났고,
이건 말도 안 되는데
여기 내 번호 있어, 그러니 전화해줄래

And all the other boys
try to chase me,
but here's my number,
so call me maybe

다른 남자애들 모두가 나를 쫓아다니려고
애쓰고 있어,
하지만 여기 내 번호가 있어,
그러니 전화해줄래

- **crazy :** (말이나 행동이) 정상이 아닌,
  말도 안 되는
- **chase :** (사귀자고) 쫓아다니다

You took your time with the call
I took no time with the fall
You gave me nothing at all
but still you're in my way
I beg and borrow and steal at first sight
and it's real
I didn't know I would feel it,
but it's in my way

너는 전화 걸기까지 시간이 좀 걸리는 것 같아
나는 바로 사랑에 빠졌는데
넌 내게 준 게 아무것도 없지만
넌 여전히 내 앞에 있어
난 애원하고 빌리고 (마음을) 훔치려고도 하네
처음 본 순간부터 그리고 그건 진짜야
내가 그런 걸 느끼게 될 줄은 몰랐어,
하지만 그건(사랑은) 내 앞에 있어

- **still :** 여전히
- **beg :** 애원하다
- **borrow :** 빌리다
- **steal :** 훔치다
- **at first sight :** 처음 본 순간

Your stare was holding,
Ripped jeans, skin was showing,
Hot night, wind was blowing,
Where do you think you're going, baby?

너의 시선은 멈춰있었어,
찢어진 청바지, 그 사이로 살갗이 보였고,
뜨거운 밤, 바람은 불었지,
넌 어디로 가고 있는 거니?

★ Repeat

Before you came into my life I missed you so bad I missed you so bad I missed you so, so bad Before you came into my life I missed you so bad And you should know that I missed you so so bad	네가 내 삶에 들어오기 전에 나는 널 아주 많이 그리워했어 나는 너를 아주 많이 그리워했어 나는 너를 아주, 아주 많이 그리워했어 네가 내 삶에 들어오기 전에 난 너를 아주 많이 그리워했어 그리고 너는 알아야 해 내가 너를 아주 아주 많이 그리워했다는 걸 • **bad** : 구어에서 **badly**(심하게)의 뜻으로 쓰임
( )'s ( )( )( ) right at you, baby, but here's my number, so call me maybe Hey, I just met you, and this is crazy, but here's my number, so call me maybe And all the other boys try to chase me, but here's my number, so call me maybe	널 똑바로 쳐다보는 것은 정말 힘들어 하지만 여기 내 번호가 있어, 그러니 전화해줄래 헤이, 난 방금 너를 만났고, 이건 말도 안 되는데 여기 내 번호 있어, 그러니 전화해줄래 다른 남자애들 모두가 나를 쫓아다니려고 애쓰고 있어, 하지만 여기 내 번호가 있어, 그러니 전화해줄래
Before you came into my life I missed you so bad I missed you so bad I missed you so, so bad Before you came into my life I missed you so bad And you should know that so call me maybe	네가 내 삶에 들어오기 전에 나는 널 아주 많이 그리워했어 나는 너를 아주 많이 그리워했어 나는 너를 아주, 아주 많이 그리워했어 네가 내 삶에 들어오기 전에 난 너를 아주 많이 그리워했어 그리고 너는 그걸 알아야 해 그러니 내게 전화해줄래

73 It ~ to … 가주어 진주어

It ~ to … 가주어 진주어란

- 주어로 쓰인 to 부정사가 긴 경우, it을 주어 자리에 쓰고, to 부정사 구문은 문장의 뒤로 보낸다. 이때 it을 '가주어', to 부정사 이하를 '진주어'라 한다.
- 진주어부터 해석하고 '가주어' it은 해석하지 않는다.

To keep the promise is important. → **It** is important **to keep the promise**.

(To keep the promise: 주어가 긴 경우 / It: 가주어 / to keep the promise: 진주어)

It의 여러 가지 쓰임

대명사	A: Where's your office? B: **It**'s on the third floor.
비인칭주어	A: I think we are late. Let's hurry. B: Relax. **It**'ll take only 10 minutes by taxi. We have enough time.
가주어	**It** is important to save money when we are young.

가사 예문

It's hard to look right at you.

널 똑바로 쳐다보는 것은 정말 힘들어.

Attention!

to 부정사의 의미상 주어 나타내기!

- 「for + 목적격」: 일반적으로 to 부정사 앞에 위치
- 「of + 목적격」: kind, nice, honest, careful, wise, foolish, rude, polite 등 사람의 성질을 나타내는 형용사가 올 경우 to 부정사 앞에 위치
- It is difficult **for me** to finish the work alone. (의미상 주어 for me)
- It is foolish **of you** to make the same mistake. (의미상 주어 of you)

Q1 다음 밑줄 친 it의 쓰임이 〈보기〉와 같은 것은? (답 2개)

〈보기〉 It is dangerous to drive a bike without a helmet.

① It is not easy to change our habits.

② I don't want to talk about it anymore.

③ We must go home. It's almost midnight.

④ It's over 200 miles from London to Manchester.

⑤ It was very kind of him to help my homework.

Q2 다음 우리말과 의미가 같도록 it을 사용하여 문장을 완성하시오.

1. 우리에게 새로운 언어를 배우는 것은 어렵다. (hard / for us / learn a new language)

→ ______________________________

2. 영화 보기 전에 휴대폰을 끄는 것이 필요하다. (necessary / turn off / before watching movie)

→ ______________________________

3. 네가 나를 위해 문을 잡아주는 것은 매우 예의바르다. (polite / of you / hold the door for me)

→ ______________________________

Fill in the Blank It, hard to look

Question 1 ①, ⑤

Question 2 **1.** It's hard for us to learn a new language. **2.** It is necessary to turn off the cell phone before watching movie. **3.** It is very polite of you to hold the door for me.

74	How deep is your love	Bee Gees

I know your eyes in the morning sun
I feel you touch me in the pouring rain
And the moment that you wander far from me
I wanna feel you in my arms again
And you come to me on a summer breeze
Keep me warm with your love
Then you softly leave
And (　)'(　)(　)(that) you need to show
How deep is your love

당신의 눈이 아침 햇살 속에 있는 걸 알아요
쏟아지는 빗속에서 그대 손길을 느껴요
그대가 나를 떠나 배회하는 순간에도
내 품에 안긴 당신을 다시 느끼고 싶어요
그대는 여름날의 산들바람처럼 내게 다가와
그대의 사랑으로 날 따뜻하게 감싸주고는
살며시 떠나죠
당신이 보여주어야 할 사람은 바로 나예요
그대의 사랑이 얼마나 깊은지

- **pour :** 비가 쏟아지다
- **wander :** 방황하다
- **breeze :** 산들바람

★ How deep is your love,
How deep is your love,
I really need to learn
Cause we're living in a world of fools breaking us down
When they all should let us be
We belong to you and me

그대의 사랑이 얼마나 깊은지,
그대의 사랑이 얼마나 깊은지,
난 정말로 알고 싶어요
왜냐하면 우리는 우리를 헤어지게 만드는
어리석은 이들의 세상에 살고 있으니까요
세상이 우리를 있는 그대로 내버려둘 때
우리는 서로에게 속하게 되죠

- **break down :** 무너뜨리다
- **let ~ be :** ~를 가만 놔두다
- **belong to~ :** ~에 속하다

I believe in you
You know the door to my very soul
You're the light in my deepest darkest hour
You're my savior when I fall
And you may not think I care for you when you know down inside that I really do
And (   )'(   )(   )(that) you need to show
How deep is your love

난 그대를 믿어요
그대는 내 영혼으로 통하는 문을 알고 있죠
그대는 내 가장 깊고 어두운 시간에 한 줄기 빛이죠
그대는 내가 쓰러질 때 나를 구원해주는 사람이죠
그대는 내가 그대를 좋아한다고 여기지 않을지도 몰라요 내가 진실로 그대를 깊이 좋아하고 있는지 알면서도
당신이 보여주어야 할 사람은 바로 나예요
그대의 사랑이 얼마나 깊은지

- savior : 구세주
- very : 바로 그
- care for~ : ~를 좋아하다

★ Repeat

And you come to me on a summer breeze
Keep me warm with your love
Then you softly leave
And (   )'(   )(   )(that) you need to show
How deep is your love

그대는 여름날의 산들바람처럼 내게 다가와
그대의 사랑으로 날 따뜻하게 감싸주고는 살며시 떠나죠
당신이 보여주어야 할 사람은 바로 나예요
그대의 사랑이 얼마나 깊은지

★ Repeat × 3

74 It is(was)~ that… 강조 구문

It is(was)~ that… 강조 구문이란

- It is(was)와 that 사이에 강조할 부분을 넣는다.
- 강조하는 대상에 따라 that 대신 who, whom, which, when, where 등의 관계대명사나 관계부사로 바꿔 쓸 수 있다.

I	met	Psy	at the club	yesterday.
① 주어		② 목적어	③ 장소	④ 시간부사

① 주어 강조	**It** was **I that** (who) met Psy at the club yesterday.
② 목적어 강조	**It** was **Psy that** (whom) I met at the club yesterday.
③ 장소 강조	**It** was **at the club that** (where) I met Psy yesterday.
④ 시간부사 강조	**It** was **yesterday that** (when) I met Psy at the club.

가사 예문

It's me (that) you need to show. How deep is your love.

그대가 보여주어야 할 사람은 바로 나예요. 그대의 사랑이 얼마나 깊은지.

Attention!

It ~ that… 구문에서 that은 생략이 되기도 한다.

It ~ that… 구문에서 동사는 강조할 수 없다.

Q1 다음 밑줄 친 부분을 강조하는 문장으로 바꿔 쓰시오.

1. Columbus discovered America in 1492.

→ ______________________________

2. I have loved Kelly since I was 10 years old.

→ ______________________________

3. The graduation ceremony was held last Friday.

→ ______________________________

4. I took this picture in front of the Louvre Museum.

→ ______________________________

Q2 다음 우리말과 의미가 같도록 괄호 안의 말을 이용하여 문장을 완성하시오.

1. 그들이 결혼한 해는 바로 2005년이었다. (in 2005 / get married)

→ ______________________________

2. 만유인력의 법칙을 발견한 사람은 바로 Newton이다. (find / the Law of Gravitation)

→ ______________________________

3. APEC 정상회담이 열렸던 곳이 바로 누리마루였다. (Nurimaru / APEC summit / take place in)

→ ______________________________

4. 나의 선생님이 이 프로젝트에서 강조하는 것은 바로 협력과 조화이다.
   (cooperation and harmony / emphasize / in this project)

→ ______________________________

Fill in the Blank It's me

Question 1

1. It was Columbus that (who) discovered America in 1492.
2. It is Kelly that (whom) I have loved since I was 10 years old.
3. It was last Friday that (when) the graduation ceremony was held.
4. It was in front of the Louvre Museum that (where) I took this picture.

Question 2

1. It was in 2005 that (when) they got married.
2. It is Newton that (who) found the Law of Gravitation.
3. It was Nurimaru that (where) APEC summit took place in.
4. It is cooperation and harmony that (which) my teacher emphasizes in this project.

75 Listen — Beyonce

Listen to the song here in my heart
A melody I started, but can't complete

내 마음에서부터 나오는 이 노래를 들어주세요
내가 시작했지만, 내가 끝낼 수는 없는 노래예요

- complete : ① 끝내다 ② 완전한

Listen to the sound from deep within
It's only beginning to find release
Oh, the time has come for my dreams to be heard
They will not be pushed aside and turned into your own
All 'cause you won't listen...

내 마음 깊은 곳에서부터 나오는 소리를 들어주세요
탈출구를 찾는 시작인 그 소리를
내 꿈에 귀를 기울여야 할 때가 오네요
내 꿈은 무시되지도 당신의 것이 되지도 않을 거예요
당신이 들으려 하지 않을 거니까요…

- release : ① 석방하다 ② 발표하다 ③ 방출 ④ 해방
- push aside : 밀쳐내다
- turn into~ : ~으로 변하다

☆ Listen, I am alone at a crossroads
I'm not at home in my own home
And I've tried and tried to say what's on my mind
You should have known

들어주세요, 난 중요한 기로에 혼자 서 있어요
난 내 것이 아닌 집에 있었죠
난 마음속에 있는 말을 하려고 노력하고 또 노력했어요
당신은 그걸 알았어야만 했어요

- at the crossroads : (중요한) 기로에 서 있는
- should have p.p(~) : ~했었어야 했다

★ Oh, now I'm done believing you
You don't know ①(   ) ( )'( ) (   )
I'm more than what you made of me
I followed the voice you gave to me
But now I gotta find my own

난 이제 당신을 믿지 않으려고 해요
당신은 내가 무슨 감정을 느끼는지 몰라요
난 당신이 만든 나보다 더 나은 존재예요
난 당신이 내게 준 소리를 따랐었지요
하지만 이제 나는 나 자신의 소리를 찾을 거예요

- done : 다 끝난, 완료된
- gotta : (구어) got to의 줄임말, 해야 한다

You should have listened There is someone here inside Someone I thought had died so long ago Oh, I'm screaming out, and my dreams will be heard They will not be pushed aside or worse into your own All 'cause you won't listen...	당신은 귀 기울였어야 했어요 이 안에 누군가가 있어요 나 자신조차 오래 전에 죽었다고 생각했던 누군가가 난 소리치고 있어요, 그리고 내 꿈이 들릴 거예요 내 꿈은 이제 무시되거나 당신 것으로 되지 않을 거예요 당신이 들으려 하지 않을 거니까요… • scream out : 고함치다

☆ Repeat

★ Repeat

I don't know ②( ) ( ) ( ) But I'll be moving on If you don't, if you won't...	난 지금 내가 어디에 속해있는지 모르겠어요 하지만 앞으로 나아가려고 해요 당신이 듣지 않고, 듣고 싶어 하지 않는다면… • move on : 옮기다, 넘어가다

Listen to the song here in my heart A melody I started, but I will complete	내 마음에서부터 나오는 이 노래를 들어주세요 내가 시작했지만 내가 끝맺을 거예요

★ Repeat

75 간접의문문

간접의문문이란

- 의문문이 문장의 일부로 포함되어 쓰일 때, 이것을 간접의문문이라고 한다.
- 주로 Do you know~?, I (don't) know~, Tell me~, I wonder~ 등과 같은 어구와 함께 쓰이며 문장의 주어, 목적어, 보어로 쓰인다.

간접의문문의 어순

1. 의문사가 있는 간접의문문	의문사가 있는 의문문이 다른 문장의 일부로 포함될 때, **「의문사 + 주어 + 동사」**로 바뀐다. - "Could you tell me?" + "What time is it?" →"Could you tell me **what time it is**?" - I asked him + "What did she say?" → I asked him **what she said**.
2. 의문사가 없는 간접의문문	의문사가 없는 의문문이 다른 문장의 일부로 포함될 때, **if / whether (~인지 아닌지) + 주어 + 동사**로 바뀐다. - "Do you know?" + "Is she married?" → "Do you know **if (whether) she is married**?" - I asked him + "Did you pass the exam?" → I asked him **if (whether) he passed the exam**.
3. 의문사가 있는 의문문과 Do you think? 등이 결합된 간접의문문	의문사가 있는 의문문에 Do you think?, Do you believe?, Do you suppose?, Do you guess? 등이 결합되어 간접의문문을 만들 때는 **의문사가 맨 앞으로 이동**한다. - "Do you think?" + "What does it mean?" → "**What** do you think **it means**?" - "Do you guess?" + "Where did he go yesterday?" → "**Where** do you guess **he went** yesterday?"

가사 예문

You don't know what I'm feeling.
당신은 내가 무슨 감정을 느끼는지 몰라요.

I don't know where I belong.
난 지금 내가 어디에 속해있는지 모르겠어요.

Q1 다음 두 문장을 한 문장으로 만들 때 빈칸에 알맞은 말을 쓰시오.

1. I wonder. + How much is it?

→ ______________________________

2. Can you tell me? + What time is it?

→ ______________________________

3. I don't know. + Where does she live?

→ ______________________________

4. I am not sure. + Is she interested in me?

→ ______________________________

5. Do you think? + Who is the most popular singer in Korea?

→ ______________________________

6. Do you believe? + What is the most important thing in your life?

→ ______________________________

Q2 다음 우리말과 의미가 같도록 괄호 안의 단어들을 배열하여 문장을 완성하시오.

1. 어느 팀이 그 경기에서 이겼는지 나에게 말해줄 수 있니? (won / the game / which team)

→ Can you tell me ______________________________?

2. 내일 비가 올지 궁금하다. (tomorrow / whether / will / it / rain)

→ I wonder ______________________________.

3. 나는 그녀의 전화번호를 알고 싶어. (her / is / phone number / what)

→ I want to know ______________________.

4. 나는 그가 결과에 만족하는지 확실치 않아. (he / if / is / with / satisfied / the result)

→ I am not sure ______________________.

5. 몇 시에 그 가게 문이 연다고 추측하니? (guess / do / you / what time)

→ ______________________ the store opens?

6. 그곳에 도착하는 데 얼마나 걸릴 거라고 생각하니? (you / do / think / how long)

→ ______________________ it will take to get there?

7. 나는 올림픽 개막식에서 누가 노래를 부를지 궁금해.
(at the opening ceremony / is going to / who / sing / of the Olympics)

→ I wonder ______________________.

Q3 다음 문장을 어법상 알맞게 고쳐 다시 쓰시오.

1. Do you think where is Jessica from?

→ ______________________

2. Can you tell me where you did get the money?

→ ______________________

3. Do you think whether will he apply for the company?

→ ______________________

Fill in the Blank ① what I'm feeling ② where I belong

Question 1 **1.** I wonder how much it is. **2.** Can you tell me what time it is? **3.** I don't know where she lives. **4.** I am not sure if (whether) she is interested in me. **5.** Who do you think the most popular singer is in Korea? **6.** What do you believe the most important thing is in your life?

Question 2 **1.** which team won the game **2.** whether it will rain tomorrow **3.** what her phone number is **4.** if he is satisfied with the result **5.** What time do you guess **6.** How long do you think **7.** who is going to sing at the opening ceremony of the Olympics

Question 3 **1.** Where do you think Jessica is from? **2.** Can you tell me where you got the money? **3.** Do you think whether he will apply for the company?

76 You raise me up

Westlife

*작사: Brendan Graham, 작곡: Rolf Lovland

When I am down and oh my soul so weary,
When troubles come and my heart burdened be,
Then I am still and wait here in the silence
Until you come and sit awhile with me

내 마음이 우울하고 내 영혼이 지칠 때,
고통이 밀려와서 나의 마음이 번민으로 가득할 때,
나는 여기서 가만히 당신을 기다릴 거예요
당신이 오셔서 내 곁에 자리하실 때까지

- When~ : ① 언제 ② ~할 때
- down : 우울한
- weary : 지친
- burden : 부담감
- still : 정지한
- awhile : 잠시

You (   ) me (   ), so I can stand on mountains
You (   ) me (   ) to walk on stormy seas
I am strong when I am on your shoulders
You (   ) me (   ) to more than I can be

당신이 나를 일으켜주시기에, 나는 산에 우뚝 서 있을 수 있고
당신이 나를 일으켜주시기에 나는 폭풍의 바다도 건널 수 있습니다
당신이 나를 떠받쳐줄 때 나는 강인해집니다
당신은 나를 일으켜 나보다 더 큰 내가 되게 합니다

- raise somebody up : ~를 일으켜 세우다
- stormy : 폭풍우의
- more than~ : ~보다 더

You (   ) me (   ), so I can stand on mountains
You (   ) me (   ) to walk on stormy seas
I am strong when I am on your shoulders
You (   ) me (   ) to more than I can be

당신이 나를 일으켜주시기에, 나는 산에 우뚝 서 있을 수 있고
당신이 나를 일으켜주시기에 나는 폭풍의 바다도 건널 수 있습니다
당신이 나를 떠받쳐줄 때 나는 강인해집니다
당신은 나를 일으켜 나보다 더 큰 내가 되게 합니다

You raise me up, so I can stand on mountains You raise me up to walk on stormy seas I am strong when I am on your shoulders You raise me up to more than I can be	당신이 나를 일으켜주시기에, 나는 산에 우뚝 서 있을 수 있고 당신이 나를 일으켜주시기에 나는 폭풍의 바다도 건널 수 있습니다 당신이 나를 떠받쳐줄 때 나는 강인해집니다 당신은 나를 일으켜 나보다 더 큰 내가 되게 합니다

You raise me up, so I can stand on mountains You raise me up to walk on stormy seas I am strong when I am on your shoulders You raise me up to more than I can be	당신이 나를 일으켜주시기에, 나는 산에 우뚝 서 있을 수 있고 당신이 나를 일으켜주시기에 나는 폭풍의 바다도 건널 수 있습니다 당신이 나를 떠받쳐줄 때 나는 강인해집니다 당신은 나를 일으켜 나보다 더 큰 내가 되게 합니다

You raise me up to more than I can be	당신은 나를 일으켜 나보다 더 큰 내가 되게 합니다

76 구동사 1

구동사란

- 구동사(phrasal verb)란 두 개 이상의 어휘가 구(phrase)를 이루어 하나의 동사처럼 기능하는 것을 말한다.
- '일어나다'라는 의미로 말하기 위해서 동사 get과 up을 함께 썼으며 이때, get up은 구동사이다.

구동사	예문
get up : 일어나다	What time do you usually **get up** in the morning?
give up : 포기하다	It wasn't easy for him, but he didn't **give up**.
calm down : 진정하다	Listening to a nice music can help you **calm down**.
show up : 나타나다	I arrived on time for the meeting, but no one **showed up**.
fall off : 떨어지다	Be careful! You might **fall off** the ladder.
come back : 돌아오다	They **came back** to their nests after the storms had passed.
run away : 달아나다	If a stranger offers you a ride somewhere, say 'No' and **run away**.
work out : (일이) 잘 풀리다 / 운동하다	Things didn't **work out** as I had hoped in the final round. Many people decide to **work out** regularly in the New Year.

가사 예문

You raise me up, so I can stand on mountains.

당신이 나를 일으켜 주시기에, 나는 산에 우뚝 서 있을 수 있습니다.

You raise me up to walk on stormy seas.

당신이 나를 일으켜 주시기에 나는 폭풍의 바다도 건널 수 있습니다.

Attention!

구동사 뒤에 전치사를 함께 써서 목적어를 취할 수 있다!

- That's the limit. I decided to **break up with** him.
- Don't be nervous. If you **get along with** new friends, everything will go well!

Q1 다음 주어진 구동사를 사용하여 문장을 완성하시오. (필요한 경우 동사 변형)

〈보기〉 watch out give in break down look around

1. Someone called my name, and I ______________.
2. ______________! A city bus is in front of your car.
3. He could not hand in his report because his computer ______________.
4. We tried to win the battle, but after several hours we just ______________.

Q2 다음 우리말과 의미가 같도록 괄호 안의 말을 이용하여 빈칸에 알맞은 말을 쓰시오.

1. 한 달에 몇 번 외식하니? (How many times, eat out)

→ ______________________________

2. 난 커서 신경과 의사가 되고 싶어. (neurologist, grow up)

→ ______________________________

3. 기다리시겠습니까, 나중에 다시 거시겠습니까? (hold on, call back later)

→ ______________________________

4. 그녀는 강의 후에 친구들하고 커피숍에서 시간을 보낸다. (hang out with, after the lecture)

→ ______________________________

Fill in the Blank raise up

Question 1 **1.** looked around **2.** Watch out **3.** broke down **4.** gave in

Question 2 **1.** How many times do you eat out? **2.** I want to be a neurologist when I grow up.
3. Would you hold on or call back later?
4. She hangs out with her friends in a coffee shop after the lecture.

77 Wake me up before you go go | Wham

Jitterbug Jitterbug
Jitterbug Jitterbug

지르박 춤을 춥시다 지르박 춤을 추어요
지르박 춤을 춥시다 지르박 춤을 추어요

- Jitterbug : ① 지르박
  (1940년대 유행하던 빠른 춤)
  ② 지르박을 추다
  ③ 신경질적인 사람

You put the boom-boom into my heart
You send my soul sky high when your loving starts
A Jitterbug into my brain
It goes bang-bang-bang till my feet do the same

당신이 나에게 사랑을 표현할 때
당신은 내 마음을 쿵쾅거리게 하고
나의 영혼을 하늘 높이 보내죠
지르박이 내 머릿속으로 들어와
쾅쾅쾅 울렸어요
나의 발까지 똑같이 '쾅' 하고 터져버릴 것 같았죠

- boom : ① 쿵 하고 울리는 소리 ② 호황
- go bang : 쾅 하고 울리다

But something's bugging me
Something ain't right
My best friend told me what you did last night
You left me sleeping in my bed
I was dreaming but I should have been with you instead

그러나 무언가가 나를 괴롭히고 있어요
무언가가 잘못되고 있는 거예요
나의 가장 친한 친구가 당신이 어젯밤 무얼 했는지 나에게 말해주었어요
당신은 침대에서 자는 나를 두고 떠나버렸어요
난 꿈을 꾸고 있었지만 난 당신과 함께 있었어야 했어요

- bug : ① 벌레 ② 괴롭히다
- should have been : 있어야 했다

★( )( )( ) before you go-go
Don't leave me hanging on like a yoyo yoyo
( )( )( ) before you go-go
I don't wanna miss it when you hit that high
( )( )( ) before you go-go
'Cause I'm not planning on going solo
( )( )( ) before you go-go
Take me dancing tonight

당신이 떠나기 전에 나를 깨워주세요
요요처럼 매달리는 나를 떠나지 마세요
당신이 떠나기 전에 나를 깨워주세요
난 당신이 주목받는 것을 놓치고 싶지 않아요
당신이 떠나기 전에 나를 깨워주세요
왜냐하면 난 혼자가 되고 싶은 생각이 없으니까요
당신이 떠나기 전에 나를 깨워주세요
오늘밤 나와 춤을 춰요

I wanna hit that high
yeah yeah

나도 그렇게 주목받고 싶어요
예 예

You put the grey skies out of my way
You make the sun shine brighter than Doris Day
You turned a bright spark into a flame (yeah, yeah)
My beats per minute never been the same
'Cause you're my lady I'm your fool
It makes me crazy when you act so cruel
Come on baby, let's not fight
We'll go dancing
Everything will be alright

당신은 내 앞길을 막고 있는 회색빛 하늘을 걷어주고
당신은 Doris Day보다 더 화창한 햇빛을 비춰주었어요
밝은 섬광을 활활 타오르는 불꽃으로 바꿔주었지요 (예, 예)
내 심장 박동이 예전같지 않아요
당신이 내 여인이 되었으니 난 당신의 바보예요
당신이 내게 잔인하게 행동할 때면 난 화가 나죠
부탁인데 그대여, 우리 싸우지 말고
춤추러 가는 거예요
모든 것이 괜찮아질 거예요

- **Doris Day** : 1960년대 미국 인기 영화배우이자 가수
- **turn A into B** : A를 B로 바꾸다
- **cruel** : 잔인한

★ Repeat

I wanna hit that high yeah yeah	나도 그렇게 주목받고 싶어요 예 예
Jitterbug Jitterbug	지르박 춤을 춥시다 지르박 춤을 추어요
Cuddle up, baby Move in tight We'll go dancing tomorrow night It's cold out there but it's warm in bed They can dance We'll stay at home instead	꽉 껴안아줄 테니, 그대여 꼭 안겨보세요 우리는 내일 밤에 춤추러 가요 바깥은 춥지만 침대 속은 따뜻하지요 그들은 춤추지만 우리는 그 대신 집에 머물러요 • cuddle up : 꼭 껴안다 • instead : 대신에
Jitterbug	지르박 춤을 춥시다

★ Repeat × 2

77 구동사 2

구동사의 특징

• 구동사는 목적어와 함께 쓰일 수 있는데, 명사인 목적어는 구동사의 가운데 또는 뒤에 위치할 수 있다.

구동사	예문		
turn on ~ : ~을 켜다	Please **turn on the TV**.	또는	Please **turn the TV on**.
turn off ~ : ~을 끄다	He **turned off the computer**.		He **turned the computer off**.
put on ~ : ~을 입다	She **put on the jacket**.		She **put the jacket on**.
take off ~ : ~을 벗다	Would you **take off your hat**?		Would you **take your hat off**?
put off ~ : ~을 연기하다	They **put off the meeting**.		They **put the meeting off**.
try on ~ : ~을 입어보다	Can I **try on those shoes**?		Can I **try those shoes on**?
throw away ~ : ~을 버리다	Don't **throw away a cigarette butt** on the floor.		Don't **throw a cigarette butt away** on the floor.

가사 예문

Wake me up before you go go. Don't leave me hanging on like a yoyo yoyo.
당신이 떠나기 전에 나를 깨워주세요. 요요처럼 매달리는 나를 떠나지 마세요.

Attention!

구동사의 목적어로 명사가 아닌 it, them 등의 대명사를 쓰는 경우에는 구동사의 가운데 위치시키고 뒤에 쓰지 않는 것에 유의!

- **Wake me up** before you go go. (O) / **Wake up me** before you go go. (X)

Q1 다음 주어진 구동사를 사용하여 문장을 완성하시오.

〈보기〉	let down	fill out	call off	ask out

1. He didn't ____________ his trip, he just postponed it.
2. Don't forget to ____________ the form before handing it.
3. Why don't you ______ her ______ if you like her so much?
4. I will try my best this time. I don't want to ______ you ______.

Q2 문맥에 어울리도록 주어진 표현들을 배열하여 문장을 완성하시오. (대문자에 유의)

1. I'm so depressed. (my ex-girlfriend / over / I / get / can't /.)

→ ____

2. She's a good musician, but (to show / off / likes / her talents / too much / she /.)

→ ____

3. This is a sensitive situation. (let me / over / it / think) before giving my answer.

→ ____

4. You don't have to look up the dictionary. You can use context (to figure / the word meaning / out /.)

→ ____

Fill in the Blank Wake me up

Question 1 **1.** call off **2.** fill out **3.** ask out **4.** let down

Question 2
1. I can't get my ex-girlfriend over. / I can't get over my ex-girlfriend.
2. She likes to show off her talents too much. / She likes to show her talents off too much.
3. Let me think it over
4. to figure out the word meaning. / to figure the word meaning out.

78	Because you loved me	Celine Dion

For all those times you stood by me
For all the truth that you made me see
For all the joy you brought to my life
For all the wrong that you made right
For every dream you made come true
For all the love I found in you
I'll be forever thankful, baby

당신이 내 곁에 함께했던 그 모든 시간들
당신이 내게 일깨워준 그 모든 진실들
당신이 내 삶에 가져다준 그 모든 기쁨들
당신이 바로잡아 주었던 그 모든 잘못들
당신이 실현될 수 있게 해준 모든 꿈들
당신에게서 발견했던 그 모든 사랑
난 영원히 고마워할 거예요, 그대여

- **make ~ :** (사역동사로) ~하게 하다

You're the one who held me up
Never let me fall
You're the one who saw me through
through it all

당신은 나를 지켜주었던 유일한 사람입니다
절대로 나를 쓰러지게 하지 않았어요
당신은 나를 꿰뚫어보던 한 사람입니다
나의 전부를

- **hold up :** 지키다
- **see through :** 간파하다
- **let ~ :** (사역동사로) ~하게 하다

★ You ①(　　) my strength when
I (　　) weak
You ②(　　) my voice when I
(　　　　) speak
You ②(　　) my eyes when I
(　　　　) see
You ③(　　) the best there (　　) in me
④(　　) me up when I (　　　　) reach

당신은 내가 힘들 때 내게 힘이 되어주었죠
당신은 내가 말할 수 없을 때 나의 목소리가
되었죠
당신은 내가 볼 수 없을 때 나의 눈이 되었죠
당신은 내 안의 좋은 점들만 보았죠
내가 닿을 수 없을 때 나를 일으켜주었죠

You ⑤(   ) me faith 'coz you
(   )
I'm everything I am because
you loved me

당신은 믿었기에 내게 믿음을 주었어요
지금의 내 모습 전부는 당신이 날 사랑했기
때문에 존재하는 거예요

- faith : 믿음
- 'coz = because

You ⑥(   ) me wings and (   ) me
fly
You ⑦(   ) my hand I (   )
touch the sky
I ⑧(   ) my faith, you (   ) it back to
me
You ⑨(   ) no star (   ) out of reach
You ⑩(   ) by me and I (   ) tall
I ⑪(   ) your love I (   ) it all
I'm grateful for each day you gave me
Maybe I don't know that much
But I know, this much is true
I ⑫(   ) blessed because I (   ) loved
by you

당신은 내게 날개를 주고 날 수 있게 해주었죠
당신은 내 손이 하늘에 닿을 수 있게 해주었죠
내가 믿음을 잃었을 때, 당신은 다시
찾아주었고요
당신은 손에 닿지 않는 별은 없다고 했어요
당신이 내 곁에 있어서 난 당당할 수 있었어요
난 당신의 사랑을 가졌어요 그 사랑 전부를요
당신이 내게 준 하루하루에 대해서 난 감사해요
아마도 내가 아는 게 많지는 않지만
알아요, 이게 진실이라는 걸
난 축복받은 거죠 내가 당신의 사랑을
받았으니까요

- stand by : 지지하다
- stand tall : 자신을 가지고 일어서다
- be grateful for~ : ~를 고맙게 여기다
- be blessed : 축복받다
- be loved by~ : ~에 의해 사랑받다

★ Repeat

You were always there for me
The tender wind that carried me
A light in the dark shining your love
into my life
You've been my inspiration
Through the lies you were the truth
My world is a better place
because of you

당신은 항상 나를 위해 그곳에 있었어요
당신은 나를 이끌어준 부드러운
바람이었어요
당신은 내 삶에 당신의 사랑을 비추는
어둠 속의 빛이었어요
당신은 나의 영감이었어요
거짓 속에 당신은 진실이었어요
내 삶은 당신으로 인해 더 나아졌죠

- **shine A into B:** A를 B에 비추다
- **inspiration :** 영감

★ Repeat × 2

I'm everything I am
Because you loved me

지금의 내 모습 전부는
당신이 날 사랑했기 때문에 존재하는
거예요

78 시제 일치

시제의 일치란

- 주절의 시제에 따라서 종속절의 시제를 맞추어주는 것을 말한다.

주절의 시제	종속절의 시제	예문
현재	어떠한 시제라도 가능	- I think he was true. (O) - I think he had been true. (O) - I think he is true. (O) - I think he will be true. (O)
과거시제	과거 또는 과거완료시제만 가능	- I thought he was true. (O) - I thought he had been true. (O) - I thought he is true. (X) - I thought he will be true. (X)

가사 예문

You were my strength when I was weak.

당신은 내가 힘들 때 내게 힘이 되어줬죠.

Attention!

시제 일치의 예외를 알아둘 것!

- 종속절의 내용이 **불변의 진리, 속담, 격언, 현재의 습관** 등을 나타낼 때는 주절의 시제와 상관없이 **종속절에는 항상 현재시제** 사용
- Columbus **believed** that the earth **is** round.
  (→ 종속절이 '지구가 둥글다'는 불변의 진리이므로, 현재시제로 표현)
- My father always **said** that the early bird **catches** the worm.
  (→ 종속절이 '일찍 일어나는 새가 벌레를 잡는다'는 속담이므로, 현재시제로 표현)

Q1 다음 문장의 괄호 안에서 알맞은 것을 고르시오.

1. I believed he (is / was) honest.
2. He didn't think anyone (will believe / would believe) him.
3. Mark told me that he (took / takes) a shower three times a day.
4. My homeroom teacher said that every cloud (has / had) a silver lining.

Q2 주어진 우리말과 같도록 빈칸에 알맞은 표현을 쓰시오.

1. 나는 그들이 몰래 연애하고 있다는 것을 눈치챘다. (be)

→ I noticed that they secretly ________ in love with each other.

2. 너는 온실 가스가 지구 온난화를 야기할 거란 것을 아니? (cause)

→ Do you know that greenhouse gases ________ ________ global warming?

3. 그녀는 일을 떠나기로 결심하기 전에 매우 곰곰이 생각했다. (decide)

→ She thought very hard before she ________ to leave her job.

4. 과학시간에 우리는 물이 섭씨 100도에서 끓는 것을 배웠다. (boil)

→ In science class, we learned that water ________ at 100 degree celsius.

Q3 다음 문장의 주절의 시제가 바뀔 때, 빈칸에 알맞은 표현을 쓰시오.

1. My professor tells us where there is a will, there is a way.

→ My professor told us ______________________________.

2. I guess from his expression that he already knows about the accident.

→ I guessed from his expression that ______________________________.

Fill in the Blank ① were, was ② were, couldn't ③ saw, was ④ lifted, couldn't ⑤ gave, believed ⑥ gave, made ⑦ touched, could ⑧ lost, gave ⑨ said, was ⑩ stood, stood ⑪ had, had ⑫ was, was

Question 1 **1.** was **2.** would believe **3.** takes **4.** has

Question 2 **1.** were **2.** will cause **3.** decided **4.** boils

Question 3 **1.** where there is a will, there is a way **2.** he already knew(had known) about the accident

79	If I had a million dollars	Barenaked Ladies

If I ①(　　) a million dollars,
Well, I ②(　　　)(　　) you a house
If I ①(　　) a million dollars,
I ②(　　　)(　　) you furniture
for your house
Maybe a nice Chesterfield or
an Ottoman
If I ①(　　) a million dollars,
Well, I ②(　　　)(　　) you a K-car
A nice reliant automobile
If I ①(　　) a million dollars,
I ②(　　　)(　　) your love

내가 만약 백만 달러가 있다면,
네게 집을 한 채 사줄 텐데
내가 만약 백만 달러가 있다면,
너의 집에 들어갈 가구를 사줄 텐데
멋진 체스터필드나 오토맨(가구명) 같은 거 말이지
내가 만약 백만 달러가 있다면,
네게 K-car를 사줄 텐데
멋지고 믿을 만한 차
내가 만약 백만 달러가 있다면,
너의 사랑을 살 텐데

- million : 백만
- reliant : 믿을 만한
- K-car : 크라이슬러 사의 고급차
- automobile : 자동차

If I ①(　　) a million dollars,
I ③(　　　)(　　　) a tree fort in our yard
If I ①(　　) a million dollars,
You could help, it wouldn't be that hard
If I ①(　　) a million dollars,
Maybe we ④(　　　)(　　) a little tiny
fridge in there somewhere
You know, we could just go up there
and hang out like open the fridge and
stuff
There'd already be foods laid out for us

내가 만약 백만 달러가 있다면,
우리 정원에 나무로 요새를 지을 텐데
내가 만약 백만 달러가 있다면,
네가 요새 만드는 데 날 좀 도와줄 수 있겠지, 그렇게 힘들진 않을 거야
내가 만약 백만 달러가 있다면,
작고 조그만 냉장고 하나쯤 그 요새 어딘가에 들여놓을 수 있을 텐데
있잖아, 우린 거기 올라가서 냉장고랑 그런 것들을 열고 즐거운 시간을 보낼 수 있을 텐데
거기엔 이미 우리가 함께 먹을 음식들이 쫙 깔려 있을 거야

Like little pre-wrapped sausages and things, Um
They have pre-wrapped sausages,
but they don't have pre-wrapped bacon
Well, Can you blame them? Uh, Yeah!

작은 포장 소시지 뭐 그런 거 말야. 음…
소시지는 바로 그냥 먹을 수 있게 미리 싸놓은 건 있는데, 베이컨은 그냥 먹을 수 있게 포장해 놓은 게 없대
짜증나지? 그래, 맞아!

- fort : 요새
- tiny = small
- fridge : 냉장고 = refrigerator
- hang out : 놀다
- stuff : 물건
- pre-wrapped : 미리 포장해놓은

If I ①(   ) a million dollars,
I ②(   )(   ) you a fur coat
But not a real fur coat, that's cruel
If I ①(   ) a million dollars,
Well, I ②(   )(   ) you an exotic pet
Yep, like a llama or an emu
If I ①(   ) a million dollars,
Well, I ②(   )(   ) you John Merrick's remains
Ooh, all them crazy elephant bones
If I ①(   ) a million dollars,
I ②(   )(   ) your love

내가 만약 백만 달러가 있다면,
네게 모피코트를 사줄 텐데
하지만 진짜 모피코트는 안 돼, 너무 잔인하잖아
내가 만약 백만 달러가 있다면,
네게 이국적인 애완동물을 사줄 텐데
라마나 에뮤 같은 것 말이지
내가 만약 백만 달러가 있다면,
John Merrick의 유물들을 사줄 텐데
그 괴상한 상아로 만든 것들 있잖아
내가 만약 백만 달러가 있다면,
너의 사랑을 살 텐데

- cruel : 잔인한
- exotic : 이국적인
- remains : 유물

If I ①(   ) a million dollars,
We ⑤(   )(   )(   ) walk to the store
If I ①(   ) a million dollars,
I ⑥(   )(   ) a limousine

내가 만약 백만 달러가 있다면,
가게까지 걸어가지 않아도 될 텐데
내가 만약 백만 달러가 있다면,
리무진을 타고 다닐 텐데

cause it costs more
If I ①(   ) a million dollars,
We ⑤(   )(   )(   ) eat Kraft dinner
But we ⑦(   )(   ) Kraft dinner
Of course, we would, we'd just eat more
And buy really expensive ketchups with it
That's right, all the fanciest
Dijon ketchups, Um~!

왜냐면 비싸잖아
내가 만약 백만 달러가 있다면,
우린 kraft 저녁을 먹지 않아도 될 텐데
하지만 그래도 우린 Kraft 저녁을 먹을 거잖아
당연하지, 더 많이 먹을 수 있겠지
진짜 비싼 케첩을 뿌려 먹겠지
맞아, 가장 끝내주는 디종 케첩, 흠~!

- **Kraft dinner :** 저렴한 인스턴트 음식의 대표 브랜드
- **fanciest :** 가장 고급스러운

If I ①(   ) a million dollars,
Well, I'd buy you a green dress
But not a real green dress, that's cruel
If I ①(   ) a million dollars,
Well, I ②(   )(   ) you some art
A Picasso or a Garfunkel
If I ①(   ) a million dollars,
Well, ②(   )(   ) you a monkey
Haven't you always wanted a monkey?
If I ①(   ) a million dollars,
I ②(   )(   ) your love
If I ①(   ) a million dollars,
I ⑧(   )(   ) rich

만약 내가 백만 달러가 있다면,
네게 녹색 드레스를 한 벌 사줄 텐데
하지만 진짜 녹색 드레스는 안 돼
그건 너무 잔인하잖아
내가 만약 백만 달러가 있다면,
예술 작품을 좀 사줄 텐데
피카소의 작품이나 아님 가펑클의 것으로
내가 만약 백만 달러가 있다면,
네게 원숭이를 사줄 텐데
너 항상 원숭이 하나 원하지 않았어?
내가 만약 백만 달러가 있다면,
너의 사랑을 살 텐데
만약 내게 백만 달러가 있다면,
난 부자가 될 텐데

- **cruel :** 잔인한
- **Haven't you always wanted~? :** 과거에서 지금까지 항상 ~ 원하지 않았니? (현재완료)

79 가정법 과거

가정법 과거란

- 현재 사실에 반대되는 가정을 나타낸다.
- If절의 동사가 be동사인 경우, 주어의 인칭과 수에 상관없이 were를 주로 쓴다.

〈형태〉 If + 주어 + 동사의 과거형(~), 주어 + 조동사의 과거형(would / could / should / might) + 동사원형(…)

〈뜻〉 만약 ~한다면, …할 텐데 (속뜻 : ~하지 않아서 …할 수 없다)

가정법	- If I **had** enough money, I **could buy** her the dress. 내게 돈이 많다면, 그녀에게 그 드레스를 사줄 텐데.
직설법	= As I don't have enough money, I can't buy her the dress. 속뜻 : 내가 충분한 돈이 없기 때문에, 그녀에게 그 드레스를 사줄 수 없음

가사 예문

If I had a million dollars, I would buy you a house.

만약 내가 백만 달러가 있다면, 너에게 집을 사줄 텐데.

Attention!

단순 조건절과 가정법 과거의 차이!

실제로 가능한 일을 가정할 때는 단순 조건절을,

가능성이 희박하거나 불가능한 일을 가정할 때는 가정법 과거를 쓴다.

- If it **rains** tomorrow, our field trip **will** be cancelled. - 단순 조건절 (현실 가능)
- If I **won** the lottery, I **would** travel around the world. - 가정법 과거 (가능성 희박)

Q1 다음 두 문장의 의미가 같도록 〈보기〉와 같이 빈칸에 알맞은 말을 쓰시오.

〈보기〉 If I were rich, I could travel around the world.
→ As I **am not** rich, I **cannot travel** around the world.

1. If I were a bird, I could fly to you.

→ As I ______ ______ a bird, I ______ ______ ______ to you.

2. If I were over 18, I could drive a car.

→ As I ______ ______ over 18, I ______ ______ ______ a car.

3. If I had more time in LA, I could visit Hollywood.

→ As I ______ ______ more time in LA, I ______ ______ ______ Hollywood.

Q2 우리말과 일치하도록 괄호 안에 주어진 단어를 이용하여 문장을 완성하시오.

1. 만약 내가 차가 있다면, 내가 너를 태워줄 텐데. (have a car / give you a ride)

→ ______________________________

2. 내가 프랑스어를 구사한다면, 파리를 여행할 텐데. (speak French / travel Paris)

→ ______________________________

3. 내가 만일 판사라면, 그 나쁜 사람을 처벌할 텐데. (be a judge / punish that bad guy)

→ ______________________________

4. 내가 너라면, 그녀를 위해서 깜짝파티를 열어줄 텐데. (be you / throw a surprise party for her)

→ ______________________________

Fill in the Blank ① had ② would buy ③ would build ④ could put ⑤ wouldn't have to ⑥ would take ⑦ would eat ⑧ would be

Question 1 **1.** am not, can not fly **2.** am not, can not drive **3.** don't have, can not visit

Question 2 **1.** If I had a car, I would(could) give you a ride.
2. If I spoke French, I would(could) travel Paris.
3. If I were a judge, I would(could) punish that bad guy.
4. If I were you, I would(could) throw a surprise party for her.

80	Lucky	Jason Mraz & Colbie Caillat

Do you hear me? I'm talking to you
Across the water, across the deep blue ocean
Under the open sky, oh my, baby I'm trying

내 얘기 들려요? 당신에게 말하고 있어요
강을 건너고, 깊고 푸른 바다를 건너
탁 트인 하늘 아래서, 당신에게 말하고 있어요

- across : ~을 건너서

Boy, I hear you in my dreams
I feel your whisper across the sea
I keep you with me in my heart
You make it easier when life gets hard

그대여, 꿈속에서 난 당신의 얘기가 들려요
바다를 건너 당신의 속삭임을 느끼죠
난 당신을 내 마음속에 간직해요
당신은 삶이 힘들 때 날 위로해주죠

- whisper : ① 속삭이다 ② 속삭임
- make it easy : 편하게 하다

☆ Lucky I'm in love with my best friend
Lucky to have been where I have been
Lucky to be coming home again

내 가장 가까운 친구와 사랑에 빠진 건 행운이에요
내가 그곳에 있었던 것은 행운이에요
집에 다시 돌아온 건 행운이에요

They don't know how long it takes waiting for a love like this
Every time we say goodbye
I (   )(   )(   ) one more kiss
I wait for you, I promise you, I will

이런 사랑이 찾아오기까지 얼마나 오랜 시간이 걸리는지 사람들은 모르죠
우리가 작별인사를 할 때마다
난 우리가 한 번 더 입맞춤하기를 원해요
난 당신을 기다려요, 약속해요, 그럴게요

☆ Repeat

★ Lucky we're in love in every way
Lucky to have stayed where we have stayed
Lucky to be coming home someday

우리가 사랑에 푹 빠진 건 행운이에요
우리가 이렇게 예전처럼 머물러서 행운이에요
언젠가 집에 돌아오게 되는 건 행운이에요

And so I'm sailing through the sea
to an island where we'll meet
You'll hear the music, fill the air
I'll put a flower in your hair

그래서 난 바다를 건너 항해를 하고 있어요
우리가 만날 섬으로 가고 있죠
당신은 음악을 듣게 될 거고, 하늘을 가득 채울 거예요
당신의 머리에 꽃을 꽂아줄게요

- **through~** : ~을 통해

And though the breezes through trees
move so pretty, you're all I see
As the world keeps spinning round
You hold me right here right now

나무 사이로 산들바람이 기분 좋게 불어와도
당신이 내가 보는 전부예요
세상이 계속 돌아가고
당신은 바로 여기서 지금 나를 안아주죠

- **though~** : 비록 ~하지만
- **breeze** : 산들바람

☆ Repeat

★ Repeat

80 I wish 구문

I wish + 주어 + 동사의 과거

• 상황이 현재와 다르기를 바란다고 말할 때 「I wish + 주어 + 과거시제」를 쓴다.

〈형태〉 I wish + 주어 + **동사의 과거형** ~ (be동사의 경우 were)
〈뜻〉 ~하면 좋을 텐데

I wish + 주어 + 과거형	I share a room with my older sister. **I wish I had** my own room. 나는 언니와 방을 같이 쓴다. 내 방을 가지면 좋을 텐데.
속뜻	→ I am sorry that I don't have my own room. 내가 나의 방을 가지지 못해서 유감이다.

I wish + 주어 + 동사의 과거완료

• 상황이 과거와 달랐기를 바란다고 말할 때 「I wish + 주어 + 과거완료시제」를 쓴다.

〈형태〉 I wish + 주어 + **동사의 과거완료형** ~
〈뜻〉 ~했다면 좋았을 텐데

I wish + 주어 + 과거완료	The traffic is bumper to bumper on the road. **I wish we had taken** another road. (bumper to bumper : 차가 꽉 막힌) 길에 차가 꽉 막혀있어. 우리가 다른 길을 택했어야 하는데….
속뜻	→ I am sorry that we did not take another road. 우리가 다른 길을 택하지 못했던 것이 유감이다.

가사 예문

Every time we say goodbye, I wish we had one more kiss.

우리가 헤어질 때마다, 나는 우리가 한 번 더 입맞춤을 하기를 원해요.

Q1 다음 괄호 안에 주어진 동사를 이용하여 문장을 완성하시오.

1. I wish I ________________ your conversation but I did. (not overhear)
2. I wish I ________________ a house of my own however humble it might be. (have) (however humble it might be : 아무리 누추하다 할지라도)
3. I wish you ________________ to me when I raised an objection to your opinion. (listen)
4. I wish we ________________ Martin. He spends work time chatting on his cell phone. (not hire)

Q2 우리말과 일치하도록 I wish와 주어진 표현을 이용하여 문장을 완성하시오.

1. 나는 세계일주 여행을 할 수 있으면 좋을 텐데. (travel, around the world)

→ ________________________________

2. 내가 그녀만큼 영어를 잘할 수 있으면 좋을 텐데. (speak English, as well as she does)

→ ________________________________

3. 내가 젊었을 때 돈을 모았더라면 좋았을 텐데. (save some money, when I was young)

→ ________________________________

4. 내가 그에게 '사랑해'라는 말을 더 자주 했더라면 좋았을 텐데. (say 'I love you', more often)

→ ________________________________

Fill in the Blank wish we had

Question 1 **1.** had not overheard **2.** had **3.** had listened **4.** had not hired

Question 2 **1.** I wish I could travel around the world.
2. I wish I could speak English as well as she does.
3. I wish I had saved some money when I was young.
4. I wish I had said 'I love you' more often to him.